Studies in Finance an[illegible]

The 'Studies in Finance and Accounting' series publishes contemporary research findings in the fields of accounting and finance. It embraces a broad range of research methods, with a strong emphasis on empirical work, whether quantitative or qualitative. The series includes theoretically grounded and innovative dissertations that are of interest to both the academic community and business practitioners.

Frederic Lammers

The Role of Executive Characteristics in Financial Decision-Making

Springer Gabler

Frederic Lammers
Chair of Finance
ESCP Business School
Berlin, Germany

ISSN 3059-3468 ISSN 3059-3476 (electronic)
Studies in Finance and Accounting
ISBN 978-3-658-51854-7 ISBN 978-3-658-51855-4 (eBook)
https://doi.org/10.1007/978-3-658-51855-4

This Springer Gabler imprint is published by the registered company Springer Fachmedien Wiesbaden GmbH, part of Springer Nature.
The registered company address is: Abraham-Lincoln-Str. 46, 65189 Wiesbaden, Germany

Acknowledgments

The completion of this dissertation would not have been possible without the support and encouragement of those around me, to whom I owe my deepest gratitude.

I wish to thank my supervisor, Ulrich Pape, for his invaluable support and guidance throughout these recent years. His mentorship allowed me to develop both professionally and personally, always offering understanding and continuous support, especially during challenging periods.

My heartfelt appreciation goes to my family and friends, who have consistently had my back. A special mention is dedicated to my father, whose memory remains a constant source of strength and inspiration.

To Sarah, I extend my deepest appreciation for her unwavering love and support. Her presence has been a cornerstone of my journey, providing reassurance whenever needed.

Thank you for everything.

Contents

Abbreviations

CEO	Chief Executive Officer
CFO	Chief Financial Officer
M&A	Mergers & Acquisitions
NIE	New Institutional Economics
TMT	Top Management Team
UET	Upper Echelons Theory

List of Tables

Introduction 1

Abstract

This dissertation investigates how top management team (TMT) members shape strategic decision-making in the corporate finance context, drawing on Upper Echelons Theory (UET) as its theoretical foundation. While behavioral perspectives have long established that senior executives exert meaningful influence on organizational outcomes, corporate finance research continues to rely on frameworks with insufficient behavioral foundations, a gap this work seeks to address. The dissertation comprises three interrelated research manuscripts. The first examines how Chief Financial Officers with greater managerial power contribute to value creation in mergers and acquisitions. The second and third manuscripts shift focus to CEOs, exploring how narcissistic tendencies drive the use of impression management in M&A contexts and how this relationship is moderated by the degree of communication constraints executives face. Together, the manuscripts advance understanding of both functional TMT members and CEO psychology as drivers of corporate strategic behavior, enriching theoretical frameworks at the intersection of strategic management and corporate finance.

Companies' strategic decision-making shapes economic, social, and environmental landscapes, often with lasting consequences for stakeholders and society at large. For example, entering the smartphone market with the iPhone not only fueled Apple's growth (Apple Inc., 2009, 2024), transforming it into one of the world's largest mobile phone vendors, but also played a pivotal role in revolutionizing daily life by making mobile apps and internet access ubiquitous (International Data Corporation, 2024). Similarly, Google's acquisition of YouTube, widely regarded as one of the most successful tech acquisitions of

F. Lammers, *The Role of Executive Characteristics in Financial Decision-Making*, Studies in Finance and Accounting, https://doi.org/10.1007/978-3-658-51855-4_1

all time, reshaped online media consumption and cemented Google's dominance across video streaming and digital advertising, with YouTube now contributing approximately 10% of Alphabet's total revenue (Alphabet Inc., 2024). Moreover, General Electric's aggressive strategic shift away from its industrial core toward rapid growth through diversification into high-margin financial services exposed critical vulnerabilities, triggering massive financial losses that necessitated a government bailout and ultimately undermining the stability of what was once among the world's most valuable and admired firms (Wheelen et al., 2017).

From market disruptions to bold acquisitions, real-world examples like the ones above abound, demonstrating the profound and often ripple effects corporate strategic actions might have—for better or worse. In light of these far-reaching impacts, it is hardly surprising that researchers across various economic disciplines have devoted considerable effort to better understanding organizational behavior, particularly strategic decision-making (Gavetti et al., 2012; Hagen et al., 2024). Within the assessment of this topic, one matter that continues to spark considerable scholarly interest relates to the role of firms' leadership, i.e., its top management team (TMT),[1] in steering strategic behavior at the corporate level (Bromiley & Rau, 2016; Carpenter, 2011; Wowak et al., 2017). While it appears intuitively reasonable to assume that the TMT, given its position at the apex of the firm's hierarchy and ultimate responsibility over resource allocation, plays a pivotal role in shaping the firm's trajectory (Busenbark et al., 2016; Crossland et al., 2014; Hodgkinson et al., 2023), this perspective is vigorously debated across competing theoretical positions (Finkelstein et al., 2009). Several classic economic perspectives, which remain highly influential, presume that firm behavior is predominantly determined by external forces such as organizational inertia, path dependence, and institutional pressures toward conformity (Bertrand & Schoar, 2003; Hambrick & Quigley, 2014).[2] Firms are conceptualized as unified actors whose behaviors represent collective adaptations to external constraints, implying that managers hold little sway over organizational outcomes.

[1] In line with existing literature in the field (e.g., Crossland et al. (2014); Fang et al. (2018); Popli et al. (2022)), the term "leadership" is used to denote a firm's TMT. Typically, this includes the Chief Executive Officer (CEO) and a relatively small group of the most senior managers who bear overall responsibility for managing the entire enterprise, rather than only a subsidiary or business unit (Cuypers et al., 2022). Thus, the term implies substantive strategic decision-making responsibilities, extending beyond the interpersonal or social dimensions commonly associated with the term leadership alone (Hambrick, 1989).

[2] Please see Chapter 2 for a more detailed discussion of the role of managers within various schools of economic thought.

However, as behavioral economics gained traction, this omission of managers from explanations of organizational behavior was increasingly deemed an unfeasible proposition (Aharoni et al., 2011; Augier & Teece, 2009; Mintzberg et al., 2009). Scholars began advocating a more realistic, manager-centered view of organizational decision-making (Powell et al., 2011; Zacharias et al., 2015), reinforced by leading voices such as Hambrick (2007), who pointed out that "if we want to understand why organizations do the things they do, or why they perform the way they do, we must consider [...] their most powerful actors—their top executives" (p. 334). The underlying premise of the behavioral perspective views organizations as distinct social entities, with the TMT driving overall strategic initiatives and thereby influencing firm behavior (Foss & Mazzelli, 2025; King et al., 2010). The inherent emphasis on managers has, over time, profoundly influenced numerous economic disciplines, particularly strategic management and related fields of social scientific inquiry. Its core concepts such as bounded rationality (Simon, 1957), conflicts of interest (Amason, 1996), and organizational learning (Miller & Lin, 2010), are now commonplace and form a foundational basis for a variety theoretical and empirical studies on organizational phenomena (Augier & March, 2008; Gavetti et al., 2012).

Although the emphasis on top managers' influence is recognized as valuable for advancing our understanding of corporate behavior, this perspective has only marginally carried over into the discipline of corporate finance, where research continues to heavily rely on theories of intraorganizational decision-making that lack adequate behavioral foundations (Bamber et al., 2010; Bertrand & Schoar, 2003; Hertrampf et al., 2025; White & Borgholthaus, 2022). Indeed, commonly employed frameworks remain somewhat parochial in their explanations of firm heterogeneity, often providing insufficient consideration for managerial influence (Greve & Argote, 2015; Powell et al., 2011). For instance, traditional agency theory (Jensen & Meckling, 1976), a cornerstone of financial theorizing, typically confines its analysis to rational agents (usually CEOs) focusing narrowly on their self-interest and risk preferences (Bendickson et al., 2016; Bosse & Phillips, 2016). This approach, however, largely neglects broader behavioral factors that shape managerial decisions and actions (Finkelstein et al., 2009). The restrictive emphasis significantly curtails its relevance for explaining the complex dynamics driving managerial behavior and influence in diverse organizational contexts (Aharoni et al., 2011; Foss & Mazzelli, 2025). A deeper incorporation of insights regarding top managers and their influence on corporate outcomes into corporate financial research thus holds considerable potential to bridge disciplinary divides, enrich theoretical frameworks, and enhance our comprehensive understanding of organizational decision-making processes.

More generally, the growing necessity for rigorous research is further evidenced by the rapid expansion of scholarly literature on this topic, particularly over the past few years, as highlighted by recent reviews (Hodgkinson et al., 2023; White & Borgholthaus, 2022; Wowak et al., 2017). This heightened attention aligns with scholarly evidence suggesting that the scale of managerial impact on corporate outcomes has substantially expanded in recent decades (Mackey, 2008; Quigley & Hambrick, 2015). Thus, considering both the research trajectory and phenomenological significance, sustained scholarly focus on this area appears increasingly important (Neely et al., 2020).

Against this backdrop, the objective of this dissertation is to deepen the understanding of how TMT members influence strategic decision-making within the corporate finance context. Theoretically, this research is grounded in Upper Echelons Theory (UET) (Hambrick & Mason, 1984), which conceptualizes corporate behaviors as reflections of the characteristics and experiences of TMT members (Cuypers et al., 2022; Neely et al., 2020). UET has established itself as a predominant framework within the behavioral perspective of organizational theory, supported by an extensive body of literature that deepens our understanding of the pivotal role played by senior executives in determining organizational trajectories (Abatecola & Cristofaro, 2018; Carpenter et al., 2004; Neely et al., 2020; White & Borgholthaus, 2022).

Central to this dissertation are three research manuscripts, each addressing a distinct yet interconnected facet of strategic decision-making. Research Manuscript 1 examines how Chief Financial Officers (CFOs) with greater managerial power within the firm contribute to adding value to mergers and acquisitions (M&A) throughout the entire takeover process, from initiation to closure. The study therefore advances the understanding of the influence of functional members within the TMT, addressing a critical gap in the literature that has traditionally concentrated on the CEO role in shaping strategic decision outcomes (Bedard et al., 2014; Menz, 2012).

Acknowledging the established focus on the CEO's central role in existing research (Quigley & Hambrick, 2015), the subsequent manuscripts explicitly shift focus to CEOs, exploring their distinctive psychological and behavioral influences on strategic processes. Specifically, research manuscripts 2 and 3 contribute to a growing area of organizational research by advancing our understanding of how TMTs actively seek to influence stakeholder reactions to corporate events through impression management (Bolino et al., 2016; Brauer & Vandepoele, 2023). Specifically, manuscript 2 examines the relationship between CEO narcissistic tendencies and the firm's use of impression management in the context of M&A. Building on this, research Manuscript 3 proposes that the effect of CEO narcissism on the use of impression management techniques is particularly evident in situations where CEOs face less communication constraints. By focusing on the psychological trait of narcissism, these manuscripts also align with recent developments in upper-echelons research, advocating for the integration of more complex constructs in the study of executive behavior.

The remainder of this dissertation is organized as follows. Chapter 2 lays the theoretical foundation by outlining firm behavior through various economic lenses, providing a conceptual basis for the analysis. Chapter 3 provides an overview of the three research manuscripts and elaborates on the fundamental theory-of-science assumptions underlying this research. Chapters 4 through 6 present the three research manuscripts: Chapter 4 contains the first manuscript, Chapter 5 the second, and Chapter 6 the third. Finally, Chapter 7 discusses the overall contributions of the dissertation, highlights its practical implications, and reflects on its limitations, offering directions for future research.

Theoretical Perspectives on Firm Behavior

2

Abstract

This chapter traces the evolution of economic perspectives on organizational behavior and the role of top management. Beginning with early behavioral approaches that positioned senior executives as central to strategic decision-making, the neoclassical paradigm displaced this view by reducing firms to passive "black boxes" and treating managers as interchangeable inputs. New Institutional Economics partially countered this reductionism by highlighting institutional environments, yet similarly constrained managerial influence through isomorphic pressures and agency-theoretic governance mechanisms. Behavioral economics broke decisively with these assumptions, foregrounding bounded rationality, organizational coalitions, and iterative decision-making as key drivers of firm behavior. Building on these foundations, Upper Echelons Theory formalized the link between executives' cognitive frameworks and organizational outcomes, establishing top management as a legitimate and consequential unit of analysis, and has since expanded its reach into accounting and finance research.

2.1 Traditional Economics

Amid shifting economic paradigms, scholarly views on the determinants of organizational behavior and actions have undergone significant changes. Early work emphasized the behavioral role of individuals, positioning top management at the center of strategy formulation and central to strategic decision-making (Augier & March, 2008; Corr & Plagnol, 2023; Thaler, 2016). These efforts were also prominently reflected in foundational frameworks such as the Harvard model,

F. Lammers, *The Role of Executive Characteristics in Financial Decision-Making*, Studies in Finance and Accounting, https://doi.org/10.1007/978-3-658-51855-4_2

emphasizing that strategy involves the integration of corporate functions, directed by top management to achieve overarching organizational goals (Foss & Mazzelli, 2025). This notion changed, however, with the rise of more mechanistic economic theories that prioritized mathematical modeling based on clear, predefined variables (Augier & March, 2008). As a result, organizations were effectively embodied, and the role of top managers was largely dismissed (Finkelstein et al., 2009), as economists increasingly viewed managerial behaviors as inconsistent and unreliable metrics for analyzing economic phenomena (Camerer et al., 2004).

As part of this development, the rise of neoclassical economics as the dominant theoretical framework, prominently represented by scholars such as Hicks (1939), Samuelson (1947), and Friedman (1953), marked a significant turning point. Neoclassical economics, also referred to as mainstream economics (Corr & Plagnol, 2023), primarily focuses on attaining an optimal equilibrium model of the overall market economy (Elsner et al., 2015). Strongly influenced by the intellectual tradition of physics as a scientific ideal (Drakopoulos, 2021), neoclassical theory conceptualizes human economic activities as governed by "natural" forces of supply and demand, largely isolated from societal influences and the natural environment (Campling et al., 2000). In doing so, neoclassical theory offers a rather abstract and simplified conceptualization of firms and their behavior. Firms are established as exogenously given production mechanisms that transform inputs into outputs (Frantz et al., 2017). Economic agents—that is, households and firms—are assumed to act rationally. Households aim to maximize utility, while firms seek to maximize profit. Markets achieve equilibrium through the interaction of supply and demand (Bardmann, 2011). Business operation is conducted independently under perfect competition (Tsoulfidis & Tsalikē, 2019), with no single firm's decisions exerting a significant influence on market outcomes, as their impact is considered so marginal that it can be neglected in market analysis (Elsner et al., 2015). The simplified role of firms also becomes evident in their assumed role as "price takers," whose decision-making is purely reactive to changes in the household preferences and production technologies, which are assumed to be uniformly available (Campling et al., 2000).

It follows that neoclassical theory conceptualizes firms as "black boxes" (Frantz et al., 2017), operating in a social vacuum, leaving little room for management to exert unique or idiosyncratic influence on corporate outcomes (Bamber et al., 2010). A firm's management is considered a homogeneous and selfless input in the production process, functioning merely as perfect substitutes for one another (Bardmann, 2011; Bertrand & Schoar, 2003). In a now classic paper, Baumol (1968) laments the elusiveness of management in neoclassical economics, pointing out that "the management group becomes a passive calculator that reacts mechanically to changes imposed on it by fortuitous external developments over which it does not exert, and does not even attempt to exert, any influence" (p. 67).[1] By focusing on market forces as the primary units of analysis, neoclassical theory relegates the role of managers to the background (Foss & Mazzelli, 2025). Ultimately, this omission may also be attributable to the analytical challenges of incorporating non-standardized, heterogeneous managerial influence into the economic models of neoclassic, which often seek the precision of clockwork mechanics (Endres & Woods, 2006; Rocha, 2012).

2.2 New Institutional Economics

Partly as a response to the dominance of neoclassical theory, New Institutional Economics (NIE) emerged as an alternative framework in economic thought (Crossland & Hambrick, 2011), emphasizing the influence of social factors in shaping organizational behavior (Yeung et al., 2011). NIE posits that firms operate in institutional environments, which form through individuals' shared understanding and collective interpretation of acceptable norms governing group activities (North, 1991; Suddaby et al., 2010). Within this paradigm, firms are presumed to seek legitimacy and avoid negative sanctions (North, 1990; Webb et al., 2013), by adhering to prevailing societal norms and expectations (Waddingham et al., 2025; Yeung et al., 2011). For instance, a firm's engagement in corporate social responsibility and adherence to sound ethical principles may not be explained by strategic choice in anticipation of positive organizational outcomes (e.g., enhanced prestige) but rather because such behavior adheres to the dominant practices within the organization's institutional fields. Under strong pressure to conform to institutional environment, these practices come to be seen as the only

[1] Others have voiced similar criticisms. For instance, Nobel laureate Ronald Coase observed that "economists have tended to neglect the main activity of the firm, running a business" (Coase, 1988, p. 38). It is noteworthy, however, that some economists in the neoclassical era made efforts to incorporate the role of decision-makers within a firm, albeit within the constraints of static equilibrium analysis. Knight (1921), exemplified this perspective by emphasizing the entrepreneur as the bearer of uncertainty in the pursuit of profit. Accordingly, entrepreneurs earn profits as compensation for assuming uninsurable uncertainty, thereby portraying the firm's actions as driven by entrepreneurial risk-taking and judgment (Langlois & Cosgel, 1993). Similarly, Schumpeter (1942) identified the entrepreneur as an innovator whose decisions propel economic development, once again highlighting the role of an individual decision-maker—though still within the framework of profit-driven innovation. For a more detailed review, see Campling et al. (2000).

conceivable, "obvious," or "natural" way to carry out organizational activities (Oliver, 1991).

This perspective implies that managers play a relatively limited role in shaping corporate outcomes, as organizational behavior is primarily driven by the subconscious adoption of institutionalized values and practices (Scott, 2014). While firms are recognized as being embedded within complex social systems rather than merely described by production functions, managerial influence remains heavily constrained by the institutional environment, thereby limiting TMTs impact on organizational outcomes (Chin et al., 2013). External pressure to align with institutional environments gives rise to institutional isomorphism (Ang et al., 2015; Judge et al., 2008), which fosters similarities in organizations structure, thought, and action, ultimately leading to the "unspoken assumption that all organizations are essentially the same" (Greenwood et al., 2014, p. 1207). Any observed heterogeneity among firms is then presumed to manifest primarily across distinct organizational fields. For instance, firms operating in different countries face unique institutional pressures, leading to variations in organizational practices (Delmas & Toffel, 2008).

Over the years, several subdomains have emerged from NIE, with agency theory becoming the most prominent, particularly within the finance discipline (Bendickson et al., 2016; Schreyögg & Geiger, 2016).[2] The central premise of agency theory is the "agency problem in corporate control," (Boivie et al., 2011, p. 551) arising from the misalignment of interests between a firm's management (agents) and its shareholders (principals) (Jensen & Meckling, 1976).[3] Agency theory assigns a less extreme yet limited role to individual managers in shaping corporate outcomes (Bamber et al., 2010). The theory acknowledges that the agent has the ability to influence corporate policies and is assumed to act opportunistically, advancing their personal goals at the expense of the principal (Chin et al., 2013). To mitigate this problem, principals implement monitoring mechanisms and incentive structures (e.g., compensation schemes) designed to align managerial actions with shareholder interests. However, such controls give

[2] Other prominent subdomains include the property rights theory (Demsetz, 1967), which examines how the allocation and definition of property rights affect economic behavior, and the transaction cost theory (Coase, 1937; Williamson, 1975), which focuses on the costs associated with market transactions and the resulting emergence of firms and other organizational structures.

[3] Although often applied to shareholder–management relationships, principal–agent theory extends to a wide range of contexts, including conflicts between shareholders and bondholders (Smith & Warner, 1979), principal–knowledge worker dynamics (Mitchell & Meacheam, 2011), and other stakeholder relationships (Bendickson et al., 2016; Hill & Jones, 1992).

rise to agency costs, including expenses associated with monitoring and bonding activities as well as residual losses arising from suboptimal managerial decisions (Boivie et al., 2011), highlighting the inherent trade-off between mitigating agency conflicts and ensuring efficient corporate governance. When such mechanisms are effectively in place, managers are modeled as representative agents (Stiglitz, 2011), behaving in a homogeneous manner that reflects the aligned interests of principals (Aharoni et al., 2011; Bamber et al., 2010). Under this notion, variations in corporate practices or performance are attributed not to individual managers but rather to differences in the strength of governance mechanisms across firms, that is, the extent to which firms can effectively monitor and control managerial behavior (Bertrand & Schoar, 2003; Busenbark et al., 2016; Jensen & Zajac, 2004). Ultimately, agency theory simplifies the decision-making problem by shifting analytical attention from the decision-making processes themselves toward evaluating the effectiveness of governance mechanisms (Aharoni et al., 2011).

Summarizing the evolution of economic models, early economic perspectives recognized the significant role of managerial influence in shaping strategic decision-making and corporate behavior. This emphasis, however, declined with the emergence of the neoclassical approach, which prioritized mathematically rigorous methodologies and depicted firms as passive entities responding mechanically to market forces. Such a reductionist viewpoint largely excluded managerial roles from economic analyses. In reaction to the limitations inherent in neoclassical assumptions, the NIE framework arose, highlighting the importance of institutional environments in influencing organizational behavior. Although NIE incorporates broader social and contextual dimensions into economic theory, it continues to assume that managers have relatively limited influence, emphasizing instead that firms predominantly adapt to institutional norms and external pressures to maintain legitimacy. Within this context, agency theory further underscores the limited scope of managerial impact on corporate outcomes, attributing differences in firm performance and strategic results primarily to variations in governance effectiveness across organizations.

2.3 Behavioral Economics

While neoclassical and institutional economics largely rest on the premise of rational and self-interested agents, behavioral economics takes a decisive step away from these idealized assumptions. According to the behavioral perspective, individuals are prone to numerous cognitive biases, rendering the conventional economic assumption of near-perfect rationality unrealistic, as Nobel laureate Richard Thaler vividly remarked during an interview: "For the last 50 or 60 years, economists have devoted themselves to studying fictional creatures [...] They might as well be studying unicorns" (Thaler, 2015). After early considerations of human behavior were largely displaced by neoclassical models, Herbert Simon and his colleagues laid the foundations for a renewed behavioral perspective during the 1950s and 1960s, establishing what became widely known as the Carnegie School (Augier & Teece, 2009). Adopting an interdisciplinary approach that integrates sociology and social psychology with economic theory, Carnegie theorists emphasized that individuals and organizations must navigate the complex "uncertainties and ambiguities of life" (March & Simon, 1993, p. 2), compelling behaviors that diverge substantially from the idealized omniscience attributed to neoclassical agents (Augier, 2010; Frantz et al., 2017).

Central to the behavioral paradigm is the concept of bounded rationality which acknowledges that individuals face inherent cognitive constraints influenced by a variety of unique factors, such as personal goals, evaluation criteria, and identity (Aharoni et al., 2011; Gavetti et al., 2007; Hagen et al., 2024). Consequently, although individuals might not act randomly or arbitrarily, their behaviors are shaped by subjective interpretations of their environments, which can differ considerably from one person to another (Finkelstein et al., 2009; Wheeler, 2024). Given the inherent constraints of bounded rationality, actual decision-making diverges notably from theoretical models that posit instantaneous, fully informed choices made by perfectly rational actors (Corr & Plagnol, 2023; Frantz et al., 2017). Economic agents rarely select from a predetermined, comprehensive set of alternatives; rather, feasible options typically emerge through an active search process (Gavetti et al., 2007). Decisions, therefore, unfold iteratively as individuals systematically search for alternatives, explore potential solutions, and ultimately commit to a chosen course of action. Thus, the behavioral approach emphasizes the importance of the processes through which individuals search for and evaluate possible actions, rather than assuming that economic agents already possess complete knowledge of all available options and their potential outcomes (Earl, 2022).

The process-oriented view of decision-making in behavioral economics has spawned a distinct perspective on firms, placing them at the heart of examining economic activity, as Cyert and March (1963) outline in their seminal work, *A Behavioral Theory of the Firm*: "We believe that, in order to understand contemporary economic decision making, we need to supplement the study of market factors with an examination of the internal operation of the firm" (p. 1). Rather than opaque black boxes, firms are conceived as collective social systems composed of coalitions of individuals, including shareholders, managers, employees, or customers (Surdu et al., 2021), each pursuing diverse and potentially conflicting goals (Augier & Teece, 2009; Greve & Argote, 2015; Mooney & Amason, 2011). Some goals, such as the organizational survival, are likely shared universally across coalitions (Bidwell, 2012). Other goals, however, stem directly from specific coalitions' attempts to advance their unique interests, perspectives, and priorities, potentially creating internal conflicts (Greve, 2008). In contrast to traditional economic assumptions, goal attainment is evaluated not by utility maximization, but relative to aspiration levels, defined as "the smallest outcome that would be deemed satisfactory by the decision maker" (Schneider, 1992, p. 1053). These aspiration levels, in turn, are influenced by an organization's past performance as well as the performance of relevant peer organizations (Hagen et al., 2024). Decision-making based on such aspiration levels arises from the bounded rationality of actors, who seek to simplify the evaluation process and subsequent course of action by transforming a continuous measure of performance into a discrete assessment of success or failure (Gaba & Joseph, 2013; Greve, 2003). Actions that lead to satisfying outcomes above the firm's aspiration level are positively reinforced, whereas outcomes below the aspiration level trigger a problemistic search for solutions, aimed at closing the performance-aspiration gap (Desai, 2016; Gavetti et al., 2007). Over time, firms adjust their aspirations and refine their search strategies, facilitating organizational learning through adaptive behavior. In this manner, experience is accumulated and embedded within stable routines and rules, which have consistently generated effective solutions (Gavetti et al., 2012; Greve & Argote, 2015; Surdu et al., 2021). Thus, many organizational actions are not solely outcomes of deliberate calculation; rather, they reflect enactments of established routines (Greve & Argote, 2015). Organizational learning occurs at multiple levels: locally, such as within individual departments, as well as corporately, as different participants interpret and evaluate similar events uniquely based on their distinct perspectives (Hagen et al., 2024). Ultimately, these institutionalized processes enable firms to adapt, innovate, and evolve over time by leveraging their accumulated collective knowledge and practices.

In this behavioral theory framework, the TMT of a firm is commonly viewed as the "dominant coalition" positioned at the organization's apex and wielding disproportionate influence over its behavior (Miller & Lin, 2010; Morgan, 2006; van Doorn et al., 2022). The dominant coalition embodies the firm's collective cognition, perceptions, and decision-making processes, and holds ultimate responsibility for defining the firm's overall strategic direction (Bartlett & Ghoshal,

1993; Crossland et al., 2014). According to the prevalent model wherein the dominant coalition comprises the firm's senior-most executives (Cuypers et al., 2022; Foss & Mazzelli, 2025; Hambrick, 2010), these individual top managers often represent distinct departmental or stakeholder interests (Bruneel et al., 2020). Consequently, strategic decisions emerge primarily through negotiation and bargaining processes often resulting in compromises, rather than through purely analytical optimization (Kanihan et al., 2013). The chosen strategy than reflects a balance that sufficiently addresses the essential demands of coalition members to at least a minimally acceptable standard (Ben-Shahar et al., 2023). The inherent hierarchical structure across coalitions grants the dominant coalitions the formal authority necessary to implement the strategy, manage arising conflicts among subordinate coalitions, and foster cooperation throughout the organization. This authority typically manifests in mechanisms such as controlling access to critical resources, thereby aligning diverse coalition priorities with the firm's overarching objectives (Augier & Teece, 2009; Bidwell, 2012). The dominant coalition of top managers also plays an essential role in establishing evaluative standards that trigger problemistic searches when the organizational strategy falls short of expectations. These aspiration levels are disseminated throughout the organization and become integrated into the practices of other coalitions. Consequently, these coalitions internalize the established standards, aligning their behaviors and directing their efforts toward the achievement of the firm's collective goals (Gaba & Joseph, 2013).

In summary, the behavioral perspective views organizations as a system of coalitions continuously shaped by interactions among the coalition members whose interests are diverse and often conflicting. This paradigm fosters sustained heterogeneity among organizations in terms of their strategies, structures, and decision-making processes. By acknowledging the bounded rationality of actors and the critical influence of top managers comprising the dominant coalition, the behavioral perspective challenges traditional economic models of organizational behavior and draws attention to the significance of internal dynamics and iterative decision-making. Behavioral economics' micro-foundational insights have substantially influenced fields such as evolutionary economics, organizational learning, and strategic management. As such, behavioral theory provides a comprehensive and nuanced framework for analyzing the complexity and variability inherent in organizational behavior, serving as a vital foundation for ongoing theoretical development and practical application.

2.4 Upper Echelons Theory

The foundational insights drawn from behavioral economics have sparked considerable scholarly interest in gaining a deeper understanding of how top executives shape the structure and fate of organizations (Foss & Mazzelli, 2025). The UET, developed by Hambrick and Mason (1984), marked a significant milestone in this development by proposing that organizational behavior inherently mirrors the values, cognitive biases, experiences, and backgrounds of senior executives. Strategic decision-making is therefore understood as predominantly interpretive rather than purely technical, as executives are presumed to evaluate their circumstances and choices through individualized lenses (Chin et al., 2013).

At its core, the theory centers on the premise that top managers encompasses a complex array of internal and external stimuli as a result by an organization's strategic context. Due to their limited cognitive capacities, executives perceive and interpret only a subset of these stimuli (Finkelstein et al., 2009). To cope with such cognitive limitations, they simplify the situation by filtering and distorting available information through a three-stage process influenced by their individual cognitive frameworks and values (Carpenter et al., 2004; Hambrick, 2007). First, the executives' *field of vision* delineates the subset of stimuli to which they are attentive. Second, *selective perception* further narrows this subset, identifying those stimuli actively perceived and processed. Third, *interpretation* occurs when executives assign meaning to these selected stimuli. Although psychological constructs underpin this process, Hambrick and Mason (1984) acknowledge the practical challenges involved in observing these constructs directly. Consequently, they suggest utilizing observable demographic characteristics as proxies to capture these underlying psychological dimensions (Plöckinger et al., 2016). These cognitive distinctions among executives shape their individual perceptions of strategic contexts, significantly influencing their decision-making behaviors and ultimately manifest in organizational outcomes (Herrmann & Datta, 2002; Miner et al., 2011).

Since its introduction, UET has progressed from its nascent stage into a systematic research stream, which has been continuously evolving ever since (Wowak et al., 2017). Executives' demographic characteristics and their ability to reflect underlying cognitive processes have been of particular academic interest in this respect. While initial studies primarily focused on a rather narrow set of demographic indicators, subsequent research has progressively expanded the analytical scope to incorporate diverse factors such as foreign experience (Conyon et al., 2019; Quan et al., 2023), celebrity status (Hayward et al., 2004; Lovelace et al., 2018), and birth order (Campbell et al., 2019), among others. These developments have facilitated a more nuanced and comprehensive understanding of executive influence.

However, as research matured, increasing criticism emerged regarding the lack of attention paid to the cognitive and psychological aspects through which executive characteristics translate into organizational decisions and outcomes (Carpenter et al., 2004; Cragun et al., 2020; Menz, 2012). Critics frequently describe this issue as a proverbial "black box," highlighting researchers' tendency to demonstrate correlations between executives' demographics and organizational outcomes without adequately clarifying the underlying causative processes, ultimately limiting the conceptual, and especially the practical, contributions of the theory (Neely et al., 2020). In response, prior work has progressively shifted its attention beyond strategic and organizational outcomes to more explicitly address the psychological and cognitive processes linking executives' socio-demographic characteristics with those outcomes (Abatecola & Cristofaro, 2018). More recent research has begun utilizing less overt indicators of executive traits, extending proxy variables to encompass measures related to personality, cognition, and values (Bromiley & Rau, 2016; Neely et al., 2020). For example, scholars increasingly employ comprehensive personality frameworks, such as the Five-Factor Model (Barrick & Mount, 1991; Colbert et al., 2014; Nadkarni & Herrmann, 2010), or focus on specific traits including humility (Petrenko et al., 2019), charisma (Wowak et al., 2016), overconfidence (Malmendier & Tate, 2005), and narcissism (Bromiley & Rau, 2016; Buyl et al., 2019; Cragun et al., 2020). Aimed at further attributing to the efforts of opening the black box, recent studies have also opted for integrating executive values, including political ideology (Chin et al., 2013; Elnahas & Kim, 2017), and cognitive attributes, such as temporal dispositions (e.g., Chen & Nadkarni, 2017), thus continuing to expanding the theory's explanatory power concerning executive demographics (Campbell et al., 2019). Advances in technology (e.g., content analysis and machine learning) have notably facilitated this evolution by providing researchers with detailed and sophisticated data, allowing more precise assessments of executives' inherent psychological processes (White & Borgholthaus, 2022).

Efforts to establish appropriate demographic proxies for underlying psychological characteristics have been complemented by conceptual developments addressing diverse moderating relationships within the UET. Carpenter et al. (2004) emphasize this advancement, asserting that "the understanding of such contingencies is perhaps the single greatest advance in UE theorizing and application" (p. 764). To this end, managerial discretion (Hambrick & Finkelstein, 1987) emerged early in UET as one of its initial and most influential boundary conditions, moderating how executives' characteristics affect organizational outcomes. In this context, executives' interpretations of strategic choices translate into tangible actions contingent upon the decision-making latitude available within their organizations (White & Borgholthaus, 2022). Although managerial discretion remains consistently acknowledged as a pivotal moderator (Wangrow et al., 2015), recent scholarship advocates broadening the analytical scope to encompass additional contextual variables. In this regard, reflecting the increasingly globalized nature of business operations, scholars have shifted attention toward institutional factors as significant moderators within UET (Yamak et al., 2014). These factors, such as political risk, governance standards, ownership dispersion, and legal frameworks, have been shown to critically shape executive influence on organizational strategies and trajectories (Crossland & Hambrick, 2007, 2011; Neely et al., 2020). Concurrently, research has increasingly opened new frontiers regarding the structural characteristics of TMTs, scrutinizing relational dynamics at the board level—including board size, diversity, and independence—as critical moderators affecting upper-echelons relationships (Cuypers et al., 2022). Incorporating such moderators has significantly enhanced scholarly understanding of variations in UET's explanatory power across diverse organizational and environmental contexts. Indeed, there now appears to be widespread scholarly agreement that integrating organizational and environmental contingencies markedly improves the robustness and generalizability of theoretical predictions drawn from upper-echelons research (Carpenter et al., 2004).

Another important development in upper-echelons research relates to the significant diversity in the assessment of who constitutes the TMT, a topic that has attracted considerable scholarly attention (Nielsen, 2010). Substantial variation exists regarding who should be considered the unit of analysis, with some studies exclusively focus on executives ranked above board vice-president, whereas others adopt a broader view, including all board members and influential senior managers actively involved in corporate governance (Abatecola & Cristofaro, 2018; Carpenter, 2011; Ma et al., 2022).[4] Because the notion "coalition" is generally not understood to refer to a single actor (van Doorn et al., 2022), it might seem surprising that one of the most prevalent conceptualizations of a firm's TMT within the literature centers exclusively on the CEO. Indeed, a substantial body of literature has attempted to quantify what is commonly referred to as the "CEO effect" (Quigley & Hambrick, 2015), arguing that this focus on CEOs is

[4] See van Doorn et al. (2022) for a recent review of the most prevalent models on the composition of the dominant coalition.

justified because they often serve as the public face of the organization (Love et al., 2017) and typically exercise considerable influence over firm performance (Busenbark et al., 2016; Hiebl, 2014; White & Borgholthaus, 2022). Methodological constraints, particularly the greater availability of comprehensive data on CEOs, may have further reinforced this focus, as frequently used databases such as S&P ExecuComp and BoardEx offer extensive historical information on CEOs but relatively limited data on other C-suite members (Plöckinger et al., 2016).

Despite these challenges, recent literature increasingly emphasizes the importance of considering other senior executives within the TMT, particularly recognizing the potential contributions and influence of functional executives on specific strategic decision-making processes (Abatecola & Cristofaro, 2018). Accordingly, scholars have begun to examine the roles of executives like CFOs, reflecting a broader acknowledgment of diverse executive influences on key firm outcomes (Menz, 2012).

Over time, UET has served as a critical catalyst in exploring how executives' characteristics and experiences shape diverse organizational outcomes, progressively growing in both influence and scholarly recognition (Hodgkinson et al., 2023; Neely et al., 2020).[5] The theoretical insights generated through the UET framework have considerably broadened, originating within the broader discipline of management and subsequently extending into related fields (Whitler et al., 2021). In the case of mainstream finance, research has predominantly emphasized market forces, rational decision-making models, and impersonal factors, such as capital costs and information asymmetry, over individual managerial attributes. As a result, explicit incorporation of UET into finance research remains relatively uncommon (Ali et al., 2022). While scholars have recently begun to adopt UET perspectives more actively (Hiebl, 2014; Plöckinger et al., 2016), contemporary finance scholarship frequently frames related studies under terminologies such as "CEO effects" or "behavioral corporate finance" rather than explicitly citing UET (Plöckinger et al., 2016). Notably, an upper-echelons perspective has begun to prominently emerge at the intersection of accounting and finance, where studies highlight how CEO and CFO characteristics significantly impact financial reporting practices, influencing earnings management, disclosure tone, and accounting decisions (e.g., Allee, 2015; Bedard et al., 2014; Hiebl, 2014).

---

[5] The unabated scholarly interest in the UET is further underscored by a recent review conducted by White and Borgholthaus (2022). Their analysis of 811 studies revealed that more than 50 percent were published after 2018, indicating rapid growth in publication volume. Importantly, this increasing quantity of research is paralleled by a rise in publications appearing in top-tier journals.

Research Manuscripts Overview 3

Abstract

This chapter introduces the three research manuscripts forming the empirical core of this thesis, each grounded in Upper Echelons Theory and investigating the influence of managerial characteristics on finance-related firm outcomes. Following this overview, the chapter outlines the positivist research paradigm underpinning all three studies, discussing its key ontological, epistemological, and methodological implications for the conducted research.

As outlined above, three research manuscripts form the core of this thesis. Each manuscript is grounded in UET and distinctly investigates the influence of managerial idiosyncrasies on finance-related firm outcomes. Table 3.1 provides an overview of the research manuscripts, summarizing their main research question, underlying sample and methods.

3.1 Summary

Research Manuscript 1, "The Impact of Powerful CFOs in M&A: Evidence from U.S. Acquisitions," addresses the previously mentioned gap within upper-echelons research concerning the influence of executives other than the CEO. Responding to scholars' frequent calls to investigate the strategic roles and impacts of functional TMT members (Carpenter et al., 2004; Menz, 2012; Welch et al., 2020), this manuscript specifically examines the influence of powerful CFOs in M&A, recognized as among the most significant and visible strategic decisions made by companies (Renneboog & Vansteenkiste, 2019). Although

F. Lammers, *The Role of Executive Characteristics in Financial Decision-Making*, Studies in Finance and Accounting, https://doi.org/10.1007/978-3-658-51855-4_3

Table 3.1 Overview of the research manuscripts

	Manuscript 1	Manuscript 2	Manuscript 3
Title	The Impact of Powerful CFOs in M&A: Evidence From U.S. Acquisitions.	The Influence of CEO Narcissism on Firms' Impression Management During Acquisitions.	CEO Narcissism and Linguistic Complexity in Earnings Conference Calls.
Main research question	Do CFOs create value in the acquisition process through their functional finance background?	Are highly narcissistic CEOs less likely to engage in impression management strategies during acquisitions?	Do more narcissistic CEOs use less complex language during earnings conference calls?
Sample	2,336 U.S. acquisitions from 1996 to 2018.	648 U.S. acquisitions from 2009 to 2018.	3,931 U.S. firm-quarter observations from 2010 to 2018.
Methods	• OLS regression • Logistic regression • Propensity score matching • Instrumental variables estimation	• Binomial regression • Propensity score matching • OLS regression	• OLS regression • Principal component analysis • Stacked difference-in-difference regression

anecdotal evidence frequently underscores the strategic advantage of CFOs' financial expertise in M&A processes (Agrawal et al., 2020; Fuhrer et al., 2017; Jöhnk et al., 2020), rigorous empirical studies in this area remain limited.

Utilizing Finkelstein's (1992) managerial power framework, the study's primary hypothesis asserts that powerful CFOs who have the discretion to influence crucial decisions throughout the deal process, might leverage their specialized financial knowledge to enhance M&A performance. Recognizing that transaction complexity often escalates with deal size, the study further hypothesizes that financial expertise is increasingly valuable in larger transactions, suggesting a positive moderating role for deal size. To uncover the specific mechanisms underlying value creation, the manuscript includes five additional hypotheses examining value-creation channels spanning from deal initiation to post-merger integration. Empirical analyses reveal no direct effect of CFO power on M&A performance; however, findings highlight the moderating importance of deal size, demonstrating that CFO expertise significantly influences performance outcomes in larger, more complex acquisitions. These results remain robust after rigorous tests addressing potential endogeneity issues. Furthermore, detailed examination of value-creation channels indicates that CFO experience notably contributes to reducing takeover premiums and third-party advisory fees.

Research Manuscript 2, "The Influence of CEO Narcissism on Firms' Impression Management During Acquisitions," investigates the role of CEO narcissism as a potential determinant of a firm's decision to engage in impression management. Initially developed within psychological literature (Leary, 1996; Schlenker, 1980), the concept of impression management has recently garnered considerable interest among economic scholars (Bolino et al., 2016), who recognize its significance in shaping stakeholders' perceptions of various corporate events, including poor performance disclosures (Noh & Zhou, 2022), workforce downsizing (Brauer & Vandepoele, 2023; Nègre et al., 2017), and acquisition announcements (Gamache et al., 2019; Graffin et al., 2016). Although prior research has made considerable headway in exploring the effectiveness and economic implications of impression management, the underlying determinants remain poorly understood.

Manuscript 2 addresses this gap by proposing that narcissistic CEOs—characterized by an inflated self-perception and low motivation to avoid negative outcomes—are less inclined to utilize impression management strategies for remediation during acquisition announcements compared to less narcissistic counterparts. Additionally, the manuscript explores the moderating effects of public attention directed toward CEOs and the extent of managerial power, two factors highlighted in recent literature as influential in amplifying narcissistic tendencies (Borgholthaus et al., 2023; Cragun et al., 2020). The empirical findings do not indicate a direct relationship between CEO narcissism and overall firm impression management behavior. However, consistent with previous work suggesting that reputation intensifies narcissistic tendencies (Aabo et al., 2022), the analysis reveals that highly narcissistic CEOs with elevated reputational status exhibit an increased propensity to engage in impression management. Supplementary tests further indicate that shareholders' and analysts' assessments of acquisitions remain unaffected by firms' impression management efforts.

Research manuscript 3, "CEO Narcissism and Managerial Obfuscation in Earnings Conference Calls," contributes to the expanding literature examining linguistic narratives as effective tools for impression management. Previous research has consistently demonstrated that variations in corporate communication, such as sentiment, boilerplate language, and euphemisms, significantly influence key stakeholders, including investors (Bushee & Huang, 2024), financial analysts (Lehavy et al., 2011), and rating agencies (Bonsall & Miller, 2017). Addressing ongoing calls for incorporating an upper-echelons perspective, this study specifically explores the link between CEO narcissism and the deliberate use of complex, obfuscatory language in earnings conference calls, recognized as a critical channel through which organizations communicate their current and anticipated performance (Allee, 2015). In contrast to regulatory filings, which typically adhere to standardized formats, earnings conference calls represent dynamic platforms where executives can strategically select information for disclosure and directly respond to stakeholder inquiries (Bae et al., 2023). Recent research underscores that this interactive context is especially conducive to impression management, allowing executives to obscure negative performance disclosures by employing unnecessarily complex language (Amicis et al., 2021; Bushee & Huang, 2024). Drawing on recent psychological insights that narcissistic individuals are inclined toward impression management primarily in image-enhancing rather than image-threatening scenarios (Buyl et al., 2019; Patel & Cooper, 2014), this study hypothesizes a negative association between CEO narcissism and linguistic complexity. Empirical findings partially support this hypothesis, revealing a significant negative relationship between CEO narcissism and linguistic complexity in the Q&A section—but not the presentation segment—of earnings conference calls. The results prove robust to several tests, including alternative specifications of linguistic complexity and a stacked difference-in-differences analysis.

3.2 Research Paradigm

Conducting research within social science does not occur in isolation but is guided by explicit or implicit beliefs regarding the nature of the social world and suitable methodologies for its exploration (Burrel & Morgan, 1979; Lather, 1986; Phoenix et al., 2013). Collectively, these theoretical orientations constitute the research paradigm, serving as the backbone of all scholarly inquiry, with great bearing on the selection of research topics, methodological approaches, and interpretations of research outcomes (Kivunja & Kuyini, 2017; Pretorius, 2024). Guba and Lincoln (1994) underscore the critical importance of paradigms, asserting that: "Paradigm issues are crucial; no inquirer, we maintain, ought to go about the business of inquiry without being clear about just what paradigm informs and guides his or her approach" (p. 116).

Central to the conceptualization of paradigms are underlying philosophical assumptions addressing ontology, epistemology, and methodology (Crotty, 1998; Phoenix et al., 2013; Schnelker, 2006). Ontological assumptions pertain to fundamental beliefs regarding the nature and structure of reality—specifically, whether reality exists objectively, independent of human perceptions, or is socially constructed, emerging from human experiences and interactions (Sugden, 2016). Epistemology addresses the nature and justification of knowledge, focusing on how research is enacted as a situated practice, shaping the researcher's role and their interactions with research subjects (Leavy, 2014). Lastly, methodological assumptions concern the systematic strategies and principles utilized in the pursuit of knowledge. These philosophical assumptions are intrinsically interconnected, as beliefs about the nature of reality (ontology) logically influence assumptions about the nature and scope of knowledge (epistemology), which in turn guide the choice of methodological approaches. Consequently, each research paradigm represents an integrated set of assumptions that consistently directs the design, implementation, interpretation, and applicability of research findings in a cohesive and meaningful manner (Guba & Lincoln, 1994; Schnelker, 2006).

Researchers' adoption of a research paradigm is influenced by socialization within their disciplinary or institutional contexts, shaping their perceptions of which topics are considered important, legitimate, and reasonable to investigate (Phoenix et al., 2013). Aligning with a long-standing tradition in social science research (Guba & Lincoln, 1994), the three manuscripts included in this dissertation adopt a positivist paradigm. Positivism posits that the social world can be objectively examined, and truths about it can be established with a considerable degree of certainty (Brand, 2009; Mackenzie & Knipe, 2006; Mertens, 1998). This paradigm is rooted in the ontological assumption that reality exists independently of human perception and is governed by natural laws and mechanisms. Consequently, research guided by positivism aims to uncover objective truths without relying on subjective interpretations (Scotland, 2012). This reality, perceived as stable and consistent, provides a solid foundation for formulating theories and developing predictive models to explain social phenomena (Pretorius, 2024).

From an epistemological standpoint, positivism emphasizes empirical observation, measurement, and verification as the primary methods for comprehending human behavior, thus viewing these approaches as the only legitimate pathways for knowledge advancement (Comte, 1865; Kivunja & Kuyini, 2017). Additionally, positivist research assumes generalizability, meaning that findings derived in one context can reliably be extended to other contexts through inductive reasoning (Kivunja & Kuyini, 2017). To preserve objectivity and credibility, positivism views the researcher and the research object as independent entities, thereby minimizing the risk of results being influenced by the researcher's personal values or biases (Guba & Lincoln, 1994). Methodologically, positivism mandates rigorous knowledge verification through adherence to the scientific method, employing either analytical techniques for inherently verifiable phenomena (such as mathematical equations) or empirical data collection for concepts not intrinsically verifiable (Brand, 2009; Crotty, 1998). Quantitative methodologies are thus prioritized over qualitative ones, guided by a deductive framework emphasizing hypothesis formulation, systematic testing, and precise, valid measurements of clearly operationalized variables (Easterby-Smith et al., 2012; Leavy, 2014; Phoenix et al., 2013).

Implementing this research approach requires meticulous data collection processes to create robust datasets suitable for empirical analysis. Given that each manuscript relies, to varying extents, on manually collected data unavailable in established databases (e.g., proxy data for CEO narcissism), the sample primarily consists of publicly listed U.S. firms, chosen due to their superior data availability. The structure of these datasets is inherently hierarchical, with lower-level data—such as executive-specific details—nested within higher-level, firm-specific information. Data collection across all manuscripts involved integrating established databases with manual extraction from primary sources, such as firm annual reports, proxy statements, and conference call transcripts. Consistent with established practice in the field (e.g., Bamber et al., 2010; Bertrand & Schoar, 2003; Custódio & Metzger, 2013), firm-level data were primarily sourced from reputable databases, including Compustat for fundamental financial information, LSEG Eikon for M&A, CRSP for stock prices, and IBES for analyst forecasts.

Executive demographic characteristics were gathered using BoardEx and ExecuComp, with cross-validation conducted between databases to ensure accuracy and reliability.

Beyond these common data sources, each manuscript required unique datasets tailored specifically to its research objectives. For instance, Manuscript 1 involved manually extracting CFO shareholdings from firms' annual proxy statements (DEF 14A), while data regarding deal initiators and deal duration were obtained from the "Background of the Merger" sections found in DEFM 14A, PREM 14A, or S-4 filings. Manuscript 2 assessed CEO narcissism through several methods, including manually collecting and categorizing CEO photograph sizes in firm annual reports and analyzing self-referential pronouns in CEO speech transcripts. Additionally, press releases were systematically collected and classified via Nexis Uni to evaluate corporate impression management strategies. In Manuscript 3, earnings conference call transcripts featuring executives and analysts were analyzed to create a proxy measure for the strategic use of obfuscatory language. CEO narcissism in this manuscript was further assessed by manually extracting data from diverse sources, including 10-K reports, DEF 14A proxy statements, and Dow Jones Factiva. Detailed information about the data and their collection processes can be found in the respective manuscripts.

Research Manuscript 1

4

The Impact of Powerful CFOs in M&A: Evidence From U.S. Acquisitions

Abstract

Practitioners and researchers have long been interested in gaining a better understanding of the factors driving Mergers & Acquisitions (M&A) outcomes. While studies are increasingly adopting an upper-echelons perspective in this regard, the role of individual decision-makers, other than the chief executive officer (CEO), remains poorly understood. In this study, we investigate how acquiring companies' chief financial officers (CFOs), who possess greater managerial power to influence crucial decisions in the acquisition process, can affect M&A outcomes. We expect greater decision authority to enable CFOs to contribute valuable financial expertise at different stages of a deal, ultimately enhancing the takeover's overall value creation. Utilizing a large sample of U.S. transactions that occurred from 1996 to 2018, our results suggest that more powerful CFOs improve M&A performance in large deals where shareholders presume CFO financial expertise will be especially valuable. Further analyses of specific mechanisms through which CFOs improve M&A outcomes reveal the importance of distinguishing between the multiple dimensions through which CFOs gain influence in a firm. In this context, we

This chapter is based on the article: Lammers F., & Pape U. (2024). The Impact of Powerful CFOs in M&A: Evidence from U.S. Acquisitions. Review of Managerial Science, 19(6), 1669–1710.
DOI: https://doi.org/10.1007/s11846-024-00803-8. Reproduced with permission from Springer Nature.

Supplementary Information The online version contains supplementary material available at https://doi.org/10.1007/978-3-658-51855-4_4.

F. Lammers, *The Role of Executive Characteristics in Financial Decision-Making*, Studies in Finance and Accounting, https://doi.org/10.1007/978-3-658-51855-4_4

find that CFOs' M&A experience (i.e., their expertise power) is the most persistent dimension of improved deal outcomes, as reduced takeover premiums and lower third-party advisory fees make clear.

4.1 Introduction

Mergers and acquisitions (M&A) are among the most important investment decisions for a company's top management. Representing valuable means for corporate growth, M&A allow companies to realize operating and financial synergies, implement strategic realignment, diversify their line of business, or achieve an increase in market power (Renneboog and Vansteenkiste 2019; Welch et al. 2020). Over the past two decades, U.S. companies have spent nearly $30 trillion in more than 256,000 deals,[1] underscoring the economic importance of the M&A market. Despite their managerial appeal, many acquisitions fail to meet expectations, with some studies indicating failure rates ranging from 70% to 90% (Christensen et al. 2011). In light of their economic importance and substantial number of failures, gaining a better understanding of what drives M&A performance appears crucial. Existing literature has made considerable efforts in this regard, but it still lacks a clear understanding of the factors that determine successful acquisitions (Aktas et al. 2016; DePamphilis 2019; Renneboog and Vansteenkiste 2019). Importantly, while the prevailing discourse utilizes deal-, firm-, or market-level antecedents to explain M&A outcomes (Bertrand and Schoar 2003), research on the influence of individual actors remains scarce and predominantly focuses on chief executive officers (CEOs). Scholars have increasingly raised concerns about the lack of appreciation for the impact of other decision-makers on acquisition outcomes, leading to recurring calls for studies that incorporate the roles of other top management team (TMT) members (Bedard et al. 2014; Han et al. 2016; Wang and Yin 2018). For example, in their comprehensive literature review on M&A research, Welch et al. (2020) note that the majority of studies consider the acquiring firm a single and monolithic entity, concluding that "... it is necessary to carefully dissect the locus of actions and decisions and extend beyond the simplistic assumption of the firm as a unitary actor or of the CEO" (p. 22).

The present study aims to contribute to filling this theoretically and practically important gap by examining the influence of powerful chief financial officers (CFOs) on M&A performance and the mechanisms through which they affect a

[1] See https://imaa-institute.org/mergers-and-acquisitions-statistics/united-states-ma-statistics.

deal's outcome. While CFOs' responsibilities originally centered around finance and accounting activities (Zorn 2004), academics and practitioners increasingly highlight the importance of CFOs' functional role in strategic decision-making, particularly emphasizing their contribution to shaping an organization's acquisition strategy (Agrawal et al. 2020). Since acquisitions involve a large number of finance-related objectives and tasks (Finkelstein 1992), CFOs' finance background presumably enables them to serve as impartial advisors in various deal stages, ultimately preventing CEOs' potential misjudgments (Firk et al. 2023). While we argue that their financial expertise is likely to benefit acquisitions, we acknowledge that CFOs do not exhibit unlimited discretion in their decisions. Rather, we hypothesize that the degree to which their knowledge and advice become evident in M&A outcomes is a function of the managerial power they hold, i.e., their ability to influence crucial decisions during the takeover process. By following Finkelstein's (1992) well-established power framework, we account for the multiple dimensions through which an executive might gain power in a company. We distinguish between prestige power (the number of outside board memberships a CFO holds), ownership power (the percentage of a firm's outstanding shares a CFO owns), expertise power (a CFO's M&A experience), and structural power (a CFO's annual compensation relative to the annual compensation of the firm's most highly paid executive).

We test our predictions utilizing a sample of 2,336 acquisitions by 959 U.S. firms, from 1996 to 2018. Our results suggest that powerful CFOs assist in improving M&A performance in the context of larger deals where their financial expertise is especially crucial. Examining the underlying mechanisms through which CFOs may positively affect M&A performance, we observe notable differences in the predictive ability of each power dimension. On the one hand, our results suggest that CFOs' M&A experience (i.e., their expertise power) is the most consistent predictor of acquisition improvements throughout the deal process. In this context, we document the association of more experienced CFOs with lower takeover premiums paid and lower external advisory fees. On the other hand, focusing on the remaining power dimensions reveals that while the structural and ownership dimensions do not seem to impact M&A, the power that CFOs acquired through the prestige dimension (i.e., number of external board seats) actually shows an association with less favorable deal outcomes. This influence becomes evident in paying higher premiums and an enhanced likelihood of conducting large loss acquisitions. It also aligns with existing research arguing that the responsibilities that accompany multiple directorships affect the quality of managerial oversight (Ahn et al. 2010).

Our specific research contribution to the literature is threefold. First, our paper adds to the M&A literature. To date, a considerable body of literature has examined several factors that influence whether undertaking an acquisition creates or destroys shareholder value.[2] While studies increasingly focus on the role of individual decision-makers and their characteristics in the M&A process, research in this area remains very limited in terms of both quantity and the focus on the CEO as the major unit of analysis. This is striking, given that researchers have consistently emphasized the role of other decision-makers, arguing that CEOs do not exert the sole influence on M&A (El-Khatib et al. 2015; Finkelstein and Hambrick 1990; Welch et al. 2020). We follow the literature's recurrent calls to extend this area of research to other executives (Carpenter et al. 2004; Menz 2012; Welch et al. 2020). Second, our findings contribute to the growing literature in the field of behavioral corporate finance by providing new insights into the impact of directors' personal traits on investment decisions and firms' economic performance. Related evidence indicates that management style influences investment, financing, and other strategic decisions, suggesting that managers' characteristics impact corporate outcomes (Bertrand and Schoar 2003). Most of this evidence is CEO-specific and pertains to personal traits (e.g., Adams et al. 2018; Aktas et al. 2016; Malmendier and Tate 2008), education (e.g., Wang and Yin 2018), or career experience (e.g., Custódio et al. 2013; Custódio and Metzger 2014). We extend this work by examining the effect of the CFO's functional finance background on M&A, arguably one of the most important investment decisions that a company will make. Finally, our study adds to upper-echelons and managerial-power research. Most existing studies rely on composite-index power indices by aggregating several power proxies. This approach tends to create a "black box" phenomenon, limiting the ability to explain the underlying factors driving the results (Finkelstein et al. 2009). Drawing upon the well-established power framework that Finkelstein (1992) proposed, we provide evidence for the importance of distinguishing between various dimensions through which executives gain influence in a company.

[2] See Renneboog and Vansteenkiste (2019) for a comprehensive review of factors leading to failure and success in M&A.

4.2 Theoretical Arguments and Related Literature

4.2.1 Influence of Executives' Characteristics on M&A

The basis of our study is the assumption that executives' decisions influence firms' outcomes (Hambrick 2007; Hambrick and Mason 1984). In their tasks, managers often face an overload of information, ambiguous cues, and competing goals, particularly pertinent to strategic decision-making of the type that acquisitions involve, where the process's complexity and ambiguity commonly result in decision challenges (Carpenter et al. 2004). How managers respond to such challenges and the decisions they ultimately make depend on how they interpret the situation. In turn, their personal characteristics, such as age, education, and functional or career experiences, strongly influence that interpretation (Finkelstein and Hambrick 1990).

A range of empirical literature has documented the notion that individual managers matter for strategic decisions and ultimately, corporate outcomes.[3] In the context of M&A, research indicates that personal traits, such as a director's promotion focus (Gamache et al. 2015), overconfidence (Billett and Qian 2008; Malmendier and Tate 2008), and extraversion (Malhotra et al. 2017), relate to M&A outcomes. Other work suggests that educational paths and career experiences are crucial in shaping acquisitions. For example, Custódio and Metzger (2013) find that bidder CEOs with previous experience in the target's industry negotiate better deals, resulting in a lower takeover premium and higher acquirer deal-announcement returns. Similarly, Field and Mkrtchyan (2017) examine the effect of directors' acquisition experience and find an association between the bidder's board acquisition experience and higher acquisition-announcement returns. Other notable traits include directors' gender (Huang and Kisgen 2013), age (Yim 2013), tenure (Bergh 2001; Zhou et al. 2020), and social networks (El-Khatib et al. 2015; Schmidt 2015).

[3] See Carpenter et al. (2004), Menz (2012), and Welch et al. (2020) for reviews of studies researching the effect of TMTs on organizational outcomes and Wang et al. (2016) for a meta-analysis of studies focusing on the impact of CEO characteristics.

4.2.2 CFOs' Role and Value during Corporate Takeovers

While empirical literature consistently supports the notion that individual managers significantly influence M&A outcomes, research in this area has predominantly focused on the CEO (e.g., Chikh and Filbien 2011; Custódio and Metzger 2013; El-Khatib et al. 2015; Yim 2013). However, the consideration of functional TMT members is crucial (Carpenter et al. 2004; Welch et al. 2020), especially for those who are second in command, such as the CFO. These appointments are made not for their compatibility with the TMT, but rather to compensate for skills and expertise that the CEO lacks in specific functional areas (Hambrick and Cannella, Jr. 2004; Menz 2012; Nath and Vijay 2008). Next to the CEO, the CFO is the most important decision-maker in the company, with "critical say in strategic and operational decisions, [...] often second only to the chief executive officer" (Zorn 2004, p. 347). Consistent with this, research shows that the compensation of chief operating officers (COOs) is declining relative to that of CFOs (Wang 2010), as is the number of S&P and Fortune 500 companies with COOs in place (Neilson 2015). Paralleling this development, several regulatory changes have magnified the importance of the CFO in top management, including the Sarbanes-Oxley Act and its emphasis on a financial expert's role on the board of directors (Venus and Engelen 2012).

Practitioners and researchers have widely recognized the crucial role of financial expertise in the context of acquisitions, which usually involve a substantial number of finance-related objectives and tasks (Agrawal et al. 2020; Fuhrer et al. 2017; Jöhnk et al. 2020). Supporting this notion, empirical studies document associations between executives' finance backgrounds and various acquisition outcomes, including the likelihood of successfully completing deals (Huang et al. 2014), the premium paid (Porrini 2006), and overall acquisition performance (Aktas et al. 2021). As CFOs typically possess the strongest financial background among executives, we argue that their expertise enables them to enhance a company's takeover decisions across the entire process, from deal initiation to closing.

Starting with the target-screening phase, CFOs are likely to add value by defining appropriate screening criteria, assessing potential synergies, and ultimately identifying suitable targets. Thus, they provide important guidance that enables the acquirer to capture the greatest possible value from a deal (Agrawal et al. 2020; Huang et al. 2014). During the subsequent valuation process, CFOs could more effectively utilize tailored valuation techniques, helping the acquirer to conduct more rigorous due diligence (Aktas et al. 2021). This is especially crucial, as failure to conduct proper due diligence might have severe financial consequences for the deal's success (Daley et al. 2024). A CFO's financial expertise will also be particularly beneficial in negotiating finance-related issues of a deal, thereby enabling the firm to better assess the target's potential value (Mukherjee et al. 2004) and, in turn, reducing the risk of overpaying (Huang et al. 2014). Finally, recent literature suggests that the post-acquisition integration of the target plays a pivotal role in acquisition performance (Teerikangas and Thanos 2018). CFOs could leverage their financial expertise by tracking synergy targets and embedding them in financial processes, thereby supporting the acquirer's capturing long-term value from the acquisition (Agrawal et al. 2020; Jöhnk et al. 2020). Taken together, a CFO's multifaceted contributions constitute an indispensable role at every stage of the M&A process, ultimately securing the likelihood of successful outcomes and long-term value creation for the acquiring firm.

While we argue that the CFO's functional finance background benefits acquisition outcomes, we acknowledge that CFOs do not experience unlimited discretion in a firm but that the managerial power they hold determines the degree to which they can contribute valuable knowledge and expertise in the takeover process. Even though executives' power may emerge from personal traits, such as overconfidence (Malmendier and Tate 2008), TMT members' managerial power is most crucial to their ability to influence decisions and outcomes (Chin et al. 2013). Finkelstein refers to this type of power as "[…] the capacity of individual actors to exert their will" (Finkelstein 1992, p. 506), emphasizing that the distribution of TMT power is unlikely to be equal across the team. Expanding on this notion, empirical literature suggests that variations in TMT members' power reflect associations with various corporate outcomes, including compensation (Abernethy et al. 2015; Schmid et al. 2018), board structure (Joseph et al. 2014), financial reporting (Baker et al. 2019), and corporate performance (Adams et al. 2005; Han et al. 2016). In the context of M&A, Firk et al. (2023) observe that CFOs' heightened career concerns have an association with increased acquisition activity, and this relationship is more pronounced when the CFO possesses greater decision-making authority within the firm. Similarly, Agrawal et al. (2020) document that acquirers are more likely to meet targeted revenue and cost synergies when the CFO's involvement in the M&A process is more substantial. Jöhnk et al. (2020) find increased M&A success rates when the company strongly integrates the finance function during the takeover process. In a paper related to ours, Ferris and Sainani (2021) document that in the U.K., firms with more powerful CFOs close deals more frequently, accelerate the deal processing time, and more likely acquire target firms with higher earnings quality. Importantly, notable cultural differences affecting decision-making as well as differing business and legal frameworks that impact M&A outcomes (Aktas et al. 2021; Renneboog and Vansteenkiste 2019) prevent us from applying their findings to the U.S. context.

In summary, existing research has repeatedly shown managerial power to be a critical determinant in the manifestation of managerial attributes and skills in various scenarios. Against this background, we argue that CFOs provide valuable expertise to the acquisition process if they possess a certain degree of decision authority, i.e., managerial power, in the firm. The degree to which CFOs' expertise becomes evident in M&A outcomes is thereby intrinsically tied to their ability to shape critical decisions throughout the deal-making process.

Expanding upon the preceding discussion, we next develop testable hypotheses regarding the influence of CFO expertise on M&A outcomes. We begin by outlining our predictions concerning the impact of influential CFOs on a deal's performance and the moderating role of a deal's size. We then theorize specific mechanisms through which CFOs can potentially influence M&A outcomes.

4.3 Hypotheses Development

4.3.1 Announcement Returns and the Moderating Role of Large Deals

To assess the performance of an acquisition, we analyze acquiring-firm shareholder returns around the announcement of a deal (DePamphilis 2019), which reflect market anticipation regarding the deals' success or failure, i.e., the discounted future cash flows the acquisitions generate (Renneboog and Vansteenkiste 2019). Recall from Sect. 4.2.2 that CFOs' financial expertise is expected to add value at various stages of a deal, assisting the firm in capturing the maximum possible value. Assuming at least semi-strong efficient markets (Fama 1970), we hypothesize that acquiring-firm shareholders will recognize this value-enhancing role of CFOs and perceive the presence of more powerful CFOs in an acquisition as beneficial to the takeover process. We expect this to result in a more positive reaction to the deal announcement, ultimately leading to an increase in acquiring-shareholder wealth effects.

Hypothesis 1 (H1): The degree of power a bidder's CFO holds positively impacts the acquiring company's deal-announcement return.

While we argue that a CFO is likely to exert influence through managerial power, we add that the extent to which the CFO's expertise becomes evident in acquisition outcomes is likely to vary, depending on the deal size. Specifically, we expect the importance of financial expertise to become even more crucial in the context of larger-scale acquisitions, particularly emphasizing CFOs' pivotal role in navigating the complexities inherent in such transactions. First, the difficulty of assessing potential synergistic combinations increases with larger targets, highlighting the importance of financial expertise during the target-screening phase for evaluating the full range of takeover opportunities (Agrawal et al. 2020). Second, as the integration process is more complex for large businesses (Alexandridis et al. 2013), taking over larger targets demands more intricate due diligence and a thorough financial valuation. This will also be of significant value during the subsequent negotiation stage of a deal, given the association of larger targets with enhanced bargaining power (Ahern 2012). Third, researchers have claimed the association of acquiring larger companies with more complex post-merger integration, in light of the heightened challenge of tracking synergy targets and incorporating them into financial procedures (Agrawal et al. 2020; Shrivastava 1986). Finally, acquiring large targets often entails increased disclosure requirements and approvals from regulatory authorities, thus demanding a stronger financial expert advisory (DePamphilis 2019; Golubov et al. 2012).

Empirical evidence suggests that shareholders are aware of the heightened complexity associated with larger targets and the increased difficulty for acquirers of capturing the expected economic benefits, leading to significantly more negative reactions to the announcement of large deals (Alexandridis et al. 2013; Fich et al. 2018). The increased significance of the financial function in large deals leads us to expect the presence of influential CFOs to result in more favorable shareholder reactions than it would in smaller deals. Empirical evidence supports our prediction, demonstrating that the advisory role of financial experts in M&A becomes especially important and visible in larger acquisitions (Huang et al. 2014; Wang and Whyte 2010). On the basis of the preceding discussion, we formulate the following hypothesis regarding the moderating role of deal size on the relationship between powerful CFOs and acquisition performance.

Hypothesis 2 (H2): The impact of a bidder's CFO power on the deal-announcement return of the acquiring company is positively moderated by deal size.

4.3.2 Underlying Mechanisms Through Which CFOs Influence M&A Outcomes

4.3.2.1 Deal Initiation

In the usual presence of asymmetric information between the acquirer and the target, initially expressing interest in a potential business combination may provide the other party with valuable information. Potential bidders can perceive target-initiated deals as a sign of eagerness to sell, consequently strengthening a bidder's bargaining position during negotiations (Aktas et al. 2010). Conversely, the act of a bidder to initiate a deal might cause the target to update forecasts positively regarding potential economic gains (e.g., in the form of synergies the acquirer can achieve), which weakens a bidder's negotiating power (Masulis and Simsir 2018; Simsir 2008).

To better understand the antecedents of deal initiation, literature focusing on the influence of executives' characteristics has identified the functional finance background of executives as a crucial driver of deal initiation (Jensen and Zajac 2004; Palmer and Barber 2001; Song 1982). Executives with a predominant finance background tend to perceive firms as portfolios of assets, not necessarily tied to a single line of business. Consequently, they are more likely to pursue diversification and growth through acquisitions rather than relying solely on organic growth strategies (Hayes and Abernathy 1980; Jensen and Zajac 2004). Since the CFO typically possesses the strongest financial background among executives, we hypothesize that firms with powerful CFOs are more inclined to initiate acquisitions.

Hypothesis 3 (H3): The degree of power a bidder's CFO holds positively impacts the likelihood of bidder-initiated deals.

4.3.2.2 Deal-Process Length

The speed of an acquisition's completion is another mechanism through which powerful CFOs might affect a takeover, with potentially far-reaching consequences for a deal's success. To a certain extent, speed is crucial for minimizing disruption during the process, reducing uncertainty for stakeholders, and allowing less time for competitors to react (Meglio et al. 2017). However, excessively accelerated acquisition momentum may put at risk carefully and rationally considering issues of both strategic and organizational fit (Jemison and Sitkin 1986). While previous studies have found several CEO-related factors impacting the length of the acquisition process, the prediction seems ambiguous in light of the effect of powerful CFOs. On the one hand, influential CFOs' proficiency in finance-related tasks might speed up certain aspects of the deal process, such as target screening and due diligence. Consistent with this argument, existing research shows that the financial expertise of M&A teams relates negatively to a deal's negotiation length (Aktas et al. 2021). An alternative argument is that powerful CFOs may delve into more details and aspects of the deal, thereby slowing down the pace of the process (Song et al. 2013). This would also be consistent with incentivizing executives to carefully consider acquisition-related decisions, given that managers who make value-destroying acquisitions have been found to face a significantly higher probability of being replaced (Lehn and Zhao 2006). Building upon the preceding discussion, we offer a non-directional hypothesis regarding the influence of CFO power on the acquisition process length.

Hypothesis 4 (H4): The degree of power a bidder's CFO holds will positively or negatively impact the process length of a deal.

4.3.2.3 Deal Advisor

CFOs might also add value through mechanisms that relate to an acquisition's transaction costs. In the market for M&A transactions, investment banks often act as financial deal advisors and assist the acquirer in screening potential targets, making initial contact, and utilizing support in the negotiation process, in return for substantial advisory fees (Cai and Sevilir 2012; Chuang 2017; DePamphilis 2019). Significant overlaps between the responsibilities of a deal's financial advisor and those of the CFO suggest that influential CFOs might act as substitutes for the expertise of deal advisors. CFOs are likely to have deeper knowledge of the acquiring firm's business model, financing position, and goals, allowing them to provide more tailored expert advice in such areas as identifying cost-effective financing alternatives and locating targets that best meet the acquirer's strategic objective (Graham et al. 2017). Recent findings by Aktas et al. (2021) support this argument. The authors find that internal M&A teams, rather than external deal advisors, are the main source of value creation, providing crucial assistance throughout various stages. We therefore hypothesize that acquirers with powerful CFOs will be less likely to hire a financial advisor.

Hypothesis 5 (H5): The degree of power a bidder's CFO holds negatively impacts the likelihood of hiring a financial deal advisor.

4.3.2.4 Deal Premium

A frequently cited reason for the acquirers' underperformance in M&A is overpaying the target—that is, paying an excessively high takeover premium (Cai and

Sevilir 2012), leading shareholders to lower their expectations for the value the acquirer captures. Prior work has shown that acquirers often overpay as a result of insufficient synergy anticipation and poor due diligence, ultimately resulting in a target's misvaluation (Daley et al. 2024; DePamphilis 2019). A prominent example is the acquisition of the British software company Autonomy by HP for $42.11 per share, representing a premium of approximately 60% over the market price. Soon after the completion of the acquisition in 2011, serious accounting improprieties that went unnoticed—the result of poor due diligence—forced HP to write down $8.8 billion of Autonomy's value within a year (Meglio et al. 2017). Recall from Sect. 4.2.2 that their functional finance background allows CFOs to conduct more rigorous due diligence and synergy anticipation. Against this background we hypothesize that powerful CFOs can assist acquirers in better estimating the target's value and purchasing it at a lower premium, thereby reducing the risk of overpayment.

Hypothesis 6 (H6): The degree of power that a bidder's CFO holds negatively impacts the acquisition premium paid.

4.3.2.5 Large Loss Deals

Existing literature indicates that the negative abnormal announcement returns that M&A research frequently observes may be attributable to a limited number of deals, such that these few transactions experience exceptionally large losses (Fich et al. 2018; Moeller et al. 2005). While firm and deal characteristics partially explain this phenomenon, studies have repeatedly attributed CEOs' misjudgments regarding the deal's value creation potential to value-destructive deals (Chatterjee and Hambrick 2007; Malmendier and Tate 2008; Shi and Chen 2019). The combination of their financial expertise and deeper involvement in the acquisition process might enable more powerful CFOs to more effectively identify these potential misjudgments. Field and Mkrtchyan (2017) empirically support this argument by documenting the significant role that acquiring-firm directors' financial expertise plays in reducing the likelihood of large loss deals. Due to their substantial influence within the firm, more powerful CFOs may also be more likely to voice their concerns that run counter to the CEO's, thereby mitigating the likelihood of executing value-destructive deals. Therefore, we hypothesize that powerful CFOs will deter their firm from participating in significant loss-generating deals.

Hypothesis 7 (H7): The degree of power a bidder's CFO holds negatively impacts the likelihood of conducting large loss acquisitions.

4.4 Data and Methods

4.4.1 Sample and Data Collection

Our final sample of 2,336 M&A transactions is obtained from Refinitiv Eikon and includes all completed acquisitions announced between January 1, 1996, and December 31, 2018, where both the acquirer and the target were U.S. firms. We apply the standard filters the literature has used and only keep significant transactions with a deal value greater than $1 million. We restrict our sample to transactions that involved transfer of control (i.e., the acquirer must have owned less than 50% prior to the deal announcement and 100% after its completion). The acquiring firm must have been listed; the target firm could be either private or publicly held. Data on CFOs and their characteristics, including information on their job history, come from BoardEx. We identify a company's CFO using the "Individual role" data item and assign to each acquirer in our deal sample the CFO in place at the deal announcement. We exclude deals where multiple CFOs were in place or the CFO also held the CEO position. Executive compensation data come from Standard and Poor's ExecuComp. We obtain data on executives' shareholdings in the acquiring company from acquirers' annual proxy statements (DEF 14 A), using a web-scraping algorithm. Finally, we gather information on firms' financial characteristics from Compustat and take stock return data from the Center for Research in Security Prices (CRSP).

4.4.2 Independent Variables

Numerous studies have emphasized that managerial power is a complex construct encompassing many dimensions, not all of which are easily observable (e.g., Adams et al. 2005; Chin et al. 2013; Florackis and Sainani 2018; Schmid et al. 2018). We aim to account for this multidimensionality by referring to Finkelstein's (1992) well-established framework of managerial power. First, to capture the structural power dimension, we include the pay slice defined as a CFO's annual compensation (Salary + Bonus), divided by the annual compensation of the highest-paid executive, measured in the deal-announcement year. This dimension reflects the hierarchical structure and, thus, the distribution of power among formal positions within the company (Finkelstein 1992). Accordingly, we consider CFOs with a high pay slice to have more power on the board. Second, we gauge the prestige power dimension by the number of board seats outside the acquiring company that a CFO holds at the deal announcement. Prestige power refers to the influence executives have as a result of their reputation and social networks. Prestigious CFOs possess greater legitimacy and cogency, making them especially valuable during the deal-negotiation process (Chikh and Filbien 2011). Moreover, their strong social networks provide access to alternative sources of information and, thus, might constitute a competitive advantage (Haunschild and Beckman 1998). Third, the ownership power dimension is the percentage of common shares the CFO owned. Having significant shareholdings in the company increases CFOs discretion and, in turn, their influence on corporate decisions (Finkelstein et al. 2009; Han et al. 2016). Last, we account for the expertise power dimension by including the CFO's acquisition experience, measured as the number of deals in which a CFO had participated as a manager or director, outside the acquiring company. Task-specific experience increases a manager's ability to cope with the contingencies of a task environment (Finkelstein 1992). As resources for information and advice, CFOs with M&A experience will more likely influence the deal process (Field and Mkrtchyan 2017; Preston et al. 2008).

4.4.3 Dependent Variables

4.4.3.1 Acquisition Performance

To examine the impact of powerful CFOs on the shareholder responses to the deal's announcement, we employ cumulative abnormal returns (CAR), i.e., the sum of daily abnormal returns for a security over a period that captures the influence of the acquisition announcement within that timeframe (Graffin et al. 2016):

$$CAR_t(T_1, T_2) = \sum_{t=T_1}^{T_2} [R_{it} - (a_i + ß_i R_{mt})]$$

Here, R_{it} represents the return of the combined firm i on day t, while R_{mt} denotes the return of the reference market on the same day. a_i is a constant, and $ß_i$ is the beta factor of stock i. T_1 and T_2 refer to the lower and upper bounds of the event window. We compute CAR over a three-day event window [−1, + 1] around the announcement day .[4] We use the CRSP value-weighted index and the Fama and French three-factor model to estimate the market return over a 229-day estimation

[4] Results remained unchanged if we applied a [−2, + 2], [−2, + 1] or [−3, + 3] event window.

window, ending 19 days before the event window. To be included in the sample, each firm must have at least 100 days of stock return data.

4.4.3.2 Large Deal

Following Ferris and Sainani (2021), we assess large deals by creating a dummy variable *Large deal* that equals 1 if an acquisition's value exceeded the median industry deal value in the announcement year of the acquisition, and 0 otherwise.

4.4.3.3 Deal Initiation

Following recent literature on the impact of deal initiation (Fidrmuc and Xia 2019; Masulis and Simsir 2018), we define a dummy variable, *Deal initiation*, that equals 1 if the acquirer initiated the deal, and 0 otherwise. We identify the initiating party of a deal by searching the U.S. Securities and Exchange Commission (SEC) EDGAR database and extracting the information from the "Background of the Merger" section that the DEFM14A, PREM14A, or S-4 filing provide. This background section yields detailed insights into the merger process by offering a chronological description of crucial steps, including information on how executives of the two parties first met, the number of interested bidders, how negotiations proceeded, and the identity of financial advisors. Appendix A in the electronic supplementary material provides examples of bidder-initiated and target-initiated deals.

4.4.3.4 Deal-Process Length

Following Aktas et al. (2016), we define the length of a takeover process as the difference (in months) between the date on which one party initiated the deal and the public announcement date. Information on the process length of a deal appears in the SEC filings' "Background of the Merger" section. In many cases, the SEC filings do not specify the exact day of the initial contact, so we measure the takeover-process length in months rather than days.

4.4.3.5 Deal Advisor

We construct a dummy variable *Deal advisor* equal to 1 if the acquirer hired a financial advisor, and 0 otherwise (Allen et al. 2004).

4.4.3.6 Deal Premium

We calculate the deal premium as the ratio between a bidder's final offer price and the target's stock price 7 days before and, as a robustness test, 42 days before the deal announcement (Custódio et al. 2013). Computing premiums can only apply to public targets, notably reducing our sample size since only 19% of the target firms were publicly listed before their acquisition.

4.4.3.7 Large Loss Deal

We construct a large-loss indicator that took the value of 1 for a deal where shareholders had lost at least 5% of the acquirer's market value within [−1, + 1] days of the announcement of a deal, and 0 otherwise (Fich et al. 2018).

4.4.4 Control Variables

Following existing literature on M&A and TMT members' influence, we control for several firm, deal, and CFO characteristics, to account for possible alternative explanations in our analysis. We lag each control variable one fiscal year prior to the focal acquisition.

4.4.4.1 Firm Controls

Regarding acquiring-firm controls, we incorporate 10 variables in our analyses. Research has found that firm size has influenced various deal outcomes, such as announcement returns (Moeller et al. 2004) and premium paid (Aktas et al. 2016). We include *Firm size* as the logged value of the acquirer's market value of equity at day − 42 relative to the deal announcement date. Leverage has impacted acquisition outcomes, such as the likelihood of being a bidder in completed M&A (El-Khatib et al. 2015) and announcement returns (Belot and Waxin 2019). We incorporate *Leverage* into our analysis, defining it as long-term debt plus debt in current liabilities, divided by the book value of stockholder equity. Previous literature has found that firm performance relates to acquisition activities (Markides 1995). We measure performance using the firm's Return on Assets (*ROA*), i.e., net income divided by the book value of total assets. Empirical evidence suggests that a firm's liquidity (Almeida et al. 2014; Lang 1991) and growth opportunities (Guo et al. 2019; Servaes 1991) affect acquisition behavior. We include *Cash flow* in our models, defining it as income before extraordinary items plus depreciation and amortization, divided by the book value of total assets. We further control for *Cash holdings* as cash and short-term investments, divided by the book value of total assets. We capture a firm's growth opportunities using *Tobin's Q*, the ratio of market to book value of assets. To distinguish between a CFO's acquisition experience and that of the acquiring firm, we include the acquisition experience of the principal firm in a separate control. *No. of deals* is the number of deals in which a firm had participated within the 10 years prior to the announcement of a sample deal. Research has found that a bidder's stock price run-up explains differences in M&A outcomes, such as the probability of conducting large-loss acquisitions (Field and Mkrtchyan 2017). We define *Run-up* as the acquirer's buy-and-hold abnormal returns (BHAR) during the period (−230, −11).

4.4.4.2 Acquisition Controls

We incorporate six acquisition control variables that research has frequently found to impact M&A outcomes. Bidder shareholders tend to react more negatively when the target is a publicly listed company (Chang 1998). *Target listing* equals the value of 1 if the target was publicly traded, and 0 if not. Prior studies found that the form of payment affects merger outcomes (Fuller et al. 2002). We include *Cash deal* (*Stock deal*), taking the value 1 if the acquisition was financed entirely with cash (stock) and, otherwise, equaling 0. Moreover, existing literature indicates that industry-relatedness influences acquisition outcomes, including announcement returns (Renneboog and Vansteenkiste 2019), as well as the duration of the deal process (Meglio et al. 2017). We implement a dummy variable, *Diversifying deal*, taking the value of 1 if the acquirer and target had different Fama-French 12-industry classifications, and 0 otherwise. In our analysis of the factors influencing the duration of a deal's process, we also control for the presence of termination fees, recognizing their potential influence on the speed of the acquisition process. *Termination fee* equals 1 if the parties agreed upon termination fees, and 0 otherwise. Finally, we control for *Relative deal size*, measured as the deal's transaction value divided by the firm size of the acquirer (Ahern 2012).

4.4.4.3 CFO Controls

We further incorporate six controls to capture effects that related to CFO characteristics. Studies have associated an executive's age and gender with acquisition outcomes (Huang et al. 2014; Huang and Kisgen 2013). Therefore, we include *Age*, i.e., the CFO's age at the time of the deal announcement, and *Gender*, equaling 1 if the CFO was male and 0 if female. Existing literature indicates that executives' educational background influences acquisition performance (Haunschild et al. 1999; Iskandar-Datta and Shekhar 2020). We include *CPA* (*MBA*) as a binary variable, equaling 1 if the CFO held a Certified Public Accountant (Master of Business Administration) degree at the time of the deal announcement, and 0 otherwise. Given the influence of executives' tenure on deal outcomes, such as performance and target choice (Zhou et al. 2020), we utilize *Tenure*, measuring the number of years a CFO had been in place at the time of a deal announcement. Finally, we include *Board membership*, taking the value of 1 if the CFO was a member of the acquirer's board, and 0 otherwise.

4.4.4.4 CEO Controls

Finally, we account for governance-related characteristics that studies have shown to have impacted acquisitions. We include *CEO duality*, a dummy variable equaling 1 if the CEO is also the chairman of the board (Chikh and Filbien 2011; El-Khatib et al. 2015), and *Board size*, the number of directors on the acquiring firm's board (Demirtaş 2017).

4.4.5 Estimation

To measure the effect of CFO power on the acquisition performance (H1), we estimate the following ordinary least squares (OLS) regression model:

$$\begin{aligned} CAR[-1,+1]_{it} = {} & \beta_0 + \beta_1 PaySlice_{it} + \beta_2 BoardSeats + \beta_3 M\&AExperience_{it} \\ & + \beta_4 Ownership_{it} + \beta_5 FirmControls_{it} + \beta_6 AcquisitionControls_{it} \\ & + \beta_7 CFOControls_{it} + \beta_8 CEOControls_{it} + \beta_9 Industry_i + \beta_{10} Time_t + \varepsilon_{it} \end{aligned}$$

where $CAR[-1,+1]_{it}$ is the cumulative abnormal returns to combined firm i on day t. $PaySlice_{it}$, $BoardSeats_{it}$, $M\&AExperience_{it}$, and $Ownership_{it}$ represent the set of power proxies. $FirmControls_{it}$, $AcquisitionControls_{it}$, $CEOControls_{it}$, and $CFOControls_{it}$ refer to the respective control variables that Sect. 4.4.4 describes. To test the moderating role of a deal's size (H2), we interact the variable Large deal with our four power proxies. We include Fama and French 12-industry ($Industry_i$) and year dummies ($Time_t$) in all models.

The models we use to test the underlying mechanisms vary, depending on the dependent variable. We employ logistic regression to assess the influence of CFO power on the probability of deal initiation (H3), hiring a financial advisor (H5), and executing large loss deals (H7). To examine the impact on deal-process length (H4) and deal premium (H6), we utilize OLS regression. Standard errors are clustered at firm level.

4.5 Results

4.5.1 Descriptive Statistics

Panel A of Table 4.1 presents the distribution of our M&A sample across industries, on the basis of the Fama and French 12-industry classification system. Consistent with Cai and Sevilir (2012), most acquisitions in our sample occur in the business equipment industry, followed by the finance sector. The utilities and telecom industries are the least active in terms of the number of acquisitions. A closer look at the power variables reveals that on average, CFOs in the utility industry have the largest number of additional board seats but hold the lowest percentage of stocks. We also find that CFOs' M&A experience is especially pronounced in the business equipment industry. Overall, Panel A suggests that the power of CFOs across all dimensions do not cluster within a specific industry.

Panel B of Table 4.1 reports additional summary statistics of our power measurements as well as for dependent and control variables. A tabulated list of the variable definitions is provided in Table 4.1 of Appendix A in the electronic supplementary material. On average, a CFO in our sample has gained M&A experience in one prior acquisition, whereas 10% of the CFOs have been involved in four or more deals in their professional career. In contrast to the findings that Ferris and Sainani (2021) presented, our observations reveal that the majority of CFOs did not hold directorships in other companies, with only 5% served on the board of the acquiring company, underscoring the notable differences between U.K. and U.S. board structures. At the deal announcement, the average CFO was 50.7 years old and had served 3.2 years as CFO in the acquiring company. Turning to deal-specific characteristics, we observe that the average deal value amounted to 10% of the acquirer's market capitalization, and one out of four was a diversifying deal. Half of the targets in our sample, 19% of which were public firms, were exclusively paid with cash. Table 4.2 of Appendix A in the electronic supplementary material presents Pearson's correlation coefficients for our list of variables. We addressed concerns regarding potential multicollinearity by examining the Variance Inflation Factors (VIF) for our models. Most of our variables have VIF well below the accepted threshold of 10 (Cohen et al. 2002), with a mean VIF of 2, indicating that multicollinearity does not appear to be a significant issue in interpreting the parameter estimates in our models.

Table 4.1 Summary statistics

Panel A: Sample distribution by industry

		Means			
Fama and French 12- industry classification	Obs.	Pay slice	No. of board seats	M&A experience	Ownership
Consumer Nondurables	71	0.44	0.25	0.54	0.26
Consumer Durables	33	0.56	0.30	1.21	0.19
Manufacturing	237	0.47	0.22	0.84	0.27
Energy Products	66	0.44	0.35	0.38	0.20
Chemicals Products	50	0.47	0.18	0.96	0.23
Business Equipment	855	0.56	0.47	1.38	0.26
Telecom	32	0.56	0.31	0.66	0.25
Utilities	32	0.48	1.03	0.59	0.08
Wholesale and Retail	131	0.50	0.25	0.57	0.35
Healthcare	262	0.50	0.39	1.01	0.30
Finance	298	0.52	0.30	0.46	0.19
Other	269	0.52	0.29	1.14	0.24

Panel B: Sample summary statistics

				Percentiles		
Variable	Obs.	Mean	SD	10th	Median	90th
Pay slice	2336	0.52	0.18	0.32	0.51	0.75
No. of board seats	2336	0.37	0.77	0	0	1
M&A experience	2336	1.01	2.29	0	0	4
Ownership	2336	0.25	0.38	0	0.12	0.66
CAR	2336	0.08	5.12	−5.27	0.14	5.65
Large deal	2336	0.50	0.50	0	0	1
Deal premium (7 days)	399	0.37	0.36	0.04	0.29	0.81

(continued)

Table 4.1 (continued)

Deal premium (42 days)	398	0.42	0.39	0.05	0.34	0.82
Large loss deal	1136	0.11	0.31	0	0	1
Deal initiation	330	0.58	0.49	0	1	1
Deal process length	342	5.51	4.11	2	4	12
Deal advisor	2336	0.32	0.47	0	0	1
Firm size	2336	21.71	1.67	19.78	21.43	24.05
Leverage	2336	0.18	0.17	0	0.15	0.40
ROA	2336	0.05	0.08	−0.01	0.06	0.14
Cash flow	2336	0.09	0.09	0.01	0.09	0.18
Cash holdings	2336	0.19	0.19	0.02	0.13	0.49
Tobin's Q	2336	2.50	2.11	1.07	1.86	4.30
No. of deals	2336	6.34	10.18	1	4	13
Run-up	2336	0.14	0.46	−0.27	0.05	0.64
CEO duality	2336	0.52	0.51	0	1	1
Board size	2336	9.18	2.40	6	9	12
Relative deal size	2336	0.10	0.17	0	0.03	0.25
Target listing	2336	0.19	0.39	0	0	1
Cash deal	2336	0.53	0.50	0	1	1
Stock deal	2336	0.23	0.42	0	0	1
Diversifying deal	2336	0.25	0.43	0	0	1
Age	2336	50.74	6.50	42	51	59
Gender	2336	0.92	0.27	1	1	1
CPA	2336	0.49	0.50	0	0	1
MBA	2336	0.49	0.50	0	0	1
Tenure	2336	3.22	2.97	0.42	2.39	7.18
Board membership	2336	0.05	0.22	0	0	0

4.5.2 CFO Influence on Acquisition Performance

Model 1 in Table 4.2 presents multivariate regression results, including only control variables, with CAR as the dependent variable. Most of the controls have the expected sign but do not differ significantly from zero. One exception is the listing status of the target, significant at the 1% level. Accordingly, the market reacts less favorably to the announcement of an acquisition when the target is public rather than private. In Model 2, we include CFO power measures and control variables. Consistent with Ferris and Sainani (2021), none of the power coefficients is statistically significant, indicating that powerful CFOs do not generally improve acquisition performance by increasing shareholder wealth effects around the deal's announcement. Therefore, we reject Hypothesis 1.

To consider the possibility that the market does not fully incorporate some CFO effects until later (Huang et al. 2014), we further examine the relationship between CFO power and the long-term post-acquisition stock performance, by computing BHAR from one month before the announcement of a deal to 24 months after its completion. This approach is also more suitable for capturing CFOs' influence on the post-merger integration phase of the deal, which usually takes several years to complete (Teerikangas and Thanos 2018). We follow Hirshleifer et al. (2009), calculating the BHAR as the difference between the two-year buy-and-hold return of the bidding firm and that of a benchmark portfolio designed to measure the firm's post-acquisition expected return:

$$BHAR[-1,24]_i = \prod_{j=t-1}^{t+24} (1 + R_{ij}) - \prod_{j=t-1}^{t+24} (1 + R_{pj})$$

where t is the month in which the acquirer i announced the focal acquisition, R_{ij} is the return of acquirer i, and R_{pj} is the return on a size and book-to-market matching portfolio in month j. In the month preceding an acquisition, we match each of the acquiring firms in our sample with one of 25 equally weighted portfolios formed on the New York Stock Exchange (NYSE) size and book-to-market quintiles, using the bidder's market equity and book-to-market ratio, measured as book equity[5] from the last fiscal year, divided by the market equity for the previous December. We exclude deals in which the minimum number of monthly

[5] In accordance with Fama and French (1993), we calculate book equity as the book value of stockholder's equity, plus balance sheet deferred taxes and investment tax credit, minus the book value of preferred stock. Depending on availability, we use the redemption, liquidation, or par value (in that order) to estimate the book value of preferred stock.

return observations is unavailable (e.g., due to an acquirers' delisting). Model 3 of Table 4.2 presents estimation results. We observe that the coefficient of the CFO's M&A experience is significantly positive, indicating that the effect of experienced CFOs might not manifest until later deal stages. This finding echoes Teerikangas and Thanos (2018), documenting the crucial role of the finance function in capturing value during the post-acquisition phase.

We next examine the moderating effect of a deal's size on the market reaction (Hypothesis 2), by interacting the variable *Large deal* with our CFO power measures in Model 4. Consistent with Hypothesis 2, the positive and significant coefficient on *M&A experience x Large deal* suggests that the market values experienced CFOs in cases where the deal is of particular economic relevance for the acquirer. For large deals, the predicted announcement returns are 0.18 percentage points higher for each acquisition in which a CFO has previously participated. The effect is also significant in an economic sense. Based on the mean bidder market value of $13.5 billion, one additional deal in which the CFO has gained acquisition experience translates into a $24 million gain in shareholder value. As a robustness test, we assess the size of a deal using the continuous *Relative deal size* variable (Ahern 2012; Ahn et al. 2010; Aktas et al. 2010) and observe similar results.

Because our results suggest that the expertise power dimension (i.e., acquisition experience) primarily drives the effect of CFOs on acquisition performance, one could argue that it is not the CFO-specific M&A experience but rather executives' acquisition experience in general that benefits a deal. In that case, we would expect to observe similar effects in the acquisition experience of the acquirer's CEO. We explore this possibility by including the number of deals in which a CEO has participated as a manager or director outside the acquiring company in Model 5 of Table 4.2. The insignificant coefficient of the CEO's M&A experience provides further evidence that it is not merely general acquisition experience that holds importance, but rather the specific M&A expertise attributable to the CFO.

Table 4.2 Regressions of acquirers' CAR and BHAR. Robust standard errors in parentheses. *** p<0.01, ** p<0.05, * p<0.1

	(1) CAR	(2) CAR	(3) CAR	(4) CAR	(5) CAR
CFO power					
Pay slice		−0.153	0.047	−0.832	−0.694
		(0.696)	(0.095)	(0.935)	(1.049)
No. of board seats		−0.059	−0.009	0.034	0.010
		(0.194)	(0.022)	(0.238)	(0.251)
M&A experience		0.047	0.017***	−0.103	−0.081
		(0.058)	(0.006)	(0.078)	(0.099)
Ownership		0.560	0.079	0.662	0.749
		(0.377)	(0.054)	(0.431)	(0.489)
Deal size					
Large deal				−0.545	−0.496
				(0.750)	(0.795)
Pay slice x Large deal				1.439	1.417
				(1.319)	(1.396)
No. of board seats x Large deal				−0.197 (0.262)	−0.092 (0.271)
M&A experience x Large deal				0.281*** (0.101)	0.264** (0.115)
Ownership x Large deal				−0.280	−0.562
				(0.633)	(0.687)
Acquirer controls					
CEO M&A experience					−0.006
					(0.025)
CEO M&A experience x Large deal					−0.044 0.048
Firm size	−0.063	−0.014	−0.033**	−0.074	0.003
	(0.114)	(0.121)	(0.015)	(0.131)	(0.136)

(continued)

Table 4.2 (continued)

	(1) CAR	(2) CAR	(3) CAR	(4) CAR	(5) CAR
Leverage	0.238	0.163	−0.017	0.012	0.443
	(0.746)	(0.748)	(0.112)	(0.738)	(0.793)
ROA	−2.705	−3.071	−0.273	−2.968	−1.894
	(4.529)	(4.556)	(0.709)	(4.538)	(4.661)
Cash flow	5.069	5.479	0.690	5.336	3.847
	(4.212)	(4.227)	(0.666)	(4.213)	(4.420)
Cash holdings	−0.769	−0.779	0.043	−0.706	−1.183
	(0.818)	(0.827)	(0.100)	(0.832)	(0.887)
Tobin's Q	−0.146	−0.151	−0.008	−0.156*	−0.138
	(0.093)	(0.094)	(0.011)	(0.094)	(0.096)
No. of deals	0.015*	0.015	0.003***	0.016*	0.010
	(0.009)	(0.009)	(0.001)	(0.009)	(0.009)
Run-up	0.129	0.120	0.042	0.144	−0.141
	(0.340)	(0.340)	(0.040)	(0.341)	(0.377)
CEO duality	−0.263	−0.313	0.047	−0.317	−0.332
	(0.221)	(0.224)	(0.034)	(0.224)	(0.248)
Board size	−0.021	−0.012	0.001	−0.008	−0.010
	(0.057)	(0.058)	(0.009)	(0.058)	(0.065)
Acquisition controls					
Target listing	−1.266***	−1.249***	0.040	−1.246***	−1.227***
	(0.314)	(0.314)	(0.041)	(0.318)	(0.335)
Cash deal	0.392	0.401	0.010	0.369	0.437
	(0.269)	(0.270)	(0.032)	(0.271)	(0.306)
Stock deal	−0.183	−0.197	−0.058	−0.282	−0.159
	(0.357)	(0.361)	(0.048)	(0.362)	(0.399)
Diversifying deal	−0.118	−0.109	−0.036	−0.137	−0.203
	(0.257)	(0.256)	(0.034)	(0.257)	(0.282)
Relative deal size	0.709	0.713	0.032	0.337	−0.205
	(1.156)	(1.154)	(0.108)	(1.232)	(1.310)

(continued)

Table 4.2 (continued)

	(1) CAR	(2) CAR	(3) CAR	(4) CAR	(5) CAR
CFO controls					
Age	0.007	0.005	−0.003	0.005	−0.019
	(0.018)	(0.018)	(0.003)	(0.018)	(0.020)
Gender	0.169	0.145	−0.080	0.145	0.460
	(0.411)	(0.409)	(0.058)	(0.405)	(0.406)
CPA	0.182	0.197	−0.013	0.188	0.270
	(0.250)	(0.249)	(0.037)	(0.249)	(0.270)
MBA	0.052	0.050	−0.016	0.042	0.064
	(0.249)	(0.249)	(0.035)	(0.249)	(0.275)
Tenure	−0.033	−0.045	−0.001	−0.047	0.015
	(0.038)	(0.039)	(0.006)	(0.039)	(0.041)
Board membership	0.464	0.256	−0.141*	0.249	1.045*
	(0.598)	(0.602)	(0.073)	(0.612)	(0.599)
Constant	3.916	2.943	0.825**	4.723	4.136
	(2.946)	(3.129)	(0.401)	(3.352)	(3.272)
Observations	2,336	2,336	1,882	2,336	1,950
Adjusted R-squared	0.041	0.043	0.064	0.048	0.059

4.5.3 Robustness Tests

Our results thus far suggest that shareholders value the M&A expertise of CFOs in large deals. However, this evidence could also be consistent with alternative explanations. To ensure the robustness of our conclusions, in the subsequent sections we address concerns regarding sample selection bias and the potential influence of omitted variables.

4.5.3.1 Propensity Score Matching

Analyzing the effect of executives' characteristics on corporate outcomes commonly raises an important concern, namely, the potential for sample selection bias, due to the fact that managers are not randomly allocated to firms. To estimate the causal effect of powerful CFOs on the CAR, we would ideally like to randomly assign some acquirers to have high-power CFOs and others to have low-power CFOs (Reeb et al. 2012). In reality, CFOs are unlikely to be matched randomly with firms; the board of directors appoints them on the basis of specific criteria (Bertrand and Schoar 2003). Consequently, unobserved firm and/or CFO characteristics correlated with both the CAR of an acquisition and our power variables, ultimately leading to biased findings. To account for this selection bias, we follow a propensity score matching approach (Rosenbaum and Rubin 1983) and create a control group (acquirer with low-power CFO in place) and a treatment group (acquirer with high-power CFO in place) from our sample, ensuring that both groups have similarly large numbers of observable characteristics. This balance allows us to attribute observed differences in outcomes to the effect of the treatment (i.e., having a high-power CFO) vs. control (i.e., having a low-power CFO), rather than differences in covariates (Rubin 2001).

We begin by converting our four continuous power variables into dummy variables that take the value of 1 for observations greater than the industry-year median, and 0 otherwise. We construct a high-power indicator that takes the value of 1 if the sum of the four power dimension dummies exceeds the industry-year median, and 0 otherwise. We then estimate a first-stage logistic regression to calculate the likelihood (i.e., the propensity score) that a firm had a powerful CFO in place, using observable CFO and firm characteristics. In the second stage, we use the propensity scores to match each treatment observation with a control observation, based on the nearest-neighbor matching technique without replacement. We apply a covariate balance test to ensure that the treatment and control groups are similar in terms of observable characteristics. The results appear in Panel A of Table 4.3 in Appendix A of the electronic supplementary material. We observe that the standardized difference for each covariate is below the acceptable threshold of 0.25 (Imbens and Wooldridge 2009), indicating negligible differences in covariates between the treatment and control groups. In Panel B of Table 4.3, we re-run analyses (2) and (4) from Table 4.2 on the matched sample, which produces estimates of the treatment effect (i.e., having a high-power CFO in place), independent of differences in the distribution between the control and the treatment group (Yim 2013). The coefficients of both Models 1 and 2 are consistent with the evidence of our baseline regression, mitigating the concern that endogenous CFO-matching is driving our findings.

4.5.3.2 Instrumental Variable Approach

Furthermore, we adopt an instrumental variable approach in a two-stage least squares framework to ensure that other unobserved sources of variation do not drive our results. We focus on finding suitable instruments for the M&A experience of CFOs because expertise power is the most consistent dimension in our baseline specification. We utilize the instruments that Field and Mkrtchyan (2017) employ, potentially fulfilling the conditions of relevance (i.e., correlated with a CFO's M&A experience) and exogeneity (i.e., influence a deal's announcement

CAR only through its effect on the CFO's M&A experience) (Bastardoz et al. 2023; Roberts and Whited 2013; Stock and Watson 2020). The first instrument is the number of serial acquirers that a CFO has previously served as a manager or director. We conjecture that CFOs who were employed by serial acquirers have more acquisition experience, with no plausible direct effect on the CAR of a deal. Following Field and Mkrtchyan (2017), we classify a company as a serial acquirer if it has conducted at least three acquisitions within the 10 years since the previous CFO had left the firm. For our second instrument, we measure the number of urban firms that a CFO has previously served in the role of manager or director, within the 10 years since the announcement of a deal.[6] Given that previous literature confirms that firms in urban areas exhibit greater acquisition activity (Cai et al. 2016; Field and Mkrtchyan 2017), it appears reasonable to assume that CFOs affiliated with firms in urban areas have more M&A experience. However, the number of urban firms in which a manager has previously worked is unlikely to directly correlate with the announcement returns of a deal that the manager's employer at the time had made. The regression results appear in Table 4.4 of Appendix A in the electronic supplementary material. In the first stage, we examine the empirical association between a CFO's M&A experience and our instruments. The coefficient of the number of urban firms that a CFO has served is not statistically significant, suggesting that this construct is not a valid instrument for our analysis. Therefore, we exclude it from further analysis. The number of serial acquirers is highly significant and positively related to the CFO's M&A experience, thereby fulfilling the condition of relevance. Models 2 and 3 present the second-stage regression results with the CAR as the dependent variable. The coefficient of *M&A experience x Large deal* remains significant at the 5% level. In summary, these results are consistent with our baseline findings that the M&A experience of CFOs positively relates to the acquirer's CAR in complex acquisitions.

4.5.3.3 Firm Fixed Effects

Although we consider several characteristics that impact acquisition outcomes, other omitted characteristics might show associations with both M&A outcomes and a CFO's influence in a firm. Our main concern relates to omitted unobservable acquirer characteristics that have the potential to bias our findings. We account for this possibility by conducting an analysis with firm fixed effects, allowing us to control for time-invariant effects at the acquirer level. We

[6] We classify a firm as being urban if its headquarters is in one of the ten largest U.S. metropolitan regions, namely, New York, Los Angeles, Chicago, Washington/Baltimore, San Francisco, Philadelphia, Boston, Detroit, Dallas, and Houston (Field and Mkrtchyan 2017).

iteratively drop singleton observations, i.e., acquiring firms that did not conduct at least two acquisitions in our sampling period.[7] This approach allows us to compare deals executed by the same acquirer but with varying degrees of CFO influence, thereby enabling us to control for time-invariant firm-level characteristics. This narrowed our sample for this analysis to 1,888 deals made by 511 acquirers. The results of the fixed-effects model appear in Table 4.5 of Appendix A in the electronic supplementary material. Model 1 refers to the baseline specification and demonstrates that the initial results remain unchanged. In Model 2, we repeat the analysis, including our proxy for large deals. The coefficient on the *M&A experience x Large deal* interaction remains positive and significant at the 5% level. Altogether, the findings hold, suggesting that unobserved firm characteristics are unlikely to bias the estimated effect of CFO power.

4.5.3.4 Additional Robustness Test

Existing studies emphasize the unique nature of firms operating in the financial industry with respect to their financial statements and stringent regulations (Masulis and Simsir 2018). To mitigate the risk that factors related to these differences might bias our findings, we excluded all finance firms according to the Fama-French 12 industry classification system. The results of untabulated analysis corroborate the findings from our main analysis.

4.5.4 Underlying Mechanisms

4.5.4.1 Deal Initiation

Table 4.3 displays the results of the logit regression analysis for our deal initiation estimation, where the dependent variable is 1 if the acquirer initiated the deal and 0 otherwise. Surprisingly, the significant coefficient of *Ownership* suggests that firms whose CFO gained more influence due to increased shareholdings in the firm are less likely to initiate an acquisition. This finding contradicts previous scholars who indicated that executives with functional finance backgrounds more actively seek growth through acquisitions (Jensen and Zajac 2004). One potential explanation could be that CFOs with significant stakes in the firm are more prone to experience personal consequences, such as wealth loss or job displacement, in the event of underperforming acquisitions (Lehn and Zhao 2006). Because of their expertise in finance, influential CFOs may possess a heightened awareness of the financial risks of acquisitions, and the high failure rate prevents them from participating in M&A.

---

[7] Singleton observations do not impact coefficient estimates but might bias standard errors, which could lead to incorrect inferences (Correia 2015).

Table 4.3 Regression of the likelihood of deal initiation by the acquirer. Robust standard errors in parentheses. *** p<0.01, ** p<0.05, * p<0.1

	P(Deal initiation)
CFO power	
Pay slice	1.065
	(1.128)
No. of board seats	0.917
	(0.179)
M&A experience	0.952
	(0.113)
Ownership	0.240**
	(0.155)
Acquirer controls	
Firm size	0.891
	(0.153)
Leverage	0.433
	(0.732)
ROA	1.182**
	(0.093)
Cash flow	0.000**
	(0.000)
Cash holdings	2.693
	(3.208)
Tobin's Q	1.404*
	(0.273)
No. of deals	1.018
	(0.028)
Run-up	1.288
	(0.636)
CEO duality	1.730
	(0.663)
Board size	1.087
	(0.088)

(continued)

Table 4.3 (continued)

	P(Deal initiation)
Target controls	
Firm size	1.227
	(0.175)
Leverage	12.273*
	(16.100)
ROA	0.015
	(0.093)
Cash flow	1.049
	(0.064)
Cash holdings	0.493
	(0.531)
Tobin's Q	0.870
	(0.196)
CFO controls	
Age	1.012
	(0.028)
Gender	0.588
	(0.394)
CPA	0.948
	(0.313)
MBA	0.685
	(0.270)
Tenure	1.040
	(0.061)
Board membership	1.890
	(1.405)
Constant	0.845
	(3.744)
Observations	250
Adjusted R-squared	0.239

4.5.4.2 Deal-Process Length

In Table 4.4 we assess the potential impact of powerful CFOs on the takeover-process length. The coefficients on our power variables are not significantly different from zero, suggesting that powerful CFOs neither escalate nor de-escalate the momentum of a takeover process. We therefore reject Hypothesis 4. Our finding contradicts the results that Ferris and Sainani (2021) obtain, which indicate that influential CFOs tend to accelerate the deal process. This might be due to differently assessing the duration of the transaction process. Ferris and Sainani (2021) define the deal completion time as the number of days between the deal announcement and completion. This approach is likely to underestimate the true length of the deal process because the public announcement of a deal typically occurs only after the involved parties have reached a substantial level of agreement. Consequently, critical deal steps that occur prior to the public announcement of the deal and are likely to be the CFO's responsibility (e.g., financial due diligence) are not captured. Notably, the coefficient of the board membership variable, also widely used to assess a manager's structural power dimension (e.g., Baker et al. 2019; Bedard et al. 2014; Ferris and Sainani 2021), is statistically significant at the 5% level. The marginal effect of having the CFO on the board is associated with a takeover process that is three months longer.

Table 4.4 Regression of the deal-process length. Robust standard errors in parentheses. *** p<0.01, ** p<0.05, * p<0.1

	Deal-process length
CFO power	
Pay slice	−0.897
	(1.662)
No. of board seats	0.483
	(0.409)
M&A experience	−0.034
	(0.160)
Ownership	1.406
	(1.259)
Acquirer controls	
Firm size	−0.190
	(0.321)
Leverage	0.067
	(1.986)

(continued)

Table 4.4 (continued)

	Deal-process length
ROA	2.100
	(13.599)
Cash flow	0.343
	(13.298)
Cash holdings	1.112
	(1.928)
Tobin's Q	−0.112
	(0.224)
No. of deals	0.023
	(0.032)
Run-up	0.571
	(0.968)
CEO duality	−0.931
	(0.621)
Board size	−0.016
	(0.149)
Target controls	
Firm size	−0.260
	(0.281)
Leverage	0.152
	(1.388)
ROA	−1.070
	(8.861)
Cash flow	2.483
	(8.300)
Cash holdings	−1.694
	(1.777)
Tobin's Q	0.046
	(0.281)
Acquisition controls	
Relative deal size	0.539
	(1.859)

(continued)

Table 4.4 (continued)

	Deal-process length
Cash deal	−0.937
	(1.000)
Stock deal	−0.203
	(0.852)
Diversifying deal	0.745
	(1.024)
Termination fee	−1.388
	(0.964)
CFO controls	
Age	0.130***
	(0.046)
Gender	−0.348
	(1.096)
CPA	0.361
	(0.640)
MBA	0.575
	(0.658)
Tenure	−0.059
	(0.101)
Board membership	3.176**
	(1.493)
Constant	3.993
	(6.404)
Observations	259
Adjusted R-squared	0.316

4.5.4.3 Deal Advisor

We next examine the influence of powerful CFOs on the likelihood of hiring a financial deal advisor (Hypothesis 5). Model 1 of Table 4.5 displays logistic regression results where the dependent variable equals 1 if the acquirer hired a financial deal advisor, and 0 otherwise. We find that larger acquirers and those with greater liquidity are more likely to hire financial advisors for their acquisition. Moreover, larger deals and those involving listed targets exhibit a higher probability that a financial advisor would participate. Consistent with Hypothesis 5, we observe that firms with more M&A-experienced CFOs in place are less likely to hire a financial deal advisor. This suggests that the acquisition experience of CFOs serves as a substitute for the knowledge and assistance that financial deal advisors typically provide.

To gain a deeper understanding of the relationship between CFO power and the choice of financial deal advisors, we next examine whether powerful CFOs influence the quality of the hired advisor as well as the advisory fees paid. In line with M&A advisor literature (e.g., Bao and Edmans 2011; Chuang 2017), we utilize Refinitiv Eikon league tables to assess the quality of an advisor. We follow Golubov et al. (2012) and classify the top eight investment banks by the value of deals on which they advised for a focal deal-year as top-tier, with the remaining financial advisors being non-top-tier. We create a dummy variable that takes a value of 1 if the deal financial advisor was a top-tier advisor, and 0 otherwise. Model 2 of Table 4.5 illustrates the impact of our CFO power dimensions on the likelihood of hiring a top-tier financial advisor. While we document the significantly higher likelihood of retaining a top-tier advisor if the acquirer has an experienced CFO, the acquiring firm's M&A experience alone has the opposite effect, suggesting that CFOs might value the expertise of prestigious deal advisors more than the firm does. There is no evidence of a relationship between the advisor's quality and the remaining three power dimensions, confirming the outstanding role of the CFO's acquisition experience that the previous analyses suggested.

Model 3 in Table 4.5 presents the effect of our four power measurements on the fees the acquiring firm pays to financial advisors. We find that a CFO's M&A experience relates negatively to the financial advisor costs. Overall, these results suggest that CFOs can influence the outcome of a deal through their expertise power dimensions, particularly by hiring more prestigious deal advisors while, at the same time, being able to secure their services for lower fees.

Table 4.5 Regressions of financial advisor characteristics. Coefficient estimates of Model 1 and Model 2 are presented as odds ratios. Robust standard errors in parentheses. *** p<0.01, ** p<0.05, * p<0.1

	(1) P(Deal advisor)	(2) P(Top-tier advisor)	(3) Advisor fee
CFO power			
Pay slice	1.192	1.672	−0.229
	(0.536)	(0.992)	(0.335)
No. of board seats	1.056	0.825	0.094
	(0.107)	(0.111)	(0.099)
M&A experience	0.931**	1.156***	−0.053*
	(0.031)	(0.059)	(0.028)
Ownership	0.707	0.683	0.206
	(0.162)	(0.253)	(0.130)
CFO controls			
Age	0.995	0.987	0.004
	(0.012)	(0.017)	(0.009)
Gender	0.900	1.562	0.033
	(0.205)	(0.489)	(0.226)
CPA	0.962	1.926***	−0.060
	(0.139)	(0.415)	(0.132)
MBA	0.897	1.450*	0.001
	(0.129)	(0.307)	(0.125)
Tenure	1.052**	0.979	0.027
	(0.025)	(0.034)	(0.021)
Board membership	1.329	1.005	−0.573**
	(0.499)	(0.439)	(0.248)
Acquisition controls			
Relative deal size	1.119***	1.025***	0.103***
	(0.014)	(0.005)	(0.007)
Cash deal	0.896	1.802**	0.185
	(0.135)	(0.464)	(0.128)
Stock deal	1.512**	1.637*	0.576***
	(0.305)	(0.468)	(0.192)

(continued)

Table 4.5 (continued)

	(1) P(Deal advisor)	(2) P(Top-tier advisor)	(3) Advisor fee
Diversifying deal	0.946	0.937	0.118
	(0.155)	(0.236)	(0.127)
Target listing	3.844***	0.885	1.665***
	(0.655)	(0.195)	(0.243)
Acquirer controls			
Firm size	1.396***	2.512***	1.470***
	(0.097)	(0.266)	(0.089)
Leverage	0.357**	0.722	−0.313
	(0.178)	(0.526)	(0.394)
ROA	0.054	28.607	−0.941
	(0.120)	(105.807)	(2.193)
Cash holdings	5.063***	1.568	0.941***
	(2.467)	(0.915)	(0.362)
Cash flow	21.551	0.152	1.828
	(45.241)	(0.517)	(2.080)
Tobin's Q	0.964	0.934	−0.178***
	(0.047)	(0.064)	(0.036)
No. of deals	0.956***	0.948***	−0.036***
	(0.009)	(0.011)	(0.011)
Run-up	1.018	1.189	0.284**
	(0.167)	(0.275)	(0.124)
CEO duality	0.913	0.843	0.266**
	(0.123)	(0.165)	(0.123)
Board size	1.059	0.930	−0.032
	(0.038)	(0.047)	(0.032)
Constant	0.000***	0.000***	−32.619***
	(0.000)	(0.000)	(2.355)
Observations	2,336	735	1,873
Adjusted R-squared	0.332	0.255	0.617

4.5.4.4 Deal Premium

In this section, we examine the influence of powerful CFOs on M&A premium. Since data are more readily available for public targets, we also incorporate target-firm controls into these models. Models 1 and 2 of Table 4.6 illustrate the impact of our CFO power dimensions on the acquisition premium paid, specifically, the target's share price 7 days (Model 1) and 42 days (Model 2) preceding the deal announcement, respectively. Across both model specifications and in line with Hypothesis 6, our findings indicate a significant negative effect on the deal premium attributable to the CFO's acquisition experience. Accordingly, acquirers whose CFOs have superior acquisition experience pay a lower target premium of 2.6 to 2.9 percentage points, suggesting that one economic mechanism through which experienced CFOs improve acquisition performance is their ability to limit the acquirer's exposure to overpayment. Interestingly, while both models offer consistent predictions regarding the influence of CFOs' M&A experience, Model 1 suggests that firms whose CFOs have higher-level shareholdings or hold more external board seats tend to pay higher takeover premiums. While the first finding appears puzzling, one potential explanation for the latter is that time and capacity constraints resulting from holding multiple directorships may hinder a CFO's ability to provide valuable guidance during the acquisition process (Ahn et al. 2010).

We aim to gain further insights into the influence of powerful CFOs by examining whether acquirers with experienced CFOs pay lower premiums due to a CFO's superior bargaining ability, which would allow the bidder to capture a larger share of the overall value (Schmidt 2015). Following Ahern (2012), we investigate this conjecture by examining the CFO's influence on the division of gains between both parties to the acquisition. Specifically, we calculate a target's surplus obtained from an acquisition as the difference in dollar gains between the target and the bidder (measured at [−1, + 1] around the announcement date), divided by the sum of both parties' market value 50 trading days before the deal announcement:

$$\Delta\$CAR_{Target} = \frac{Market\ Value_{Target} * CAR_{Target} - Market\ Value_{Acquirer} * CAR_{Acquirer}}{Market\ Value_{Target} + Market\ Value_{Acquirer}}$$

Table 4.6 Regressions of takeover premiums (Models 1–2) and distribution of the overall value created (Model 3). Robust standard errors in parentheses. *** p<0.01, ** p<0.05, * p<0.1

	(1) Deal premium (7 days)	(2) Deal premium (42 days)	(3) Target gains
CFO power			
Pay slice	0.063	0.193*	0.019
	(0.135)	(0.117)	(0.069)
No. of board seats	0.046*	0.035	0.000
	(0.027)	(0.029)	(0.015)
M&A experience	−0.026**	−0.029***	−0.006
	(0.013)	(0.010)	(0.006)
Ownership	0.164**	0.070	0.041
	(0.079)	(0.071)	(0.046)
Acquirer controls			
Firm size	0.018	0.046*	−0.027*
	(0.030)	(0.024)	(0.014)
Leverage	−0.150	−0.107	−0.066
	(0.165)	(0.146)	(0.082)
ROA	−0.827	0.279	−0.387
	(1.201)	(0.978)	(0.563)
Cash flow	0.785	0.115	0.568
	(1.212)	(1.012)	(0.590)
Cash holdings	0.057	0.057	0.076
	(0.131)	(0.113)	(0.079)
Tobin's Q	0.034	0.004	−0.017*
	(0.021)	(0.019)	(0.010)
No. of deals	−0.002	−0.004**	−0.002*
	(0.002)	(0.002)	(0.001)
Run-up	0.035	0.006	0.002
	(0.060)	(0.049)	(0.029)
CEO duality	−0.049	−0.027	−0.035*
	(0.045)	(0.038)	(0.021)

(continued)

Table 4.6 (continued)

	(1) Deal premium (7 days)	(2) Deal premium (42 days)	(3) Target gains
Board size	0.010	−0.003	0.012**
	(0.010)	(0.009)	(0.006)
Target controls			
Firm size	−0.052**	−0.079***	0.012
	(0.025)	(0.020)	(0.011)
Leverage	0.011	0.051	0.042
	(0.151)	(0.136)	(0.063)
ROA	0.687	0.335	0.438
	(0.683)	(0.610)	(0.305)
Cash flow	−0.885	−0.497	−0.414
	(0.678)	(0.591)	(0.298)
Cash holdings	−0.099	−0.088	−0.021
	(0.139)	(0.123)	(0.074)
Tobin's Q	−0.043**	−0.014	−0.007
	(0.021)	(0.017)	(0.011)
Acquisition controls			
Cash deal	0.126*	0.125**	0.054*
	(0.069)	(0.057)	(0.030)
Stock deal	0.012	0.047	0.010
	(0.063)	(0.058)	(0.030)
Diversifying deal	0.029	0.086	0.021
	(0.069)	(0.069)	(0.042)
Relative deal size	0.021	0.069	−0.189***
	(0.125)	(0.098)	(0.061)
CFO controls			
Age	−0.005	−0.002	0.001
	(0.004)	(0.004)	(0.002)
Gender	0.013	0.085	0.050
	(0.079)	(0.057)	(0.031)
CPA	−0.086*	−0.066	−0.020
	(0.049)	(0.045)	(0.026)

(continued)

Table 4.6 (continued)

	(1) Deal premium (7 days)	(2) Deal premium (42 days)	(3) Target gains
MBA	−0.035	−0.001	−0.008
	(0.049)	(0.044)	(0.024)
Tenure	−0.005	−0.003	−0.001
	(0.007)	(0.007)	(0.004)
Board membership	−0.170**	−0.067	−0.071
	(0.084)	(0.082)	(0.052)
Constant	0.343	−0.491	0.592*
	(0.624)	(0.520)	(0.316)
Observations	314	314	301
Adjusted R-squared	0.347	0.374	0.264

The dependent variable in Model 3 of Table 4.6 measures the target's relative gain compared to the acquirer's. A significant negative (positive) coefficient would indicate the favorable effect of the deal's total gain for the acquirer (target). Consistent with the notion that larger acquirers possess stronger bargaining positions (Ahern 2012), we observe a significant inverse relationship between the acquirer's size and the relative gain of the target. However, the lack of statistical significance of the coefficient's estimates for the CFO power dimensions yields no support for the conjecture that CFOs' expertise related to better bidder negotiation outcomes.

4.5.4.5 Large Loss Deal

Table 4.7 presents the results of a logit regression with the large loss dummy serving as the dependent variable. Model 1 includes only control variables. Consistent with Moeller et al. (2005) and Field and Mkrtchyan (2017), we find that a firm's Tobin's Q and the relative deal size relate positively to the likelihood of substantial shareholder value destruction in M&A. Model 2 tests the main effect of powerful CFOs on the probability of a large loss acquisition. Turning to the CFO power dimensions, we observe that firms whose CFO holds more prestige power (i.e., service on multiple outside boards) are more likely to undertake bad deals. This reinforces our conjecture from the previous section that holding multiple directorships might diminish the quality of managerial oversight and advice that the CFO can provide. Ultimately, the remaining power dimensions' insignificant coefficients lead us to reject Hypothesis 7.

Table 4.7 Regressions of the likelihood of a large loss deal. Robust standard errors in parentheses. *** p<0.01, ** p<0.05, * p<0.1

	P(Large loss deal)	
	(1)	(2)
CFO power		
Pay slice		0.450
		(0.268)
No. of board seats		1.372**
		(0.210)
M&A experience		0.988
		(0.068)
Ownership		1.076
		(0.388)
Acquirer controls		
Firm size	1.054	1.021
	(0.097)	(0.103)
Leverage	0.571	0.476
	(0.390)	(0.327)
ROA	0.061	0.075
	(0.213)	(0.268)
Cash flow	3.271	2.812
	(10.718)	(9.398)
Cash holdings	0.366	0.343
	(0.257)	(0.238)
Tobin's Q	1.179**	1.187***
	(0.077)	(0.074)
No. of deals	0.973***	0.967***
	(0.010)	(0.012)
Run-up	0.649	0.658
	(0.189)	(0.193)
CEO duality	0.839	0.864
	(0.184)	(0.197)
Board size	0.993	0.989
	(0.063)	(0.061)

(continued)

Table 4.7 (continued)

	P(Large loss deal)	
	(1)	(2)
Acquisition controls		
Relative deal size	24.726***	24.751***
	(14.184)	(14.274)
Target listing	1.402	1.384
	(0.365)	(0.360)
Cash deal	0.663	0.667
	(0.195)	(0.201)
Stock deal	1.203	1.207
	(0.358)	(0.365)
Diversifying deal	0.839	0.825
	(0.228)	(0.223)
CFO controls		
Age	0.994	0.991
	(0.018)	(0.018)
Gender	1.906	1.974
	(0.881)	(0.892)
CPA	1.257	1.209
	(0.269)	(0.266)
MBA	1.248	1.216
	(0.296)	(0.291)
Tenure	1.043	1.038
	(0.036)	(0.037)
Board membership	0.992	0.839
	(0.495)	(0.436)
Constant	0.003**	0.008*
	(0.007)	(0.020)
Observations	1,084	1,084
Adjusted R-squared	0.179	0.185

4.6 Discussion

4.6.1 Main Findings and Contributions

Despite the emerging body of organizational literature documenting the influence of individual actors on M&A outcomes, research has stopped short of examining the influence of TMT members other than the CEO. In light of recurring calls to further consider functional TMT members (Welch et al. 2020), we propose that CFOs' functional finance background enables them to contribute valuable expertise throughout various stages of a deal. We hypothesize that the extent to which CFOs' expertise becomes evident in M&A outcomes depends on the managerial power they hold, i.e., the degree to which a CFO can shape crucial M&A decisions. To account for the diverse sources through which a CFO might gain influence on M&A-related decisions, we draw upon Finkelstein's (1992) power framework and distinguish between ownership, structural, prestige, and expertise power. In doing so, we document notable differences in the explanatory power across these dimensions, through which CFOs improve deal outcomes, with expertise power (i.e., a CFO's M&A experience) being the most persistent. For example, when assessing the influence of CFOs on acquisition performance, our results indicate that investors value the presence of CFOs with acquisition experience, particularly for large deals, as evidenced by higher announcement returns. Here, the predicted announcement returns increase by 0.18 percentage points for each acquisition in which a CFO gained experience, resulting in a $24 million gain in shareholder value based on our sample firms mean size of $13.5 billion. This resonates with recent findings indicating that the complexity of the deal amplifies the influence of financial advisors' expertise on the financial performance of the acquisition (Chemmanur et al. 2018). Focusing on long-term value effects, we document the positive association between a CFO's M&A experience and the acquiring firm's 24-month BHAR, thereby echoing qualitative evidence on the important role of CFO expertise in the post-acquisition integration process (Agrawal et al. 2020).

In our second set of analyses, we examine different mechanisms through which powerful CFOs add value to the acquisition process. We observe that firms with CFOs possessing greater M&A experience tend to pay lower takeover premiums. However, this does not appear to stem from CFOs' superior bargaining skills. In line with Aktas et al. (2021), our analysis further reveals that the M&A experience of CFOs would likely serve as a substitute for the advice that third-party financial advisors provide. We find that acquirers with more experienced CFOs are less likely to hire a financial deal advisor and pay lower fees for their services if they do. Experienced CFOs also appear to be more selective, favoring top-tier advisors for their presumed superior expertise (Golubov et al. 2012). The managerial influence gained through CFOs' ownership and structural power generally appear to have less pronounced impacts on M&A outcomes. In contrast to existing literature suggesting that executives with a financial background should engage in more acquisition activity (Jensen and Zajac 2004), our findings indicate that CFOs with greater ownership power are actually less likely to initiate a deal. This might be due to an increased awareness of the risks and failure rate associated with such acquisitions. Importantly, we observe the association between the prestige power dimension and adverse acquisition effects. Our findings reveal that acquirers whose CFOs wield greater prestige power (i.e., hold a larger number of external directorships) tend to pay higher takeover premiums and exhibit greater likelihood of conducting large value-destroying acquisitions. This finding is in line with the idea that directors serving on multiple boards may underperform in acquisitions due to becoming overly busy to provide effective advice (Ahn et al. 2010).

Our study adds to acquisition and upper-echelon research in several ways. We expand M&A literature by theorizing and empirically testing a broad range of mechanisms through which CFOs might facilitate successful acquisitions. Prior work on the influence of executive attributes has predominantly centered around CEOs, neglecting the role of other corporate-level decision-makers. By shifting the focus to CFOs, we propose and find evidence that increased decision authority enables CFOs to provide valuable deal expertise. Our study thereby responds to recent calls in the literature for a stronger incorporation of the personal characteristics and experiences of other TMT members (Welch et al. 2020).

Our study also contributes to the development of theoretical perspectives on the impact of TMT attributes on M&A outcomes. While most studies are rather exploratory in nature (e.g., Custódio and Metzger 2014; Ferris and Sainani 2021; Field and Mkrtchyan 2017), we provide theoretical reasoning as to *why* and *how* financial expertise is likely to shape acquisitions.

Moreover, we document that the mechanisms through which CFOs add value are diverse and likely to manifest throughout different deal stages. This echoes existing studies highlighting the complexity of assessing the antecedents of acquisition performance, which cannot be reduced to a single factor (Teerikangas and Thanos 2018). Our study thus adds to the adoption of a holistic perspective on examining potential drivers for M&A improvements, as previous work requested (Bauer and Matzler 2014). Finally, we shed new light on deciphering the "black box" often associated with research on managerial power. Our empirical model allows for a more nuanced analysis of the incremental predictive ability of the individual power dimensions. We find notable differences in the relative importance of our dimensions, with CFOs' acquisition experience being the most consistent predictor of deal improvements. This finding supports previous theoretical assertions, arguing that "... expertise power will have the most predictive power among TMT members" (Finkelstein et al. 2009, p. 113). By contrast, we observe adverse effects for the expertise power dimension. Our findings suggest that the puzzling results that managerial power research often obtains might find at least a partial explanation in the conflicting effects inherent in some power dimensions.

4.6.2 Limitations and Future Research

Our study is not without limitations that provide opportunities for further research. First, by focusing on the isolated influence of CFOs, we take a rather narrow view, leaving out potential influences on M&A outcomes arising from the interplay of decision-makers on the TMT. Indeed, although CFOs, along with CEOs, often bear primary responsibility for M&A decisions, we recognize the importance of taking a holistic perspective in this regard, by considering multiple actors and the interactions between them, for a better understanding of acquisition outcomes (Aktas et al. 2021; Wang et al. 2020). While this would involve significant data-related challenges in identifying relevant actors and capturing their characteristics, responsibilities, and social interactions (Welch et al. 2020), we expect that overcoming these challenges would open up fruitful avenues for future research.

Second, while our measure of managerial power is well-established in the organizational literature, we acknowledge its limitations in accurately capturing the complexity of decision authorities in organizations. Particularly, we expect that Finkelstein's (1992) framework might not adequately reflect more dynamic factors impacting managerial discretion. In support of this notion, recent literature documents that the degree to which strategic decisions involve CFOs is a function of CEOs' propensity to delegate decision authority. In turn, research has found that CEO characteristics and situational factors, such as finance background and work overload, have influenced that propensity (Graham et al. 2015). We see a promising avenue for future research in examining the robustness of our results to other measures of decision authority.

Third, throughout this study, our main argument is that the functional backgrounds of influential CFOs enable them to enhance M&A outcomes. We implicitly assume that CFOs act in the interest of the acquiring firms' shareholders. However, as it does for any other executives, self-interest, such as career concerns, may at least partially motivate CFOs' actions (Firk et al. 2023), which might actually harm the outcomes of their strategic decisions. Future research could examine factors influencing CFOs' incentives and their consequences for M&A outcomes.

Finally, although our results are robust against a battery of tests, we cannot completely rule out that omitted factors partly explain our findings. For example, insufficient within-variation prevents us from using CFO-firm fixed effects that would allow us to rule out certain alternative explanations that unobservable CFO characteristics caused. Consequently, we must be cautious regarding any causal inferences we draw from our results.

4.7 Conclusion

The continuing popularity of acquisitions as an important corporate strategy, coupled with their high failure rate, has long fueled researchers' interest in gaining an in-depth understanding of the factors determining M&A success. Prior work has focused on the influence of deal or firm characteristics, largely neglecting the impact of key decision-makers on M&A performance. Building on upper-echelons theory, we extend this discussion by empirically examining the influence of powerful CFOs and their financial expertise in the acquisition process. We argue that the extent to which their financial expertise becomes evident in measurable acquisition outcomes is partially a function of their decision authority within the firm. In essence, enhanced managerial discretion should allow CFOs to shape crucial M&A decisions, thereby contributing to improved M&A outcomes. Utilizing a sample of 2,336 U.S. acquisitions, we find that the CFOs' expertise power (i.e., their M&A experience) plays a pivotal role in improving M&A outcomes. This influence manifests through multiple mechanisms, including higher announcement returns for large deals, reduced premiums paid, and lower third-party advisory fees.

References

Abernethy MA, Kuang YF, Qin B (2015) The influence of CEO power on compensation contract design. Account Rev 90:1265–1306. https://doi.org/10.2308/accr-50971

Adams RB, Almeida H, Ferreira D (2005) Powerful CEOs and their impact on corporate performance. Rev Financ Stud 18:1403–1432. https://doi.org/10.1093/rfs/hhi030

Adams RB, Akyol AC, Verwijmeren P (2018) Director skill sets. J Financ Econ 130:641–662. https://doi.org/10.1016/j.jfineco.2018.04.010

Agrawal A, Kim E, Dinneen B, Uhlaner R (2020) The one task the CFO should not delegate: Integrations. https://www.mckinsey.com/business-functions/m-and-a/our-insights/the-one-task-the-cfo-should-not-delegate-integrations. Accessed 08 March 2024.

Ahern KR (2012) Bargaining power and industry dependence in mergers. J Financ Econ 103:530–550. https://doi.org/10.1016/j.jfineco.2011.09.003

Ahn S, Jiraporn P, Kim YS (2010) Multiple directorships and acquirer returns. J Bank Finance 34:2011–2026. https://doi.org/10.1016/j.jbankfin.2010.01.009

Aktas N, Bodt E de, Roll R (2010) Negotiations under the threat of an auction. J Financ Econ 98:241–255. https://doi.org/10.1016/j.jfineco.2010.06.002

Aktas N, Bodt E de, Bollaert H, Roll R (2016) CEO narcissism and the takeover process: From private initiation to deal completion. J Financ Quant Anal 51:113–137. https://doi.org/10.1017/S0022109016000065

Aktas N, Boone A, Witkowski A, Xu G, Yurtoglu B (2021) The role of internal M&A teams in takeovers. Rev Finance 25:1047–1088. https://doi.org/10.1093/rof/rfaa034

Alexandridis G, Fuller KP, Terhaar L, Travlos NG (2013) Deal size, acquisition premia and shareholder gains. J Corp Finance 20:1–13. https://doi.org/10.1016/j.jcorpfin.2012.10.006

Allen L, Jagtiani J, Peristiani S, Saunders A (2004) The Role of bank advisors in Mergers and Acquisitions. J Money Credit Bank 36:197–224

Almeida H, Campello M, Cunha I, Weisbach MS (2014) Corporate liquidity management: A conceptual framework and survey. Annu Rev Financ Econ 6:135–162. https://doi.org/10.1146/annurev-financial-110613-034502

Baker TA, Lopez TJ, Reitenga AL, Ruch GW (2019) The influence of CEO and CFO power on accruals and real earnings management. Rev Quant Finance Account 52:325–345. https://doi.org/10.1007/s11156-018-0711-z

Bao J, Edmans A (2011) Do Investment Banks Matter for M&A Returns? Rev Financ Stud:2286–2315. https://doi.org/10.1093/rfs/hhr014

Bastardoz N, Matthews MJ, Sajons GB, Ransom T, Kelemen TK, Matthews SH (2023) Instrumental variables estimation: Assumptions, pitfalls, and guidelines. Leadership Quart 34:101673. https://doi.org/10.1016/j.leaqua.2022.101673

Bauer F, Matzler K (2014) Antecedents of M&A success: The role of strategic complementarity, cultural fit, and degree and speed of integration. Strat Manag J 35:269–291. https://doi.org/10.1002/smj.2091

Bedard J, Hoitash R, Hoitash U (2014) Chief Financial Officers as inside directors. Contemp Account Res 31:787–817. https://doi.org/10.1111/1911-3846.12045

Belot F, Waxin T (2019) CEO-CFO educational ties and Mergers and Acquisitions

Bergh DD (2001) Executive retention and acquisition outcomes: A test of opposing views on the influence of organizational tenure. J Manag Gov 27:603–622. https://doi.org/10.1177/014920630102700506

Bertrand M, Schoar A (2003) Managing with style: The effect of managers on firm policies. Quart J Econ 118:1169–1208

Billett MT, Qian Y (2008) Are overconfident CEOs born or made? Evidence of self-attribution bias from frequent acquirers. Manag Sci 54:1037–1051. https://doi.org/10.1287/mnsc.1070.0830

Cai Y, Sevilir M (2012) Board connections and M&A transactions. J Financ Econ 103:327–349. https://doi.org/10.1016/j.jfineco.2011.05.017

Cai Y, Tian X, Xia H (2016) Location, proximity, and M&A transactions. J Econ Manag Strat 25:688–719

Carpenter MA, Geletkanycz MA, Sanders WG (2004) Upper echelons research revisited: Antecedents, elements, and consequences of top management team composition. J Manag 30:749–778. https://doi.org/10.1016/j.jm.2004.06.001

Chang S (1998) Takeovers of privately held targets, methods of payment, and bidder returns. J Finance 53:773–783

Chatterjee A, Hambrick DC (2007) It's all about me: Narcissistic Chief Executive Officers and their effects on company strategy and performance. Adm Sci Q 52:351–386. https://doi.org/10.2189/asqu.52.3.351

Chemmanur TJ, Ertugrul M, Krishnan K (2018) Is It the investment bank or the investment banker? A study of the role of investment banker human capital in Acquisitions. J Financ Quant Anal 54:587–627. https://doi.org/10.1017/S002210901800073X

Chikh S, Filbien J-Y (2011) Acquisitions and CEO power: Evidence from French networks. J Corp Finance 17:1221–1236. https://doi.org/10.1016/j.jcorpfin.2011.06.007

Chin MK, Hambrick DC, Treviño LK (2013) Political ideologies of CEOs. Adm Sci Q 58:197–232. https://doi.org/10.1177/0001839213486984

Christensen CM, Alton R, Rising C, Waldeck A (2011) The new M&A playbook. Harvard Business Review 89

Chuang KS (2017) The role of investment banks on the impact of firm performance in Mergers and Acquisitions: Evidence from the Asia-Pacific market. Rev Quant Finance Account 48:677–699. https://doi.org/10.1007/s11156-016-0564-2

Cohen J, West SG, Aiken LS, Cohen P (2002) Applied multiple regression/correlation analysis for the behavioral sciences, 3rd edn. Routledge, London

Correia S (2015) Singletons, cluster-robust standard errors and fixed effects: A bad mix

Custódio C, Metzger D (2013) How do CEOs matter? The effect of industry expertise on acquisition returns. Rev Financ Stud 26:2007–2047. https://doi.org/10.1093/rfs/hht032

Custódio C, Metzger D (2014) Financial expert CEOs: CEO's work experience and firm's financial policies. J Financ Econ 114:125–154. https://doi.org/10.1016/j.jfineco.2014.06.002

Custódio C, Ferreira MA, Matos P (2013) Generalists versus specialists: Lifetime work experience and Chief Executive Officer pay. J Financ Econ 108:471–492. https://doi.org/10.1016/j.jfineco.2013.01.001

Daley B, Geelen T, Green B (2024) Due Diligence. J Finance. https://doi.org/10.1111/jofi.13322

Demirtaş G (2017) Board involvement in the M&A negotiation process. Int Rev Financ Anal 50:27–43. https://doi.org/10.1016/j.irfa.2017.01.005
DePamphilis DM (2019) Mergers, acquisitions, and other restructuring activities: An integrated approach to process, tools, cases and solutions, 10th edn. Academic Press, Los Angeles
El-Khatib R, Fogel K, Jandik T (2015) CEO network centrality and merger performance. J Financ Econ 116:349–382. https://doi.org/10.1016/j.jfineco.2015.01.001
Fama EF (1970) Efficient capital markets: A review of theory and empirical work. J Finance 25:383–417
Fama EF, French KR (1993) Common risk factors in the returns on stocks and bonds. J Financ Econ 33:3–56
.Ferris SP, Sainani S (2021) Do CFOs matter? Evidence from the M&A process. J Corp Finance 67. https://doi.org/10.1016/j.jcorpfin.2020.101856
Fich EM, Nguyen T, Officer M (2018) Large wealth creation in Mergers and Acquisitions. Financ Manag 47:953–991
Fidrmuc JP, Xia C (2019) M&A deal initiation and managerial motivation. J Corp Finance 59:320–343. https://doi.org/10.1016/j.jcorpfin.2017.01.010
Field LC, Mkrtchyan A (2017) The effect of director experience on acquisition performance. J Financ Econ 123:488–511. https://doi.org/10.1016/j.jfineco.2016.12.001
Finkelstein S (1992) Power in top management teams: Dimensions, measurement, and validation. Acad Manag J 35:505–538
Finkelstein S, Hambrick DC (1990) Top-management-team tenure and organizational outcomes: The moderating role of managerial discretion. Adm Sci Q 35:484–503
Finkelstein S, Hambrick DC, Cannella AA, Jr. (2009) Strategic leadership: Theory and research on executives, top management teams, and boards. Oxford University Press, New York
Firk S, Gehrke Y, Richter S, Wolff M (2023) CFO Career Concerns and Strategic Decisions: An Empirical Analysis of M&As. Eur Account Rev:1–32. https://doi.org/10.1080/09638180.2023.2291405
Florackis C, Sainani S (2018) How do Chief Financial Officers influence corporate cash policies? J Corp Finance 52:168–191. https://doi.org/10.1016/j.jcorpfin.2018.08.001
Fuhrer C, Liem R, Zwald D (2017) Success factors in post-merger integration. https://www.pwc.de/de/deals/success-factors-in-post-merger-integration.pdf. Accessed 15 February 2024.
Fuller K, Netter J, Stegemoller M (2002) What do returns to acquiring firms tell us? Evidence from firms that make many acquisitions. J Finance 57:1763–1793
Gamache DL, Mcnamara MJ, Russell JE (2015) Motivated to acquire? The impact of CEO regulatory focus on firm acquisitions. Acad Manag J 58:1261–1282. https://doi.org/10.5465/amj.2013.0377
Golubov A, Petmezas D, Travlos N (2012) When it pays to pay your investment banker: New evidence on the role of financial advisors in M&As. J Finance 67:271–311
Graffin SD, Haleblian J, Kiley J (2016) Ready, aim, acquire: Impression offsetting and acquisitions. Acad Manag J 59:232–252. https://doi.org/10.5465/amj.2013.0288
Graham M, Walter TS, Yawson A, Zhang H (2017) The value-added role of industry specialist advisors in M&As. J Bank Finance 81:81–104. https://doi.org/10.1016/j.jbankfin.2017.04.010

Graham JR, Harvey CR, Puri M (2015) Capital allocation and delegation of decision-making authority within firms. J Financ Econ 115:449–470. https://doi.org/10.1016/j.jfineco.2014.10.011

Guo J, Li X, Seeger NC, Vagenas-Nanos E (2019) Social connections, reference point and acquisition premium. Br Account Rev 51:46–71. https://doi.org/10.1016/j.bar.2018.07.001

Hambrick DC (2007) Upper echelons theory: An update. Acad Manag J 32:334–343

Hambrick DC, Cannella AA, Jr. (2004) CEOs who have COOs: Contingency analysis of an unexplored structural form. Strat Manag J 25:959–979. https://doi.org/10.1002/smj.407

Hambrick DC, Mason PA (1984) Upper echelons: The organization as a reflection of its top managers. Acad Manag J 9:193–206

Han S, Nanda VK, Silveri SD (2016) CEO power and firm performance under pressure. Financ Manag 45:369–400. https://doi.org/10.1111/fima.12127

Haunschild PR, Beckman CM (1998) When do interlocks matter?: Alternate sources of information and interlock influence. Adm Sci Q 43:815–844

Haunschild PR, Henderson AD, Davis-Blake A (1999) CEO demographics and acquisitions: Network effects of educational and effects of functional background. In: Leenders R, Gabbay S (eds) Corporate social capital and liability. Springer Science+Business Media, New York, pp 266–283

Hayes RH, Abernathy WJ (1980) Managing our way to economic decline. Harvard Business Review 58:67–77

Hirshleifer DA, Lim SS, Teoh SH (2009) Driven to distraction: Extraneous events and underreaction to earnings news. J Finance 64:2289–2325

Huang J, Kisgen DJ (2013) Gender and corporate finance: Are male executives overconfident relative to female executives? J Financ Econ 108:822–839. https://doi.org/10.1016/j.jfineco.2012.12.005

Huang Q, Jiang F, Lie E, Yang K (2014) The role of investment banker directors in M&A. J Financ Econ 112:269–286. https://doi.org/10.1016/j.jfineco.2014.02.003

Imbens GM, Wooldridge JM (2009) Recent developments in the econometrics of program evaluation. J Econ Lit 47:5–86. https://doi.org/10.1257/jel.47.1.5

Iskandar-Datta M, Shekhar S (2020) Do insider CFOs deliver better acquisition performance? J Bus Res 118:240–252. https://doi.org/10.1016/j.jbusres.2020.06.040

Jemison DB, Sitkin SB (1986) Corporate acquisitions: A process perspective. Acad Manag Rev 11:145–163

Jensen M, Zajac E (2004) Corporate elites and corporate strategy: How demographic preferences and structural position shape the scope of the firm. Strat Manag J 25:507–524. https://doi.org/10.1002/smj.393

Jöhnk C, Fuhrer C, Siemes, D (2020) Value creation in deals: Finance integration and separation. https://www.pwc.de/en/deals/separation-and-integration/the-finance-function-as-the-key-to-successful-transactions.html. Accessed 10 February 2024.

Joseph J, Ocasio WC, McDonnell M-H (2014) The structural elaboration of board independence: Executive power, institutional logics, and the adoption of CEO-only board structures in U.S. corporate governance. Acad Manag J 57:1834–1858. https://doi.org/10.5465/amj.2012.0253

Lang LH (1991) A test of the free cash flow hypothesis. J Financ Econ 29:315–335

Lehn KM, Zhao M (2006) CEO turnover after acquisitions: Are bad bidders fired? J Finance 61:1759–1811
Malhotra S, Reus TH, Zhu P, Roelofsen EM (2017) The acquisitive nature of extraverted CEOs. Adm Sci Q 63:370–408. https://doi.org/10.1177/0001839217712240
Malmendier U, Tate G (2008) Who makes acquisitions? CEO overconfidence and the market's reaction. J Financ Econ 89:20–43. https://doi.org/10.1016/j.jfineco.2007.07.002
Markides CC (1995) Diversification, restructuring and economic performance. Strat Manag J 16:101–118
Masulis RW, Simsir SA (2018) Deal initiation in Mergers and Acquisitions. J Financ Quant Anal 53:2389–2430. https://doi.org/10.1017/S0022109018000509
Meglio O, King DR, Risberg A (2017) Speed in Acquisitions: A managerial framework. Bus Hor 60:415–425. https://doi.org/10.1016/j.bushor.2016.12.004
Menz M (2012) Functional top management team members. J Manag 38:45–80. https://doi.org/10.1177/0149206311421830
Moeller S, Schlingemann F, Stulz R (2005) Wealth destruction on a massive scale? A study of acquiring-firm returns in the recent merger wave. J Finance 60:757–782
Moeller SB, Schlingemann FP, Stulz RM (2004) Firm size and the gains from acquisitions. J Financ Econ 73:201–228. https://doi.org/10.1016/j.jfineco.2003.07.002
Mukherjee T, Kiymaz H, Baker K (2004) Merger motives and target valuation: A survey of evidence from CFOs. J App Finance 14:7–24
Nath P, Vijay M (2008) Chief Marketing Officers: A study of their presence in firms' top management teams. J Mark 72:65–81
Neilson GL (2015) The decline of the COO. https://www.forbes.com/sites/strategyand/2015/05/20/the-decline-of-the-coo/?sh=5b54a8827cee. Accessed 14 February 2024.
Palmer D, Barber BM (2001) Challengers, elites, and owning families: A Social class theory of corporate acquisitions in the 1960s. Adm Sci Q 46:87–120
Porrini P (2006) Are investment bankers good for acquisition premiums? Journal of Business Research 59:90–99. https://doi.org/10.1016/j.jbusres.2005.03.009
Preston DS, Chen D, Leidner DE (2008) Examining the antecedents and consequences of CIO strategic decision-making authority: An empirical study. Decis Sci 39:605–642. https://doi.org/10.1111/j.1540-5915.2008.00206.x
Reeb D, Sakakibara M, Mahmood IP (2012) Endogeneity in international business research. J Int Bus Stud 43:211–218. https://doi.org/10.1057/jibs.2011.60
Renneboog L, Vansteenkiste C (2019) Failure and success in Mergers and Acquisitions. J Corp Finance 58:650–699. https://doi.org/10.1016/j.jcorpfin.2019.07.010
Roberts MR, Whited TM (2013) Endogeneity in empirical corporate finance. In: Constantinides GM, Harris M, Stulz RM (eds) Handbook of the economics of finance, 2nd edn. North-Holland, Amsterdam, pp 493–572
Rosenbaum PR, Rubin DB (1983) The central role of the propensity score in observational studies for causal effects. Biometrika 70:41–55
Rubin DB (2001) Using propensity scores to help design observational studies: Application to the tobacco litigation. Health Serv Outcomes Res Methodol 2:169–188. https://doi.org/10.1017/CBO9780511810725.030
Schmid S, Altfeld F, Dauth T (2018) Americanization as a driver of CEO pay in Europe: The moderating role of CEO power. J World Bus 53:433–451. https://doi.org/10.1016/j.jwb.2017.12.002

Schmidt B (2015) Costs and benefits of friendly boards during Mergers and Acquisitions. J Financ Econ 117:424–447. https://doi.org/10.1016/j.jfineco.2015.02.007
Servaes H (1991) Tobin's Q and the gains from takeovers. J Finance 46:409–419
Shi W, Chen G (2019) CEO-CFO relative optimism and firm Mergers and Acquisitions. https://doi.org/10.2139/ssrn.3428760
Shrivastava P (1986) Postmerger integration. J Bus Strategy 7:65–76. https://doi.org/10.1108/eb039143
Simsir SA (2008) The information content of deal initiation in Mergers and Acquisitions
Song J (1982) Diversification strategies and the experience of top executives of large firms. Strat Manag J 3:377–380
Song W, Wei J, Zhou L (2013) The value of "boutique" financial advisors in mergers and acquisitions. J Corp Finance 20:94–114. https://doi.org/10.1016/j.jcorpfin.2012.12.003
Stock JH, Watson MW (2020) Introduction to econometrics, 4th edn. Pearson, Harlow
Teerikangas S, Thanos IC (2018) Looking into the 'black box' – unlocking the effect of integration on acquisition performance. Eur Manag J 36:366–380. https://doi.org/10.1016/j.emj.2017.06.002
Venus A, Engelen A (2012) A strategy perspective on the performance relevance of the CFO
Wang X (2010) Increased disclosure requirements and corporate governance decisions: Evidence from Chief Financial Officers in the pre- and post–Sarbanes-Oxley periods. J Account Res 48:885–920. https://doi.org/10.1111/j.1475-679X.2010.00378.x
Wang W, Whyte AM (2010) Managerial rights, use of investment banks, and the wealth effects for acquiring firms' shareholders. J Bank Finance 34:44–54. https://doi.org/10.1016/j.jbankfin.2009.07.002
Wang G, Holmes RM, Oh I-S, Zhu W (2016) Do CEOs matter to firm strategic actions and firm performance? A meta-analytic investigation based on upper echelons theory. Pers Psychol 69:775–862. https://doi.org/10.1111/peps.12140
Wang Y, Yin S (2018) CEO educational background and acquisition targets selection. J Corp Finance 52:238–259. https://doi.org/10.1016/j.jcorpfin.2018.08.013
Wang Q, Lau RY, Yang K (2020) Does the interplay between the personality traits of CEOs and CFOs influence corporate Mergers and Acquisitions intensity? An econometric analysis with machine learning-based constructs. Decis Support Syst 139. https://doi.org/10.1016/j.dss.2020.113424
Welch X, Pavićević S, Keil T, Laamanen T (2020) The pre-deal phase of Mergers and Acquisitions: A review and research agenda. J Manag 46:843–878
Yim S (2013) The acquisitiveness of youth: CEO age and acquisition behavior. J Financ Econ 108:250–273. https://doi.org/10.1016/j.jfineco.2012.11.003
Zhou B, Dutta S, Zhu P (2020) CEO tenure and Mergers and Acquisitions. Finance Res Lett 34. https://doi.org/10.1016/j.frl.2019.08.025
Zorn D (2004) Here a chief, there a chief: The rise of the CFO in the American firm. Am Sociol Rev 69:345–364

Research Manuscript 2 5

The Influence of CEO Narcissism on Firms' Impression Management During Acquisitions

Abstract

Through the use of impression management, organizations aim to shape audiences' perceptions of important corporate events, which enables them to effectively influence the behavior of crucial stakeholders such as investors, analysts, or journalists. Drawing on Upper Echelons Theory, we examine how CEO narcissism influences a firm's impression management behavior during acquisitions. Due to their grandiose nature, positive expectancy bias and low motivation to avoid undesirable outcomes, we expect more narcissistic CEOs to be less likely to engage in impression management aimed at reducing negative stakeholder reactions often accompanying large takeovers. Accounting for the multidimensionality of narcissism we further theorize that this relationship is moderated by a CEO's incentives and ability to utilize impression management. Using a dataset of 648 acquisitions, we show that the relationship between CEO narcissism and impression management is not straightforward but appears to be moderated by the CEO's reputational status. In contrast to prior research, our results suggest that shareholders' and analysts' valuations of the acquisition remain unaffected by impression management efforts. Our findings contribute to the literature on impression management, CEO narcissism and corporate governance.

Supplementary Information The online version contains supplementary material available at https://doi.org/10.1007/978-3-658-51855-4_5.

F. Lammers, *The Role of Executive Characteristics in Financial Decision-Making*, Studies in Finance and Accounting, https://doi.org/10.1007/978-3-658-51855-4_5

5.1 Introduction

In recent years, a growing body of literature has examined how organizations strategically manage stakeholders' reactions through impression management—that is, by undertaking actions aimed at manipulating or controlling the image held by a target audience (Brauer & Vandepoele, 2023; Chen & Hwang, 2022; Jin et al., 2022). These studies consistently highlight the widespread adoption of impression management across various organizational settings, including earnings announcements (Noh & Zhou, 2022), mergers and acquisitions (M&A) (Ahern & Sosyura, 2014; Graffin et al., 2016), and corporate layoffs (Brauer & Vandepoele, 2023), among others. Notwithstanding the considerable headway research has made in uncovering various impression management techniques and assessing their effectiveness, less is known about the underlying factors that drive firms to adopt these techniques (Bolino et al., 2016; McFarland et al., 2023; van Iddekinge et al., 2007). However, a deeper understanding of the antecedents of impression management is particularly critical given its widespread applicability and the significant economic implications associated with their use. Moreover, it also raises essential ethical and practical concerns, notably by diminishing transparency in corporate communication and disclosures (Arena et al., 2015). Consequently, stakeholders may experience increased difficulty in accurately interpreting corporate performance, potentially exacerbating trust deficits and information asymmetries (Bolino et al., 2016; Brauer & Vandepoele, 2023). Given these substantial implications, developing a comprehensive understanding of the factors that drive impression management behavior is both academically and practically indispensable.

Importantly, the prevailing discourse primarily attributes differences in firms' impression management behaviors to firm-level factors, often overlooking the role of individual decision-makers within organizational contexts. However, scholars have increasingly expressed concerns about this matter, emphasizing the need to examine the role of individual actors in shaping a firm's impression management behavior (Gamache et al., 2019; Graffin et al., 2011). Drawing on Upper Echelons Theory, we aim to contribute to filling this research gap by investigating the influence of a CEO's narcissistic tendencies on a firm's use of impression management. Previous studies have identified a variety of firm outcomes affected by CEO narcissism, including firm performance (Wales et al., 2013), corporate risk-taking (Buyl et al., 2019), financial disclosure (Buchholz et al., 2018; Marquez-Illescas et al., 2019) and acquisition behavior (Aktas et al., 2016; Chatterjee & Hambrick, 2007). As a personality trait, narcissism is closely linked to an inflated self-view and a strong bias towards expecting positive outcomes, leading to an exaggerated belief that one's decisions will be successful (Becker & O'Hair, 2007). Moreover, previous literature has confirmed that more narcissistic individuals generally exhibit low motivation to counteract undesirable outcomes, as evidenced, for example, by lower hedging efforts compared to their less narcissistic peers (Patel & Cooper, 2014). Narcissistic CEOs' positive expectancy bias, combined with their willingness to accept undesirable outcomes, is expected to reduce their concerns about the consequences of controversial actions, potentially diminishing their motivation to engage in impression management aimed at maintaining stakeholders' support (Campbell et al., 2004).

Recent literature on narcissism highlights that its manifestation is often contingent upon various moderating factors, with inherent CEO attributes playing a pivotal role in triggering narcissistic behavior (Brunzel, 2021). We examine two factors that previous research identified as particularly important in influencing narcissistic behavior: the public attention CEOs receive and the managerial power they hold within the firm (Cragun et al., 2020; Wangrow et al., 2015). Building on the literature documenting that narcissistic CEOs highly value media coverage and the benefits associated with such public attention (Aabo et al., 2022; Chatterjee & Pollock, 2017), we posit that the motivation for narcissistic CEOs to engage in impression management will increase with their reputation. Furthermore, we expect that the relationship between CEO narcissism and the use of impression management is more pronounced when CEOs holds greater managerial power, enabling them to exert stronger influence over the firm's impression management strategies.

We examine our predictions within the context of large corporate acquisitions. Previous research indicates that acquiring firms frequently encounter significant negative reactions from stakeholders upon announcing an acquisition (Haleblian et al., 2009; Renneboog & Vansteenkiste, 2019), which can result in tangible penalties for CEOs (Lehn & Zhao, 2006). Consequently, firms have been shown to strategically engage in impression management practices designed to positively influence stakeholders' perceptions and mitigate any negative reactions surrounding acquisition announcements (Gamache et al., 2019; Graffin et al., 2016). Based on a sample of 648 U.S. acquisitions from 2009 to 2018, our findings indicate that CEO narcissism is not directly related to impression management activities but rather contingent upon the CEOs reputational status. More specifically, we find that CEOs who achieve higher reputational status demonstrate greater motivation to engage in impression management strategies to maintain their status and the benefits associated with it. Additionally, in contrast to prior literature, our results show that impression management efforts do not significantly affect shareholders' and analysts' evaluations of the acquisitions.

The contribution of this study is threefold. First, our research complements the existing literature on impression management by specifically focusing on its antecedents, thereby contributing to resolving prevailing discrepancies regarding the prevalence of organizational impression management behavior (Graffin et al., 2016). Adopting an upper-echelons perspective, our research advances an emerging theoretical stream that seeks to uncover deeper motivations behind impression management, particularly emphasizing the influential role of corporate leaders (García-Sánchez et al., 2019; Lee et al., 2020). While prior studies have examined the types and intensity of impression management tactics employed, the underlying drivers of such behaviors have largely been overlooked. By addressing this gap, our work directly responds to calls from scholars such as Bolino and colleagues (2016), who note that "Although there have been some attempts to identify the antecedents of impression management (e.g., Barsness et al., 2005; Kacmar et al., 2004), most research on impression management has focused on the consequences of such behavior" (p. 6).

Second, our study advances existing research at the intersection of Upper Echelons Theory and impression management by examining contextual contingencies that influence narcissistic CEOs' motives for impression management (Lee et al., 2020). Recent literature underscores the importance of such contingencies in enhancing our understanding of the prevalence and implications of impression management behaviors (Bolino et al., 2008; Bolino et al., 2016). Specifically, by identifying public attention directed toward CEOs significantly shapes their motivation to engage in impression management behaviors, we contribute an essential piece to the broader theoretical puzzle, enhancing our understanding of what drives impression management among top executives (McFarland et al., 2023). Relatedly, a nuanced understanding of CEO motivations provides valuable insights for developing governance mechanisms capable of more effectively monitoring and regulating executive behavior (Carter, 2006).

Finally, we extend the growing body of research on CEO narcissism (e.g., Capalbo et al., 2017; Rijsenbilt & Commandeur, 2013) by shifting attention from its direct strategic outcomes to the situational factors influencing how narcissistic traits manifest. While existing research predominantly explores the immediate organizational impacts of CEO narcissism, our study investigates the conditions under which these behaviors are likely to emerge. By doing so, we address recent calls for more context-sensitive analyses of narcissistic leadership (Cragun et al., 2020), thereby providing a deeper understanding of the environmental and organizational triggers that activate narcissistic tendencies in CEOs.

The remainder of this paper is structured as follows: Sect. 5.5.2 reviews the related literature and develops the research hypotheses. Sect. 5.5.3 describes the methodology, including the sampling procedure and data collection process. Sect. 5.5.4 presents the main results on the impact of CEO narcissism on impression management, followed by supplemental analyses in Sect. 5.5.5 and robustness checks in Sect. 5.5.6. Finally, Chap. 7 discusses the findings.

5.2 Related Literature and Hypotheses

5.2.1 Impression Management

Originally developed in the field of social psychology, impression management describes actions that actors take to manipulate or control others' perception of them (Bozeman & Kacmar, 1997). While the majority of research on this subject over the past decade has occurred at the individual level (e.g., in the context of job interviews), studies have adopted an impression management perspective within the realm of organizational behavior (Bolino et al., 2008). Existing research has shown that organizational leaders use impression management to maintain the support of various audiences critical to the firm's effectiveness and survival, such as shareholders (Bansal & Clelland, 2004; Elsbach et al., 1998), analysts (Washburn & Bromiley, 2014; Westphal & Graebner, 2010), journalists (Westphal & Deephouse, 2011), and customers (Bouzzine et al., 2020). For instance, Washburn & Bromiley (2014) observe that CEOs attempt to influence analysts' views of the firm by issuing forecast guidance when actual performance deviates from the forecasts. More recently, Blankespoor & deHaan (2020) argue that CEO visibility is important to a firm's reputation, providing evidence that CEOs actively try to shape media coverage by strategically designing corporate press releases to gain journalists' attention.

Actors may utilize a wide range of techniques to influence audiences' perceptions, reflecting either reactive or anticipatory impression management (Busenbark et al., 2017). The purpose of reactive impression management efforts, that are applied in response to a specific event, is usually to repair an organization's reputation after a widely perceived negative event becomes publicly known (Tyler et al., 2012), by providing additional information in an attempt to dampen or even reverse negative stakeholder reactions (Graffin et al., 2016). Examples of such techniques include justifications, concessions, denials, and apologies (Bansal & Clelland, 2004).

In contrast to reactive impression management strategies, our focus is on anticipatory impression management, which seeks to address potential negative perceptions of an upcoming event (Busenbark et al., 2017; Elsbach, 2012). While much of the research in this field has focused on reactive impression management, there is also evidence supporting the use and effectiveness of anticipatory impression management techniques in various corporate contexts, such as CEO succession (Graffin et al., 2011), downsizing (Brauer & Vandepoele, 2023), and M&A (Graffin et al., 2016).

5.2.2 Mergers and Acquisitions

Mergers and acquisitions are among the most critical investment decisions undertaken by a company's top management (Custódio & Metzger, 2013). Serving as powerful catalysts for corporate growth, M&A enable companies to unlock operational and financial synergies, enhance market dominance, diversify their business portfolio, and pursue strategic repositioning (Lammers & Pape, 2024; Renneboog & Vansteenkiste, 2019; Welch et al., 2019). However, as one of the largest and most observable forms of investment, acquisitions often amplify the inherent conflicts of interest between managers and shareholders (Masulis et al., 2007). Acquiring firms frequently underperform compared to their non-acquiring peers, especially in large public takeovers (Renneboog & Vansteenkiste, 2019), with some studies suggesting failure rates of takeovers between 70% and 90% (Christensen et al., 2011). Unsurprisingly, empirical literature consistently demonstrates that acquiring firms' key stakeholders react negatively to the announcement of large acquisitions (Bradley et al., 1988; Houston et al., 2001; Renneboog & Vansteenkiste, 2019), leading to substantial penalties for CEOs, to whom the shareholders assign responsibility for the deal (Lehn & Zhao, 2006; Wang et al., 2016).

Given the evidence that acquisitions often provoke adverse stakeholder reactions and their potential consequences, an increasing body of research unsurprisingly demonstrates firms' frequent use of impression management strategies during M&A announcements. For instance, Ahern & Sosyura (2014) find that firms deliberatively increase the volume of positive press releases in stock-financed acquisitions during the period when the stock exchange ratio is determined, thereby manipulating the takeover price to their advantage. Graffin et al. (2016) document that acquirers issue significantly more positive news around acquisition announcements, resulting in a less adverse market reaction. Busenbark et al. (2017) suggest that firms intentionally provide vague information about an acquisition–in a technique called "foreshadowing"–to reduce analysts' surprise at the event, leading to a significant decrease of analyst downgrades following the acquisition announcement. Kimbrough & Louis (2011) demonstrate that firms can effectively mitigate negative market reactions by offering supplementary information about the deal through conference calls. Hu et al. (2021) similarly identify a positive association between the sentiment expressed during M&A conference calls and the reactions of acquiring firms' shareholders, indicating that executives effectively engage in impression management through strategic language use. Aktas et al. (2023) observe that acquirers reduce the clarity of their SEC forms, seemingly in an impression management effort to increase the information processing costs for shareholders and reduce their ability to understand the disclosure content.

While such studies collectively indicate that firms can effectively shape audiences' perceptions and evaluations of acquisitions through impression management, there is a scarcity of research on its antecedents (Bolino et al., 2016). Closing this gap is important as scholars have long argued that studying its antecedents is crucial to better understanding impression management behavior (e.g., Kacmar et al., 2004; van Iddekinge et al., 2007). Building on a large body of upper-echelons literature documenting that CEOs' traits and experiences affect firm behavior and outcomes (Bertrand & Schoar, 2003; Petrenko et al., 2016), this paper posits that a firm's impression management behavior is partially a function of a CEO's personal traits.

5.2.3 CEO Narcissism and Impression Management

Clinical research defines narcissism as a mental disorder that presents as "a pervasive pattern of grandiosity (in fantasy or behavior), need for admiration, and lack of empathy" (American Psychiatric Association, 2013, p. 669). Contextualizing this definition to the field of economics, literature tends to view narcissism as a multidimensional personality trait encompassing a set of psychological characteristics, rather than a mental disorder (Buchholz et al., 2020; Chatterjee & Hambrick, 2007; Emmons, 1987). Current research typically differentiates between two forms of narcissism: grandiose narcissism reflects traits related to grandiosity, attention-seeking, dominance, and exploitativeness, while vulnerable narcissists tend to have low levels of self-esteem, feel more constrained, and struggle to develop social relationships (Dickinson & Pincus, 2003; Miller et al., 2011). Although these two forms of narcissism have been found to share certain core elements, recent research suggests that both relate differently to the use of impression management techniques (Hart et al., 2017). Given that the majority of existing research conceptualizes narcissism at the CEO level primarily in terms of grandiosity rather than vulnerability (e.g., Chatterjee & Hambrick,

2007; Kim & Anderson, 2024; Reina et al., 2014), our study focuses on grandiose narcissism. This is also in line with studies suggesting that grandiose narcissism is more prevalent in higher-status occupations than vulnerable narcissism (Campbell et al., 2010; O'Reilly et al., 2014). In subsequent mentions of CEO narcissism, we are referring to its grandiose form.

Narcissism is characterized by a belief in one's own superiority (American Psychiatric Association, 2013), as reflected by enhanced self-ratings on various agentic dimensions (Chatterjee & Hambrick, 2011), such as leadership skills (Judge et al., 2006), intelligence (Campbell et al., 2002), creativity (Farwell & Wohlwend-Lloyd, 1998), and competence (Anderson & Kilduff, 2009). Due to their exaggerated self-confidence, narcissists harbor a positive expectancy bias that their decisions will be successful, leading to an upward bias in estimated payoffs (Chatterjee & Hambrick, 2007; Wales et al., 2013). Absorbed by their own sense of correctness, highly narcissistic individuals have been found to be inattentive to performance feedback, disregarding the possibility of unwanted outcomes (Aabo & Eriksen, 2018; Chatterjee & Hambrick, 2011). Given that narcissists approach situations with positive expectations and persist in their positive beliefs even when faced with negative feedback (Campbell et al., 2004), we expect them to perceive a reduced need to engage in impression management to mitigate potential negative consequences of their decisions.

Despite their inflated sense of self, narcissistic individuals possess a strong desire for public acclaim and favorable treatment (Buchholz et al., 2018), leading them to engage in bold and risky actions aimed at securing recognition and validation from others (Capalbo et al., 2017), such as claiming exaggerated compensation (O'Reilly et al., 2014) or promoting favorable media coverage (Aabo et al., 2022). In doing so, grandiose narcissists are highly focused on securing personal benefits, while being less concerned about the consequences of their decisions for others (O'Reilly et al., 2014). This also aligns with grandiose narcissists high motivation to achieve desirable outcomes while being less motivated to avoid undesirable ones. In this context, Patel & Cooper (2014) note that "the low levels of avoidance motivation of narcissistic leaders decrease their tendency to attend to and plan for potential future threats in the environment..." (p. 1530). Indeed, previous studies document that narcissistic CEOs are less likely to engage in behaviors that help counteract the risks of declining performance, such as hedging against potential threats or carefully monitoring for signs of economic downturns (Buyl et al., 2019; Patel & Cooper, 2014).

Building on the previous discussion, we propose that individuals with higher levels of narcissism are less concerned about the consequences of threats to violating expectations (Dickinson & Pincus, 2003), resulting in a reduced motivation to engage in impression management for remediation purposes compared to their less narcissistic peers. This argument is supported by empirical evidence suggesting that vulnerable but not grandiose narcissists are more likely to employ impression management techniques aimed at defending themselves against threats to their self-image (Hart et al., 2017). While previous studies suggest that negative shareholder reactions around M&A announcements incentivize executives to engage in impression management (Graffin et al., 2016), we hypothesize that the heightened self-perception, positive expectancy bias, and weak avoidance focus of more narcissistic CEOs will lead them to employ fewer impression management strategies aimed at obscuring stakeholders' perception of the deal.

Hypothesis 1 (H1): A negative relationship exists between a CEO's narcissistic tendencies and engagement in impression management behavior around an acquisition announcement.

5.2.4 Factors Moderating the Relationship Between Narcissism and Impression Management

Despite theorizing a direct effect of CEO narcissism on a firm's impression management efforts, we acknowledge that this relationship is unlikely to be consistent across all situations. Research argues that environmental factors influence the manifestation of narcissistic behavior (Cragun et al., 2020), suggesting that those might impact a narcissistic CEO's decision to engage in impression management efforts. Moreover, existing literature suggests that individuals' engagement in impression management is contingent upon their motivation. Specifically, individuals are more inclined to utilize impression management tactics when they perceive that doing so will yield sufficient benefits for them (Kacmar et al., 2004; van Iddekinge et al., 2007). We therefore theorize that environmental factors further influence the relationship between CEO narcissism and impression management, affecting their motivation as well as their ability to engage in impression management.

5.2.4.1 CEO Reputation

We contend that a CEO's reputation is an important moderator of the relationship between CEO narcissism and impression management efforts. CEOs reputation refers to the degree to which they receive a favorable emotional response from a wide-ranging public audience (Lovelace et al., 2018). Recent research indicates that narcissistic CEOs fulfill their desire for public acclaim by actively seeking high reputational status (Aabo et al., 2022; Chatterjee & Pollock, 2017). As the actions of high-reputation CEOs will receive greater media attention, potentially negative stakeholder reactions associated with an acquisition announcement are likely to cause greater reputational damage. Given narcissists' desire for public admiration and a positive image, highly narcissistic CEOs with a strong reputation are likely to have greater incentives to employ impression management tactics compared to their less-reputable counterparts. We anticipate that this will reinforce their motivations to employ impression management, aiming to retain the support of both external and internal audiences, and thereby safeguard their reputation (Cho et al., 2016). This argument is consistent with previous literature noting that public awareness of individuals' behavior encourages them to employ impression management (Chng et al., 2015). Furthermore, recall that narcissistic individuals have a grossly overdeveloped sense of entitlement to favorable treatment. Obtaining a high reputational status is associated with various personal benefits for CEOs, including higher remuneration (Graffin et al., 2008), greater managerial power (Park et al., 2014), and enhanced job security (Bednar, 2012). Having obtained the personal benefits that accrue to their reputation, the narcissistic CEO will seek to maintain them and, especially mindful of public image, will experience increased pressure to employ impression management as a means of meeting audience expectations (Lovelace et al., 2018).

In summary, we expect that their reputational status will incentivize narcissistic CEOs to engage in impression management behavior, to (i) fulfill their desire for public acclaim and (ii) protect the benefits associated with their reputation.

Hypothesis 2 (H2): The negative relationship between the narcissistic tendencies of a CEO and impression management behavior around an acquisition announcement is less pronounced for CEOs with a high reputation.

5.2.4.2 CEO Power

While we possess that a CEO's narcissistic tendencies lead to less impression management around acquisitions, we add that CEOs do not have unlimited discretion in a firm, but that the managerial power they hold is likely to influence the degree to which they can shape their firm's impression management efforts. Even though executives' power may originate from their own personal traits (e.g., being overconfident) (Malmendier & Tate, 2008), the literature especially recognizes the managerial power across top management team members (Chin et al., 2013). Finkelstein (1992) refers to this type of power as "the capacity of individual actors to exert their will" (p. 506) and argues that the distribution of power is unlikely to be equal across top management teams. Prior research has found a number of corporate outcomes that differences in managerial power affect, including compensation (Schmid et al., 2018), financial reporting (Baker et al., 2019), and corporate performance (Adams et al., 2005; Han et al., 2016). We argue that the ability of highly narcissistic CEOs to significantly influence the timing and content of corporate press releases and, therefore, to employ impression management, has a positive association with their degree of power in the firm.

Hypothesis 3 (H3): The negative relationship between the narcissistic tendencies of a CEO and the impression management behavior around an acquisition announcement is more pronounced for CEOs with higher degrees of managerial power.

5.3 Methodology

5.3.1 Dependent Variable

We assessed a firm's impression management efforts surrounding acquisitions through the technique of impression offsetting, which is defined as "actions initiated to positively influence external perceptions of the organization by releasing positive, but unrelated information, in anticipation of an event becoming known that may negatively violate external stakeholder expectations" (Graffin et al., 2016, p. 233). Empirical evidence suggests that individual top managers can exert significant influence on their firm's voluntary disclosure policy (Tsileponis et al., 2020). For instance, Bamber et al. (2010) document that managers exhibit unique disclosure styles associated with their demographic characteristics, reinforcing the choice of impression offsetting as our impression management measurement. Further, as Graffin et al. (2016) argued, employing reactive impression management tactics is unlikely to substantially influence stakeholders' perceptions following the announcement of a deal. As the majority of information is already publicly available at the time of the announcement, we do not expect that companies could positively reverse audience reactions to any meaningful extent by using reactive impression management tactics, such as additional justification.

Following previous literature, we measured *impression offsetting* as the number of positive news items the acquiring firm published via press releases, over a three-business-day event window [−1, + 1] around the announcement date of a deal (Brauer & Vandepoele, 2023; Graffin et al., 2016). We accessed Nexis Uni (previously LexisNexis Academic) to collect press releases that our sample firms issued from the four largest press release wires, namely, PR Newswire, Business

Wire, GlobeNewswire, and Marketwired. Because Nexis Uni does not link a press release to its issuer, we were required to distinguish sample firm-initiated press releases from those that only mentioned a sample firm. We applied a multilevel text-parsing approach programmed in Python, similar to Blankespoor & deHaan (2020). A press release was assumed to be issued by one of our sample firms if the firm's name appeared at the very beginning of the press release's headline or if it occurred within the first 250 characters of the body text, with the firm's primary stock market ticker symbol in parentheses immediately following. Additionally, if the company's name occurred within 100 characters of the words CONTACT or SOURCE or immediately after the phrases "Additional information about" or "More information about", we assumed that company had initiated the press release. We excluded deals for which the company did not publish a press release because we could not rule out the information on the acquisition having become publicly known outside our three-day event window. We assigned each of the acquirer published press release to one or more content categories based on the approach applied by Graffin et al. (2016). We considered the following categories to be clearly positive news and consequently coded the press releases as impression offsetting: buyback or stock split, award received from third party, customer win, new product release, and social good (e.g., donation). For press releases that could be positive, neutral, or negative news, we applied specific assignment criteria. That is, we classified a dividend announcement as being positive, neutral, or negative, depending on whether the amount of the dividend was higher, equal to, or lower than the previous one. Similarly, we classified earnings announcements and earnings guidance as positive, neutral, or negative, depending on whether the announced earnings (guidance) beat, met, or missed the most recent consensus of analysts' forecasts. Consistent with Graffin et al. (2016) we classified other announcements (e.g., executive retirement, divestiture, or the appointment of a new executive director) as impression offsetting if the company used an unambiguously positive tone in the press release to describe the event.

5.3.2 Independent Variables

5.3.2.1 CEO Narcissism

Such personal traits as narcissism are complex constructs that comprise multiple dimensions, not all of which are easily observable. We relied on archival data instead of using self-reported instruments to capture narcissism. This method ensured that a CEO's willingness, time, and self-perception to fill out surveys did not influence the data-retrieval process (Buchholz et al., 2018). To measure the narcissism of CEOs, we applied a measure based on the work of Chatterjee & Hambrick (2007), who introduced an index consisting of several indicators found to accurately capture the trait of narcissism. The index has become the most frequently used and continuously validated method for measuring CEO narcissism (Cragun et al., 2020). Our measure consisted of four items: (i) the CEO's cash compensation in relation to the cash compensation of the company's second-highest-paid executive; (ii) the CEO's non-cash compensation in relation to the non-cash compensation of the company's second-highest-paid executive; (iii) the prominence of the CEO's photograph in the company's annual report; (iv) and the ratio of the CEO's use of first-person singular (I, me, my, mine, myself) to all first-person pronouns (I, me, my, mine, myself, we, us, our, ours, ourselves).

To calculate a CEO's relative cash payment, we divided the cash payment (salary + bonus) of the CEO by the cash payment of the second-highest-paid executive in the firm (Marquez-Illescas et al., 2019; Rijsenbilt & Commandeur, 2013). Using a similar approach, we calculated a CEO's relative non-cash payment by dividing the non-cash payment (Execucomp variable TDC1 less cash payment) by the non-cash payment of the second-highest-paid executive in the firm. The prominence of the CEO photograph in the annual report was measured according to the following scale:

1. The annual report shows no photograph of the CEO.
2. The CEO is shown with one or more fellow executives.
3. The photo shows the CEO alone and occupies less than half a page.
4. The photo shows the CEO alone and occupies more than half a page.

Finally, using Nexis Uni, we collected transcripts of CEO speeches from corporate events such as analyst days, earnings calls, shareholder meetings, and industry conferences. For each event, we extracted the CEO speech from the transcripts and computed the ratio of first-person singular to collective first-person pronouns.

We calculated the average of each narcissism indicator using data for the two years preceding an acquisition and subsequently computed the *CEO narcissism* measure by taking the mean of our four indicators after standardization (Chatterjee & Hambrick, 2007; Tang et al., 2018). In line with previous literature on CEO narcissism, we omitted observations for a CEO's first year to avoid potential biases arising from CEO turnover and succession (Buchholz et al., 2020; Chatterjee & Hambrick, 2007; Olsen et al., 2014).

5.3.2.2 CEO Reputation

We used award data to measure a CEO's reputational status (Cho et al., 2016; Lee et al., 2020; Malmendier & Tate, 2009). We first retrieved personal achievement data for our sample of CEOs from BoardEx. Following Malmendier & Tate (2009), we created a list of the most prestigious business awards from the following sources: *Business Week*, *Financial World*, *Chief Executive*, *Forbes*, *Fortune*, *Industry Week*, *Morningstar*, *Financial Times*, *Time*, *Electronic Business*, and *Ernst & Young*. We excluded data on awards that only related to a CEO's wealth (e.g., ranked Xth on World's Richest People) as well as regional awards (e.g., Entrepreneur of the Year for New York region), strictly considering awards sufficiently prominent to significantly influence a CEO's reputational status. Finally, we created a *CEO reputation* dummy variable that took the value of 1 if a CEO received at least one award during the last five years before a deal announcement, and 0 otherwise (Malmendier & Tate, 2009).

5.3.2.3 CEO Power

Existing literature emphasizes that managerial power is a complex construct comprising multiple dimensions, some of which are less easy to observe than others (e.g., Florackis & Sainani, 2018; Schmid et al., 2018). We aimed to account for this multidimensionality by drawing on Finkelstein's (1992) framework of managerial power. Specifically, describing the ownership power dimension occurs in terms of CEO ownership in the company, i.e., the number of common shares the CEO held divided by the highest number of common shares held by any other executive in the company. Significant company shareholdings increase CEOs' discretion, which, in turn, magnifies their influence on corporate decisions (Finkelstein et al., 2009; Han et al., 2016). We employed the natural logarithm of this variable because it is heavily skewed to the right. We accounted for the structural power dimension by referring to a CEO's duality, signifying whether a CEO also served as chair of the board. CEOs who also hold the position of a chairperson are expected to have higher-level managerial power because chairpersons tend to wield substantial influence over strategic decision-making (Adams et al., 2005). Finally, we gauged the prestige power dimension by the number of board seats a CEO held outside the acquiring company. Prestige power refers to the influence executives wield as a result of reputation and social networks (Chikh & Filbien, 2011). We lagged each of the CEO power indicators by one year, standardized the values for each variable, and averaged them to develop our *CEO power* index.

5.3.3 Control Variables

Following existing literature on impression management and disclosure behavior, we controlled for a number of firm, deal, and CEO characteristics, to account for possible alternative explanations in our analysis (Bamber et al., 2010; Carter, 2006; Gamache et al., 2019; Graffin et al., 2016). We lagged each control variable one fiscal year prior to the focal acquisition. A full description of all variables is provided in Table 5.1 of Appendix B in the electronic supplementary material.

5.3.3.1 Acquirer Controls

Regarding acquiring firm controls, we incorporated four variables in our analyses. As larger firms are likely to issue more press releases, we included *firm size* as the logged value of the acquirer's market value of equity at day −42 relative to the deal announcement date (Aktas et al., 2016). Empirical evidence suggests that managers of firms with greater growth opportunities engage more actively in impression management (Davis & Tama-Sweet, 2012). Therefore, we included *Tobin's Q* in our models, calculated as the market value of a firm's equity divided by the equity's book value. Since firm performance has an association with impression management (Huang et al., 2014; Li, 2008), we captured performance using the firm's *return on assets*, defined as EBIT divided by the equity's book value. Finally, Graffin et al. (2016) documented that a firm's prior acquisition activity relates to its impression management behavior. We included *acquisition experience* as the number of deals in which a firm had participated within 10 years preceding the focal acquisition.

5.3.3.2 Acquisition Controls

We included five acquisition control variables frequently found to impact stakeholder reaction to acquisition announcements, which might influence a CEO's incentives to engage in impression management. Existing literature shows that shareholders of the acquiring firm react particularly negatively to the announcement of diversifying acquisitions (Renneboog & Vansteenkiste, 2019). We controlled for the industry relatedness between acquirer and target by implementing a dummy variable, *diversifying deal*, that equaled 1 if the acquirer and target differed in their Fama-French's 12-industry classification, and 0 otherwise. *Cash deal* (*stock deal*) controls for effects associated with the form of payment, taking the value 1 if the acquisition was financed entirely with cash (stock), otherwise equaling 0. Previous research suggests that analysts and shareholders tend to react negatively to an acquisition announcement if the target is a public firm (Capron & Shen, 2007). Hence, *target listing* took the value of 1 if the target was publicly traded, and 0 if not. Finally, we controlled for *relative deal size*, measured as the deal's transaction value divided by the *firm size* of the acquirer.

5.3.3.3 CEO and Governance Controls

Following previous literature on the impact of executive characteristics on impression management, we also incorporated CEO-level controls. Specifically, research suggests that *CEO age* may influence the decision to employ impression management (Gamache et al., 2019). We further controlled for *CEO gender*, coded as 1 for male and 0 for female, and *CEO tenure*, both of which research has shown to generally influence a CEO's strategic decisions (Wang et al., 2016). In terms of governance-related controls, we added *board size*, measured as the number of directors sitting on the board. Finally, we included the variables used to capture CEOs' power for testing Hypothesis 3 (i.e., *CEO duality*, *CEO no. of board seats*, and *CEO ownership*) as governance-related controls in the remaining models.

5.3.4 Sample and Data Collection

Table 5.1, Panel A, outlines the sample selection process. We sourced our acquisition data from Refinitiv Eikon, focusing on all completed acquisitions announced between 2009 and 2018, where both the acquirer and target were U.S.-based firms. Prior literature suggests an inverse relationship between transaction value and stakeholder reactions to acquisition announcements (Renneboog & Vansteenkiste, 2019). Consequently, CEOs are more likely to engage in impression management when the deal value is high. In line with this reasoning, we limited our sample to acquisitions exceeding $100 million. Concentrating on large transactions also increases the likelihood that the firm's CEO plays a central role in the decision-making process (Gamache et al., 2019; Graffin et al., 2016). Furthermore, we restricted the sample to deals involving a change of control—defined as the acquirer holding less than 50 percent of the target's shares prior to the announcement and attaining full ownership upon completion. We required that the acquiring firm be publicly listed, while the target could be either publicly or privately held. These decisions left us with an initial sample of 3,821 deals. We excluded 123 deals announced on non-trading days, as well as 572 deals involving acquirers in the financial sector, to avoid distortions arising from the unique regulatory environment of financial institutions (Busenbark et al., 2017; Marquez-Illescas et al., 2019). After these exclusions, our dataset consisted of 2,481 deals with complete control variables. Next, we collected press releases and measured impression offsetting as described in Sect. 5.3.1. We excluded deals where the acquiring firm did not publish a corresponding press release, as we could not confirm whether the announcement occurred within the three-day event window. Additionally, we removed deals where the announcement date reported in Refinitiv Eikon did not align with the press release date. This resulted in a reduced sample of 2,142 deals. We then gathered earnings release and dividend data to determine whether the press releases qualify as impression offsetting, using Refinitiv I/B/E/S, and supplemented this with acquiring firm control variables from Compustat. CEO data was obtained from BoardEx, and we matched each acquisition with the CEO in office at the time of the announcement, omitting deals where multiple CEOs were in place. This yielded a sample of 1,452 observations. Finally, we matched this dataset with our CEO narcissism measure, constructed as detailed in Sect. 5.3.2. Due to data availability constraints, our final sample comprised 648 deals executed by 362 unique acquirers. Table 5.1, Panel B, presents the distribution of the collected press releases by category. Of the 496 additional press releases identified (excluding those announcing the focal acquisitions), 197 (40%) were classified as impression offsetting.

Table 5.1 Sample selection and press release coding

Panel A: Sample selection

Step	**Observations**
Initial deal sample (2009–2018)	3,821
Less: Deals announced on non-trading days	−123
Less: Acquirers from financial industries	−572
Less: Deals with missing data on deal-level control variables	−645
	2,481
Less: Deals where the acquirer did not issue a press release	−279
Less: Deals with conflicting announcement dates between press release and Eikon	−60
	2,142
Less: Deals with missing data on acquirer controls, earnings releases, or dividend information	−581

(continued)

Table 5.1 (continued)

Less: Deals involving multiple CEOs at the time of announcement	−109
	1,452
Less: Deals with missing data on CEO narcissism measures	−804
Final sample	648

Panel B: Distribution of coded press releases issued by the sample firms according to the assignment categories proposed by Graffin et al. (2016).

Category	Positive	Neutral	Negative
Buyback or stock split	5	0	0
Attending conference	0	43	0
Dividend rate change	6	19	0
Earnings guidance	16	63	18
Earnings release	52	9	18
Seasoned equity offering	0	14	0
Shareholder meeting announcement	0	41	0
Award received from third party	9	0	0
Completion of another acquisition	0	0	3
Customer win	19	0	0
Issuance of debt	0	18	0
Divesture	0	5	0
Change in stock exchange listing	0	0	0
Executive retirement	0	2	0
Appointment of new executive director	0	14	0
New product release	51	0	0
Announcement of another acquisition	0	0	7
Product recall	0	0	0
Settlement of litigation or other legal dispute	7	3	0
Social good (e.g., donation)	7	0	0
Result of sponsored study	5	0	0
Other	20	22	0
Total	**197**	**253**	**46**

5.3.5 Analysis

We applied a negative binomial regression model because our analysis featured a nonnegative count dependent variable with a large number of zeros (deals in which no offsetting press release was published) (Greene, 2019). As the data of our impression management variable displayed overdispersion, we chose a negative binomial model over a Poisson model. Specifically, we estimated the following model to test the impact of CEO narcissism on a firm's engagement in impression management:

$$\begin{aligned} Impression\,Offsetting_{it} &= \beta_0 + \beta_1\, CEONarcissism_{it} + \beta_2\, AcquirerControls_{it} \\ &+ \beta_3\, AcquisitionControls_{it} + \beta_4\, CEOControls_{it} \\ &+ \beta_5\, GovernanceControls_{it} + \beta_6\, Industry_i + \beta_7 Time_t + \varepsilon_{it} \end{aligned}$$

where $Impression\,Offsetting_{it}$ is the number of positive news items the acquiring firm i published via press releases, over a three-business-day event window $[-1, +1]$ around the announcement date of a deal t. $CEONarcissism_{it}$ represents the level of CEO narcissism in firm i at time t. $AcquirerControls_{it}$, $AcquisitionControls_{it}$, $CEOControls_{it}$, and $GovernanceControls_{it}$ refer to the respective control variables as outlined in Sect. 5.3.4. We added Fama and French 12-industry ($Industry_i$) and year dummies ($Time_t$) to all models and used robust standard errors. As a robustness check we also applied a generalized estimated equation (GEE) to control for non-independent observations resulting from firms who account for multiple deals in our sample (Chatterjee & Hambrick, 2007). Using this specification did not change our results.

5.4 Results

Table 5.2 presents descriptive statistics for all variables, as well as their correlations. The mean narcissism score in our sample is 0.05, consistent with findings from previous research (Buyl et al., 2019; e.g.,Olsen et al., 2014). Impression management has a mean value of 0.29, indicating that most firms do not issue offsetting press releases around acquisitions, as noted by Graffin et al. (2016). The majority of the CEOs in our sample are male, with a mean age and tenure of 57 and 7 years respectively. Additionally, 78% of the deals are exclusively paid in cash, with mean deal sizes representing 24% of the acquirer's market value. The mean ROA is 9%, and the mean Tobin's Q is 2.12, both of which are consistent with findings from prior research on U.S. firms (Aabo et al., 2022; Schmidt, 2015). Based on the observed correlations, it appears that multicollinearity did not pose a significant concern when interpreting the parameter estimates in our models. Computing the variance inflation factor (VIF) shows that among all independent variables, the largest VIF is 4.5.

Model 1 of Table 5.3 presents multivariate regression results including only control variables. Contrary to the findings of Graffin et al. (2016), our results suggested that acquirers tend to engage more actively in impression management when the target is unrelated, i.e., the deal is a diversifying one. We also document older CEOs' and larger acquirers' greater degree of active engagement in impression management around the announcement of a deal. Model 2 includes our CEO narcissism variable. The results do not corroborate Hypothesis 1 that narcissistic CEOs are associated with lower-level impression management around acquisition announcements, per se. However, there still might be a positive relationship between a CEO's narcissistic tendencies and impression management, conditional on the factors described in Sect. 5.2.3.

Hypothesis 2 posits that we can expect narcissistic CEOs' reputational status to moderate their impression management behavior. To test this hypothesis, we interacted the CEO narcissism indicator with our measure for CEO reputation in Model 3 of Table 5.3. The results suggested that the reputational status of a CEO is likely to moderate the relationship between a CEO's narcissistic tendencies and the firm's engagement in impression management around acquisitions. To facilitate interpretation of the results, we illustrated the moderating effect of CEO reputation in Fig. 5.1, using low and high levels of CEO narcissism (one standard deviation below and above the mean, respectively). Figure 5.1 depicts a negative slope for CEOs with low reputation and a positive slope for those with high reputation. Notably, the positive effect of a CEOs reputational status intensifies for more narcissistic CEOs, as reflected by the steeper slope. To gain a deeper insight into the relationship between these variables we further performed a simple slope analysis. The results confirm a positive and significant association between CEO narcissism and impression management when CEO reputation is high, even for low levels of CEO narcissism ($\beta = 0.189$, $p < 0.01$). This effect is further amplified at high levels of CEO narcissism ($\beta = 0.451$, $p < 0.1$). In contrast, the association is insignificant for low-reputation CEOs ($\beta = -0.034$, n.s.). Collectively, these results highlight that a CEO's reputational status is likely to serve as a significant moderator in the relationship between their narcissistic tendencies and their motivation to engage in impression management.

Table 5.2 Summary statistics

Variables	Mean	SD	Min	Max	1	2	3	4	5	6	7	8	9	10	11	12	13	14	15	16	17	18	19	20	21	22
1 CEO narcissism	0.05	0.59	-1.45	6.18	1.00																					
2 Impression offsetting	0.29	0.63	0	4	0.02	1.00																				
3 CEO reputation	0.10	0.30	0	1	-0.06	**0.11**	1.00																			
4 CEO power	-0.02	0.62	-1.66	2.2	**0.09**	**0.10**	**0.16**	1.00																		
5 CEO gender	0.96	0.20	0	1	-0.05	-0.03	**-0.12**	0.02	1.00																	
6 CEO age	57.13	6.40	34	82	**0.18**	**0.09**	**-0.08**	**0.29**	-0.03	1.00																
7 CEO tenure	6.95	5.39	1.09	35.43	0.05	0.02	**0.15**	**0.42**	**0.08**	**0.33**	1.00															
8 CEO duality	0.44	0.50	0	1	**0.11**	0.04	0.03	**0.73**	0.07	**0.26**	**0.30**	1.00														
9 CEO no. of board seats	1.22	1.36	0	14	0.05	0.06	0.03	**0.46**	**-0.08**	**0.11**	0.05	0.075	1.00													
10 CEO ownership	1.04	1.76	-6.39	10.45	0.02	**0.09**	**0.23**	**0.73**	0.03	**0.18**	**0.41**	**0.28**	0.00	1.00												
11 Cash deal	0.78	0.41	0	1	0.01	0.01	-0.03	0.00	-0.01	0.04	0.04	-0.02	-0.01	0.03	1.00											
12 Stock deal	0.18	0.38	0	1	-0.02	-0.02	0.02	-0.01	0.05	-0.06	-0.06	0.02	-0.01	-0.02	**-0.88**	1.00										
13 Relative deal size	0.24	0.36	0	2.98	-0.07	**-0.08**	**-0.09**	-0.07	0.02	0.07	-0.03	-0.06	-0.00	-0.06	**-0.43**	**0.39**	1.00									
14 Target listing	0.29	0.46	0	1	0.03	0.04	0.04	**0.15**	0.01	0.04	**0.12**	**0.09**	**0.10**	**0.10**	**-0.29**	**0.22**	**0.20**	1.00								
15 Diversifying deal	0.29	0.45	0	1	0.05	0.075	0.071	-0.04	-0.03	-0.05	-0.07	-0.02	-0.06	-0.01	0.07	**-0.10**	**-0.10**	**-0.13**	1.00							
16 Firm size	22.60	1.58	18.96	27.32	0.07	**0.14**	**0.20**	**0.14**	0.05	0.01	-0.00	**0.12**	**0.10**	0.07	**0.14**	**-0.16**	**-0.36**	**0.13**	-0.01	1.00						
17 Tobin's Q	2.12	1.12	.76	9.96	**-0.09**	0.03	**0.16**	**0.10**	0.06	**-0.13**	**0.12**	0.01	0.01	**0.16**	0.00	0.01	**-0.20**	-0.03	0.04	**0.23**	1.00					
18 Return on assets	0.09	0.08	-1.01	.5	0.05	0.04	0.04	0.01	-0.04	**0.11**	0.04	-0.01	0.02	0.01	**0.12**	**-0.13**	**-0.19**	-0.03	0.04	**0.27**	**0.35**	1.00				
19 Acquisition experience	2.81	4.07	0	25	0.02	**0.09**	**0.10**	0.06	**0.08**	0.01	0.06	**0.11**	-0.03	0.03	**0.19**	**-0.17**	**-0.22**	-0.03	**-0.09**	**0.53**	-0.03	0.07	1.00			
20 Board size	9.48	1.96	4	16	0.05	0.04	**0.15**	0.00	-0.05	0.00	**-0.11**	0.04	**0.10**	**-0.10**	**0.11**	**-0.13**	**-0.15**	0.04	-0.03	**0.52**	**-0.12**	**0.09**	**0.27**	1.00		
21 CAR [-1,+1]	0.01	0.08	-.32	.85	-0.07	0.01	0.01	**-0.10**	0.03	0.01	0.05	-0.07	**-0.11**	-0.02	0.01	-0.01	**0.14**	**-0.17**	0.01	**-0.13**	-0.01	0.00	-0.05	-0.06	1.00	
22 Analysts forecast change	-0.01	0.06	-.51	.26	0.06	-0.02	0.01	0.05	0.04	-0.04	0.02	0.01	-0.01	**0.08**	-0.00	-0.02	-0.00	-0.04	0.02	-0.00	-0.01	-0.03	0.02	0.01	0.06	1.00

Note(s): This table presents descriptive statistics and Pearson correlation coefficients for the variables used in the estimation. Statistically significant correlations at the 5% level are highlighted in bold. Detailed definitions of all variables are provided in Table 5.1 of Appendix B in the electronic supplementary material.

In practical terms, compared to a peer with low reputational standing, a high-reputation CEO with an average narcissism score (0.05) is associated with a 37% increase in published offsetting press releases around acquisition announcements. For a robustness check, we applied more conservative measures of CEO reputation, classifying as high-reputation those CEOs who received at least one award in the last three years or within the year prior to the deal announcement. The results in both models remained unchanged.

Finally, according to Hypothesis 3, we can expect the effect of CEO narcissism on their level of impression management to be stronger if CEOs wield a higher degree of managerial power in the company. We tested this hypothesis by interacting the CEO narcissism index with the CEO power index. Model 4 of Table 5.3 presents results showing no evidence that CEO managerial power moderates the effect of their narcissism on impression management. To examine whether the moderating effect of CEO power is further influenced by CEO reputation, we estimated a model that includes a three-way interaction: *CEO narcissism × CEO reputation × CEO power*. The results, shown in Model 5 of Table 5.3, indicate that the interaction term is not significant. Ultimately, we reject the hypothesis that the impact of CEO narcissism on impression management is moderated by the CEO's managerial power.

Table 5.3 Effect of CEO narcissism on the use of impression management

	Model 1	Model 2	Model 3	Model 4	Model 5
Hypotheses-testing variables					
CEO narcissism		0.005	−0.111	−0.005	−0.121
		(0.133)	(0.161)	(0.133)	(0.152)
CEO reputation			0.197		0.038
			(0.258)		(0.295)
CEO narcissism x CEO reputation			0.945*** (0.344)		1.169** (0.486)
CEO power				0.213	0.166
				(0.146)	(0.155)
CEO narcissism x CEO power				0.020	−0.118
				(0.186)	(0.242)
CEO narcissism x CEO reputation x CEO power					−0.168 (0.539)

(continued)

Table 5.3 (continued)

	Model 1	Model 2	Model 3	Model 4	Model 5
CEO controls					
CEO gender	−0.374	−0.373	−0.199	−0.388	−0.237
	(0.420)	(0.421)	(0.375)	(0.405)	(0.364)
CEO age	0.037***	0.037***	0.039***	0.036***	0.038***
	(0.014)	(0.014)	(0.014)	(0.014)	(0.014)
CEO tenure	−0.021	−0.021	−0.016	−0.022	−0.016
	(0.018)	(0.018)	(0.018)	(0.018)	(0.018)
Deal controls					
Cash deal	−0.485*	−0.485*	−0.563**	−0.484*	−0.598**
	(0.286)	(0.286)	(0.278)	(0.288)	(0.282)
Stock deal	−0.101	−0.101	−0.190	−0.120	−0.222
	(0.310)	(0.312)	(0.312)	(0.315)	(0.313)
Relative deal size	−0.472	−0.472	−0.472	−0.462	−0.479
	(0.294)	(0.293)	(0.293)	(0.296)	(0.297)
Target listing	0.010	0.010	−0.022	0.005	−0.050
	(0.179)	(0.180)	(0.174)	(0.178)	(0.174)
Diversifying acquisition	0.484***	0.484***	0.448**	0.481***	0.454***
	(0.173)	(0.174)	(0.175)	(0.174)	(0.175)
Acquirer controls					
Firm size	0.162**	0.162**	0.152*	0.160**	0.142*
	(0.080)	(0.080)	(0.079)	(0.080)	(0.078)
Tobin's Q	−0.022	−0.022	−0.032	−0.018	−0.044
	(0.091)	(0.089)	(0.095)	(0.089)	(0.101)
Return on assets	−0.422	−0.424	−0.309	−0.383	−0.092
	(1.099)	(1.093)	(1.074)	(1.096)	(1.085)
Acquisition experience	0.005	0.005	0.009	0.003	0.007
	(0.019)	(0.019)	(0.019)	(0.019)	(0.019)

(continued)

Table 5.3 (continued)

	Model 1	Model 2	Model 3	Model 4	Model 5
Governance controls					
Board size	−0.041	−0.041	−0.041	−0.041	−0.043
	(0.049)	(0.049)	(0.049)	(0.049)	(0.050)
CEO duality	0.041	0.040	0.003		
	(0.183)	(0.183)	(0.185)		
No. of board seats	0.060	0.060	0.058		
	(0.046)	(0.045)	(0.045)		
CEO ownership	0.053	0.054	0.068		
	(0.041)	(0.042)	(0.043)		
Observations	648	648	648	648	648
Pseudo R-squared	0.0790	0.0790	0.0868	0.0785	0.0878

Note(s): This table reports the estimation results from the main analysis examining the effect of CEO narcissism on the use of impression management. Impression management is operationalized as the number of positive news items published by the acquiring firm through press releases within a three-business-day event window [−1, + 1] surrounding the deal announcement date. CEO narcissism refers to our composite measure of CEO narcissism, constructed from four individual indicators. CEO reputation is a binary variable equal to 1 if the CEO received at least one award within the five years preceding the deal announcement, and 0 otherwise. CEO power is a composite measure based on three indicators of CEO power. Full variable definitions are provided in Table 5.1 of Appendix B in the electronic supplementary material. All models include industry and year fixed effects. Robust standard errors are reported in parentheses. $^{***}p < 0.01$, $^{**}p < 0.05$, $^{*}p < 0.1$.

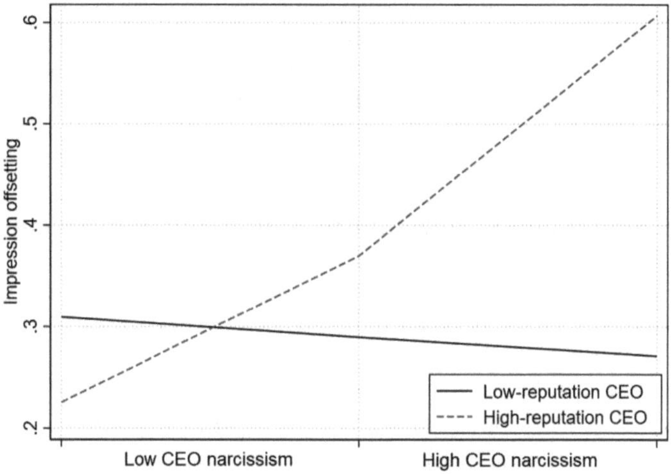

Fig. 5.1 Moderating effect of CEO reputation on the relationship between a CEO's narcissistic tendencies and the firm's engagement in impression management

5.5 Supplementary Analyses

Thus far, our results suggest that a firm whose more narcissistic CEO has a high reputational status engages more actively in impression management around the announcement of acquisitions. Next, we explore whether a firm's impression management effort actually leads to the intended effect of positively influencing the target audiences' reaction, focusing on two crucial firm stakeholders: shareholders and financial analysts.

Publishing positive but unrelated press releases will force shareholders to process the additional positive information, in turn reducing the likelihood of a strong negative market reaction to the deal announcement (Graffin et al., 2016). Averting negative stock market reactions ought to deeply concern CEOs, as these can significantly affect them in such crucial aspects as managerial reputation and compensation (Kuperman, 2003; Westphal & Clement, 2008).

The unique role of financial analysts for companies derives from their significant influence on stock market valuation and trading behavior (Westphal & Graebner, 2010). Serving as information intermediaries, analysts study firms they follow in depth, interpreting and disseminating information regarding the firm's strategic decisions, financial performance, and economic and industry trends (Westphal & Clement, 2008). Compared to analysts, shareholders tend to have less knowledge of firms' strategies and performance, so they often rely on analysts' recommendations when making investment decisions (Gamache et al., 2019). Given shareholders' and analysts' unique roles, companies engaging in impression management are likely to have a strong interest in influencing these groups' perceptions.

5.5.1 Shareholders' Reaction to Impression Management

To measure the effect of impression management on the shareholders' reaction to an acquisition, we estimated the following multivariate regression model:

$$\begin{aligned} CAR[-1,+1]_{it} = {} & \beta_0 + \beta_1 ImpressionOffsetting_{it} + \beta_2 AcquirerControls_{it} \\ & + \beta_3 AcquisitionControls_{it} + \beta_4 CEOControls_{it} \\ & + \beta_5 GovernanceControls_{it} + \beta_6 Industry_i + \beta_7 Time_t + \varepsilon_{it} \end{aligned}$$

where the dependent variable *CAR* is the cumulative abnormal return of acquirer *i* computed over a three-day event window [−1, + 1] around the announcement date of a deal *t*. We used the CRSP value-weighted index and the Fama-French three-factor model to estimate the CAR over a 200-day estimation window ending 30 days before the event window, to reduce the likelihood of a biased risk model estimation. To be included in the sample, each firm must have had at least 200 days of non-missing stock return data. Model 1 of Table 5.4 presents the multivariate regression analysis results. Contrary to the findings of Graffin et al. (2016), the results do not indicate that the publication of offsetting press releases around a deal announcement affects shareholders' perception of the acquisition.

5.5.2 Analysts' Reaction to Impression Management

We measured analyst reaction to a deal announcement as the change in the mean analyst consensus (Washburn & Bromiley, 2014). For a given deal, we subtracted the earliest average earnings per share (EPS) consensus after our [−1, + 1] announcement window from the latest average EPS consensus before the announcement window. We focused on forecasts for the first available period after the announcement of the transaction. The mean change in EPS forecast was −0.0022, indicating that, on average, analysts tend to view acquisitions rather negatively and, consequently, revise their forecasts downward following the announcement. The results of the multivariate regression analysis appear in Model 2 of Table 5.4. The results do not provide evidence that the perceptions of analysts change as a result of the publication of offsetting press releases around acquisition announcements.

Table 5.4 Effect of impression offsetting on shareholders' and analysts' reactions

	Model 1	Model 2
Impression offsetting	0.005	−0.003
	(0.004)	(0.004)
CEO controls		
CEO gender	0.010	−0.011
	(0.014)	(0.013)
CEO age	0.000	−0.000
	(0.001)	(0.000)
CEO tenure	0.001**	−0.001
	(0.001)	(0.001)
CEO duality	−0.011*	0.003
	(0.006)	(0.005)
CEO no. of board seats	−0.004**	−0.001
	(0.002)	(0.001)
CEO ownership	−0.001	0.002*
	(0.002)	(0.001)
Deal controls		
Cash deal	0.000	0.013
	(0.013)	(0.019)
Stock deal	−0.001	0.010
	(0.014)	(0.017)
Relative deal size	0.028	0.014*
	(0.020)	(0.007)
Target listing	−0.025***	−0.001
	(0.007)	(0.005)
Diversifying acquisition	−0.005	0.002
	(0.005)	(0.005)

(continued)

Table 5.4 (continued)

	Model 1	Model 2
Acquirer controls		
Firm size	−0.003	0.001
	(0.002)	(0.002)
Tobin's Q	−0.000	0.003*
	(0.004)	(0.002)
Return on assets	0.015	−0.022
	(0.039)	(0.024)
Acquisition experience	0.000	0.001
	(0.001)	(0.001)
Board size	−0.001	−0.000
	(0.002)	(0.001)
Constant	0.093	−0.036
	(0.069)	(0.046)
Observations	928	912
R-squared	0.100	0.048

Note(s): This table presents supplementary analyses. In Model 1, the association between impression management and market reaction is examined. The dependent variable is the acquirer's cumulative abnormal return over a three-day event window [−1, + 1] surrounding the deal announcement. Model 2 tests the relationship between impression management and analyst forecast revision, where the dependent variable is the change in the mean analyst consensus around the acquisition announcement. Full variable definitions are provided in Table 5.1 of Appendix B in the electronic supplementary material. All models include industry and year fixed effects. Robust standard errors are reported in parentheses. ***$p < 0.01$, **$p < 0.05$, *$p < 0.1$.

5.6 Robustness Tests

Analyses of the effect of executives' characteristics on corporate outcomes commonly express a key concern about the non-random allocation of managers to firms, which may cause sample selection bias. To accurately estimate the causal effect of narcissistic CEOs on impression management behavior, we would ideally be able to randomly assign highly narcissistic CEOs to some acquirers and to assign CEOs with a low level of narcissism to other acquirers (Reeb et al., 2012). However, in reality, random matching of CEOs with firms is unlikely. Instead, the firm's board of directors appoints them, based on specific criteria (Bertrand & Schoar, 2003). Consequently, some unobserved firm and/or CEO characteristics might correlate with both the impression management behavior around an acquisition announcement and our CEO narcissism measure, ultimately leading to biased findings. To account for this selection concern, we tested the robustness of our findings by following a propensity score matching approach (Rosenbaum & Rubin, 1983). Specifically, we created a treatment group (acquirers with highly narcissistic CEOs) and a control group (acquirers whose CEOs have a low level of narcissism) from our sample, ensuring that both groups were similar along observable characteristics. This balance allowed us to attribute observed differences in outcomes to the effect of the treatment (high level of CEO narcissism) versus the control (low level of CEO narcissism), rather than to differences in covariates (Narita et al., 2023; Rubin, 2001).

We constructed a high-narcissism indicator that took the value of 1 if our CEO narcissism measurement exceeded the industry-year median, and 0 otherwise. We then estimated a first-stage logistic regression to calculate the likelihood (as measured by the propensity score) that a firm had a highly narcissistic CEO in place, using observable CEO, deal, and firm characteristics. In the second stage, we used the propensity scores to match each treatment observation with a control observation, based on the nearest-neighbor matching technique (Malmendier & Tate, 2009). We applied a covariate balance test to ensure that the treatment and control groups were similar along observable characteristics. The results (available upon request) are consistent with the evidence of our baseline models, mitigating the concern that endogenous CEO-matching drove our findings.

Although we considered a number of firm, deal, and CEO controls in our models, it is possible that we omitted characteristics associated with both CEO narcissism and a firm's engagement in impression management. To further address this issue, we determined the extent to which an omitted variable must correlate with both the dependent variable (the number of offsetting press releases) and the independent variable (CEO narcissism), by using the impact threshold of a confounding variable (ITCV)[1] (Busenbark et al., 2022; Frank, 2000). The test indicates that to substantially bias our findings, we would need

[1] We were not able to apply this analysis to test the robustness for Hypotheses 2 and 3 because the ITCV cannot sufficiently address models including interaction terms (Busenbark et al., 2022). However, preliminary research suggests that the potential bias that omitted

to observe a correlation of 0.27 between an omitted variable and our dependent and/or independent variable. Existing research claims that an omitted variable exhibiting a correlation greater than the observed ITCV value would be highly unlikely if none (or very few) of the measured covariates exhibit such correlations (Busenbark et al., 2022). Among all the variables in our model, CEO age correlates most highly with CEO narcissism (0.18) and simultaneously exhibits a correlation of 0.09 with impression offsetting. The variable most highly correlated with impression offsetting is firm size (0.14), with a correlation of 0.08 with CEO narcissism. Given these results, we consider it unlikely that an omitted variable would exhibit a correlation with the respective variables greater than the required 0.27. Our results also hold when we consider an alternative construction of our impression management measure by computing the ratio of offsetting press releases to the total number of press releases around the acquisition announcement. Finally, we winsorized all continuous variables in our sample at the 1st and 99th percentile, to control for effects driven by outliers, and found no impact on the results reported in Sect. 5.5.5.

5.7 Discussion

Despite the emerging body of organizational literature documenting the use and consequences of strategies aimed at influencing key stakeholders' perceptions, research has stopped short of explaining the antecedents of such impression management efforts. Building on Upper Echelons Theory, we proposed that their grandiosity, positive expectancy bias and weak avoidance focus discourage narcissistic CEOs to engage in anticipatory impression management by publishing positive but unrelated press releases around acquisition announcements. Our investigation into this relationship offers notable insights. We do not observe a direct effect of CEO narcissism on impression management, indicating that more narcissistic CEOs do not inherently engage less in such activities. Instead, our findings suggest that the incentives for narcissistic CEOs to engage in impression management are likely contingent upon specific attributes of the CEOs themselves. In particular, the results indicate that more narcissistic CEOs with higher reputational status are more likely to intensify impression management efforts. This finding extends previous research highlighting narcissistic individuals' pronounced sense of entitlement to favorable treatment, which drives their

variables cause might be less pronounced in the case of interaction terms (Bun & Harrison, 2019).

strong desire to preserve the benefits associated with their reputation (Cho et al., 2016; Lee et al., 2020). The absence of evidence demonstrating a direct association between CEO narcissism and impression management is consistent with the evolving literature, which increasingly emphasizes the significance of contextual factors in influencing the manifestation of narcissistic traits (e.g., Brunzel, 2021; Cragun et al., 2020). This perspective suggests that understanding the impact of narcissism on organizational behaviors requires a nuanced consideration of the surrounding context.

Upon investigating CEO power as a potential moderating factor, we find no evidence that managerial power influences the relationship between CEO narcissism and firm impression management. This lack of moderation might be attributable to our operationalization of impression management through press releases. CEOs might generally have considerable discretion in selecting both the content and timing of corporate press releases, which may dilute the impact of their managerial power on impression management strategies.

Finally, contrary to previous literature, our results suggest that neither shareholders nor analysts valuations are affected by impression management efforts (Gamache et al., 2019; Graffin et al., 2016). One possible explanation could be the variation in the structure of press releases across the studies. Recent research by Brauer & Vandepoele (2023) on company downsizing announcements suggests that stakeholders' reactions to impression management efforts vary across different press release. Specifically, the type of news disclosed may influence how stakeholders respond to these impression management strategies.

5.7.1 Limitations and Future Research

This study has limitations that provide opportunities for further research. First, by focusing on the narcissistic behavior of CEOs, we take a rather narrow view, leaving out potential influences that relate to impression management, arising from other top management team members. Indeed, although CEOs often bear primarily responsible for strategic decisions, the literature has hinted at the role of other executives in determining corporate strategy and performance (Bedard et al., 2014). For example, the CFO widely appears to be the most important decision-maker in the company next to the CEO, with a "critical say in strategic and operational decisions,... often second only to the chief executive officer" (Zorn, 2004, p. 347). Accordingly, future studies could extend the research on the influence of other executives' managerial traits.

Second, we draw on offsetting press releases as an indicator of anticipatory impression management because the existing literature firmly grounds such an approach. However, managers choose from a large repertoire of various tools to influence the perceptions of certain audiences, such as issuing forecast guidance (Hayward & Fitza, 2016), strategically using an optimistic tone in earnings press releases (Huang et al., 2014), or applying linguistic complexity in annual reports (Li, 2008). Future research could examine whether the influence of executives' personal traits on impression management efforts varies with the applicable impression management strategy.

Third, while our measure of CEO narcissism is well-established in the organizational literature, we acknowledge its limitations in accurately capturing the multidimensionality of narcissism. Therefore, we see a fruitful avenue for future research in examining the robustness of our results to other CEO narcissism measures, such as the Narcissistic Personality Inventory (Raskin & Hall, 1979).

Finally, although our results are robust against various tests, we cannot completely rule out the possibility that omitted factors at least partially explain our findings. For example, insufficient within-variation prevents us from using CEO-firm fixed effects that would allow us to rule out certain alternative explanations that unobservable CEO characteristics cause.

5.7.2 Practical Implications

Subject to these limitations, our findings have practical implications for CEOs, stakeholders, and policymakers. While we acknowledge the challenge of monitoring psychological traits (especially one's own), CEOs capable of detached introspection might be able to leverage the positive aspects of narcissism (Petrenko et al., 2016; Rosenthal & Pittinsky, 2006) while avoiding some of its downsides. CEOs who can identify their narcissistic tendencies and recognize their potential influence on impression management behavior may deliberately incorporate steps to comprehensively assess associated risks (Gamache et al., 2015).

Stakeholders should be well informed about the combined influence of CEOs' narcissism and social status on efforts to obfuscate information. Adding to previous literature emphasizing the potentially harmful effects of a high-reputation CEO on firm performance (Malmendier & Tate, 2009), our results suggest that social status combined with narcissism distorts CEO behavior, incentivizing the CEO to employ actions in an attempt to protect personal benefits.

Finally, our ideas have corporate governance implications. We find that personal attributes of top management team members are likely to be associated with actions intended to obfuscate information. Policymakers establishing governance strategies must be aware of this relationship and attend to particular concerns about the importance of contextual factors that relate to narcissistic CEOs' personal benefits. Narcissistic behavior seems to manifest differently, depending on the setting; adopting governance practices accordingly must offset potentially harmful consequences (Desai, 2011). Carefully designed incentives might be one potential solution.

References

Aabo T., & Eriksen N. B. (2018). Corporate risk and the humpback of CEO narcissism. *Review of Behavioral Finance*, 10(3), 252–273. https://doi.org/10.1108/RBF-07-2017-0070

Aabo T., Jacobsen M. L., & Stendys K. (2022). Pay me with fame, not mammon: CEO narcissism, compensation, and media coverage. *Finance Research Letters*, 46. https://doi.org/10.1016/j.frl.2021.102495

Adams R. B., Almeida H., & Ferreira D. (2005). Powerful CEOs and their impact on corporate performance. *The Review of Financial Studies*, 18(4), 1403–1432

Ahern K., & Sosyura D. (2014). Who writes the news? Corporate press releases during merger negotiations. *The Journal of Finance*, 69(1), 241–291. https://doi.org/10.1111/jofi.12109

Aktas N., de Bodt E., Bollaert H., & Roll R. (2016). CEO narcissism and the takeover process: From private initiation to deal completion. *Journal of Financial and Quantitative Analysis*, 51(1), 113–137. https://doi.org/10.1017/S0022109016000065

Aktas N., Bodt E. de, & Dogan C. D. (2023). Do investor reactions to merger announcements shape the writing of SEC filings?

American Psychiatric Association (2013). Diagnostic and statistical manual of mental disorders, 5th edn. American Psychiatric Association, Washington

Anderson C., & Kilduff G. J. (2009). Why do dominant personalities attain influence in face-to-face groups? The competence-signaling effects of trait dominance. *Journal of Personality and Social Psychology*, 96(2), 491–503. https://doi.org/10.1037/a0014201

Arena C., Bozzolan S., & Michelon G. (2015). Environmental reporting: Transparency to stakeholders or stakeholder manipulation? An analysis of disclosure tone and the role of the board of directors. *Corporate Social Responsibility and Environmental Management*, 22(6), 346–361. https://doi.org/10.1002/csr.1350

Baker T. A., Lopez T. J., Reitenga A. L., & Ruch G. W. (2019). The influence of CEO and CFO power on accruals and real earnings management. *Review of Quantitative Finance and Accounting*, 52(1), 325–345. https://doi.org/10.1007/s11156-018-0711-z

Bamber L. S., Jiang J., & Wang I. Y. (2010). What's my style? The influence of top managers on voluntary corporate financial disclosure. *The Accounting Review*, 85(4), 1131–1162. https://doi.org/10.2308/accr.2010.85.4.1131

Bansal P., & Clelland I. (2004). Talking trash: Legitimacy, impression management, and unsystematic risk in the context of the natural environment. *Academy of Management Journal*, 47(1), 93–103

Becker J. A. H., & O'Hair D. (2007). Machiavellians' motives in organizational citizenship behavior. *Journal of Applied Communication Research*, 35(3), 246–267

Bedard J. C., Hoitash R., & Hoitash U. (2014). Chief Financial Officers as inside directors. *Contemporary Accounting Research*, 31(3), 787–817

Bednar M. K. (2012). Watchdog or lapdog? A behavioral view of the media as a corporate governance mechanism. *Academy of Management Journal*, 55(1), 131–150. https://doi.org/10.5465/amj.2009.0862

Bertrand M., & Schoar A. (2003). Managing with style: The effect of managers on firm policies. *The Quarterly Journal of Economics*, 118(4), 1169–1208

Blankespoor E., & deHaan E. (2020). Strategic disclosure and CEO media visibility. *Journal of Financial Reporting*, 5(1), 25–50. https://doi.org/10.2308/jfr-2018-0004

Bolino M. C., Kacmar K. M., Turnley W. H., & Gilstrap J. B. (2008). A multi-level review of impression management motives and behaviors. *Journal of Management*, 34(6), 1080–1109. https://doi.org/10.1177/0149206308324325

Bolino M. C., Long D., & Turnley W. (2016). Impression management in organizations: Critical questions, answers, and areas for future research. *Annual Review of Organizational Psychology and Organizational Behavior*, 3(1), 377–406. https://doi.org/10.1146/annurev-orgpsych-041015-062337

Bouzzine Y. D., Steen H., & Trautberg M. (2020). Listening to birdsong: Impression management of VW on Twitter during dieselgate. *Management Studies*, 10(3), 64–78

Bozeman D. P., & Kacmar K. M. (1997). A cybernetic model of impression management processes in organizations. *Organizational Behavior and Human Decision Processes*, 69(1), 9–30. https://doi.org/10.1006/obhd.1996.2669

Bradley M., Desai A., & Kim E. H. (1988). Synergistic gains from corporate acquisitions and their division between the stockholders of target and acquiring firms. *Journal of Financial Economics*, 21(1), 3–40

Brauer M., & Vandepoele L. (2023). Managing the "downside" of downsizing: Firms' impression offsetting around downsizing announcements. *Journal of Management Studies*, 61(8), 3684–3716. https://doi.org/10.1111/joms.13024

Brunzel J. (2021). Overconfidence and narcissism among the upper echelons: a systematic literature review. *Management Review Quarterly*, 71(3), 585–623. https://doi.org/10.1007/s11301-020-00194-6

Buchholz F., Jaeschke R., Lopatta K., & Maas K. (2018). The use of optimistic tone by narcissistic CEOs. *Accounting, Auditing & Accountability Journal*, 31(2), 531–562. https://doi.org/10.1108/AAAJ-11-2015-2292

Buchholz F., Lopatta K., & Maas K. (2020). The deliberate engagement of narcissistic CEOs in earnings management. *Journal of Business Ethics*, 167(4), 663–686. https://doi.org/10.1007/s10551-019-04176-x

Bun M. J. G., & Harrison T. D. (2019). OLS and IV estimation of regression models including endogenous interaction terms. *Econometric Reviews*, 38(7), 814–827. https://doi.org/10.1080/07474938.2018.1427486

Busenbark J. R., Lange D., & Certo S. T. (2017). Foreshadowing as impression management: Illuminating the path for security analysts. *Strategic Management Journal*, 38(12), 2486–2507. https://doi.org/10.1002/smj.2659

Busenbark J. R., Yoon H. E., Gamache D. L., & Withers M. C. (2022). Omitted variable bias: Examining management research with the Impact Threshold of a Confounding Variable (ITCV). *Journal of Management*, 48(1), 17–48. https://doi.org/10.1177/01492063211006458

Buyl T., Boone C., & Wade J. B. (2019). CEO narcissism, risk-taking, and resilience: An empirical analysis in U.S. commercial banks. *Journal of Management*, 45(4), 1372–1400. https://doi.org/10.1177/0149206317699521

Campbell W. K., Rudich E. A., & Sedikides C. (2002). Narcissism, self-esteem, and the positivity of self-views: Two portraits of self-love. *Personality and Social Psychology Bulletin*, 28(3), 358–368. https://doi.org/10.1177/0146167202286007

Campbell W. K., Goodie A. S., & Foster J. D. (2004). Narcissism, confidence, and risk attitude. *Journal of Behavioral Decision Making*, 17(4), 297–311. https://doi.org/10.1002/bdm.475

Campbell W. K., Hoffman B. J., Campbell S. M., & Marchisio G. (2010). Narcissism in organizational contexts. *Human Resource Management Review*, 21(4), 268–284

Capalbo F., Frino A., Lim M. Y., Mollica V., & Palumbo R. (2017). The impact of CEO narcissism on earnings management. *Abacus*, 54(2), 210–226. https://doi.org/10.1111/abac.12116

Capron L., & Shen J. C. (2007). Acquisitions of private vs. public firms: Private information, target selection, and acquirer returns. *Strategic Management Journal*, 28(9), 891–911. https://doi.org/10.1002/smj.612

Carter S. M. (2006). The interaction of top management group, stakeholder, and situational factors on certain corporate reputation management activities. *Journal of Management Studies*, 43(5), 1145–1176. https://doi.org/10.1111/j.1467-6486.2006.00632.x

Chatterjee A., & Hambrick D. C. (2007). It's all about me: Narcissistic Chief Executive Officers and their effects on company strategy and performance. *Administrative Science Quarterly*, 52(3), 351–386. https://doi.org/10.2189/asqu.52.3.351

Chatterjee A., & Hambrick D. C. (2011). Executive personality, capability cues, and risk taking. *Administrative Science Quarterly*, 56(2), 202–237. https://doi.org/10.1177/0001839211427534

Chatterjee A., & Pollock T. G. (2017). Master of puppets: How narcissistic CEOs construct their professional worlds. *Academy of Management Review*, 42(4), 703–725. https://doi.org/10.5465/amr.2015.0224

Chen H., & Hwang B.-H. (2022). Listening in on investors' thoughts and conversations. *Journal of Financial Economics*, 145(2), 426–444. https://doi.org/10.1016/j.jfineco.2021.09.004

Chikh S., & Filbien J. Y. (2011). Acquisitions and CEO power: Evidence from French networks. *Journal of Corporate Finance*, 17, 1221–1236. https://doi.org/10.1016/j.jcorpfin.2011.06.007

Chin M. K., Hambrick D. C., & Treviño L. K. (2013). Political ideologies of CEOs. *Administrative Science Quarterly*, 58(2), 197–232. https://doi.org/10.1177/0001839213486984

Chng D. H. M., Rodgers M. S., Shih E., & Song X.-B. (2015). Leaders' impression management during organizational decline: The roles of publicity, image concerns, and incentive

compensation. *The Leadership Quarterly*, 26(2), 270–285. https://doi.org/10.1016/j.leaqua.2014.12.003
Cho S. Y., Arthurs J. D., Townsend D. M., Miller D. R., & Barden J. Q. (2016). Performance deviations and acquisition premiums: The impact of CEO celebrity on managerial risk-taking. *Strategic Management Journal*, 37(13), 2677–2694. https://doi.org/10.1002/smj.2468
Christensen C. M., Alton R., Rising C., & Waldeck A. (2011). The new M&A playbook. *Harvard Business Review*, 89(3)
Cragun O. R., Olsen K. J., & Wright P. M. (2020). Making CEO narcissism research great: A review and meta-analysis of CEO narcissism. *Journal of Management*, 46(6), 908–936. https://doi.org/10.1177/0149206319892678
Custódio C., & Metzger D. (2013). How do CEOs matter? The effect of industry expertise on acquisition returns. *The Review of Financial Studies*, 26(8), 2007–2047
Davis A. K., & Tama-Sweet I. (2012). Managers' use of language across alternative disclosure outlets: Earnings press releases versus MD&A. *Contemporary Accounting Research*, 29(3), 804–837. https://doi.org/10.1111/j.1911-3846.2011.01125.x
Desai V. M. (2011). Mass media and massive failures: Determining organizational efforts to defend field legitimacy following crisis. *Academy of Management Journal*, 54(2), 263–278
Dickinson K., & Pincus A. L. (2003). Interpersonal analysis of grandiose and vulnerable narcissism. *Journal of Personality Disorders*, 17(3), 188–207
Elsbach K. D. (2012). A framework for reputation management over the course of evolving controversies. In: Barnett ML, Pollock TG (eds) The Oxford handbook of corporate reputation. Oxford University Press, Oxford, pp 466–486
Elsbach K. D., Sutton R. I., & Principe K. E. (1998). Averting expected challenges through anticipatory impression management: A study of hospital billing. *Organization Science*, 9(1), 68–86
Emmons R. A. (1987). Narcissism: Theory and measurement. *Journal of Personality and Social Psychology*, 52(1), 11–17
Farwell L., & Wohlwend-Lloyd R. (1998). Narcissistic processes: Optimistic expectations, favorable self-evaluations, and self-enhancing attributions. *Journal of Personality*, 66(1), 65–83. https://doi.org/10.1111/1467-6494.00003
Finkelstein S. (1992). Power in top management teams: Dimensions, measurement, and validation. *Academy of Management Journal*, 35(3), 505–538
Finkelstein S., Hambrick D. C., & Cannella A. A., Jr. (2009). Strategic leadership: Theory and research on executives, top management teams, and boards. Oxford University Press, New York
Florackis C., & Sainani S. (2018). How do Chief Financial Officers influence corporate cash policies? *Journal of Corporate Finance*, 52, 168–191. https://doi.org/10.1016/j.jcorpfin.2018.08.001
Frank K. A. (2000). Impact of a confounding variable on a regression coefficient. *Sociological Methods & Research*, 29(2), 147–194
Gamache D. L., McNamara G., Mannor M. J., & Johnson R. E. (2015). Motivated to acquire? The impact of CEO regulatory focus on firm acquisitions. *Academy of Management Journal*, 58(4), 1261–1282

Gamache D. L., McNamara G., Graffin S. D., Kiley J., Haleblian J., & Devers C. E. (2019). Impression offsetting as an early warning signal of low CEO confidence in acquisitions. *Academy of Management Journal*, 62(5), 1307–1332. https://doi.org/10.5465/amj.2017.0158

García-Sánchez I.-M., Suárez-Fernández O., & Martínez-Ferrero J. (2019). Female directors and impression management in sustainability reporting. *International Business Review*, 28(2), 359–374. https://doi.org/10.1016/j.ibusrev.2018.10.007

Graffin S. D., Wade J. B., Porac J. F., & McNamee R. C. (2008). The impact of CEO status diffusion on the economic outcomes of other senior managers. *Organization Science*, 19(3), 457–474. https://doi.org/10.1287/orsc.1080.0354

Graffin S. D., Carpenter M. A., & Boivie S. (2011). What's all that (strategic) noise? Anticipatory impression management in CEO succession. *Strategic Management Journal*, 32(7), 748–770. https://doi.org/10.1002/smj.906

Graffin S. D., Haleblian J., & Kiley J. (2016). Ready, aim, acquire: Impression offsetting and acquisitions. *Academy of Management Journal*, 59(1), 232–252. https://doi.org/10.5465/amj.2013.0288

Greene W. H. (2019). Econometric analysis, 8th edn. Prentice Hall, New Jersey

Haleblian J., Devers C. E., McNamara G., Carpenter M. A., & Davison R. B. (2009). Taking stock of what we know about mergers and acquisitions: A review and research agenda. *Journal of Management*, 35(3), 469–502. https://doi.org/10.1177/0149206308330554

Han S., Nanda V. K., & Silveri S. D. (2016). CEO power and firm performance under pressure. *Financial Management*, 45(2), 369–400. https://doi.org/10.1111/fima.12127

Hart W., Adams J., Burton K. A., & Tortoriello G. K. (2017). Narcissism and self-presentation: Profiling grandiose and vulnerable Narcissists' self-presentation tactic use. *Personality and Individual Differences*, 104, 48–57. https://doi.org/10.1016/j.paid.2016.06.062

Hayward M. L. A., & Fitza M. A. (2016). Pseudo-precision? Precise forecasts and impression management in managerial earnings forecasts. *Academy of Management Journal*, 60(3), 1094–1116. https://doi.org/10.5465/amj.2014.0304

Houston J. F., James C. M., & Ryngaert M. D. (2001). Where do merger gains come from? Bank mergers from the perspective of insiders and outsiders. *Journal of Financial Economics*, 60(1), 285–331

Hu W., Shohfi T., & Wang R. (2021). What's really in a deal? Evidence from textual analysis of M&A conference calls. *Review of Financial Economics*, 39(4), 500–521. https://doi.org/10.1002/rfe.1126

Huang X., Teoh S. H., & Zhang Y. (2014). Tone management. *The Accounting Review*, 89(3), 1083–1113. https://doi.org/10.2308/accr-50684

Jin J., Li H., & Hoskisson R. (2022). The use of strategic noise in reactive impression management: How do market reactions matter? *Academy of Management Journal*, 65(4), 1303–1326. https://doi.org/10.5465/amj.2018.1054

Judge T. A., LePine J. A., & Rich B. L. (2006). Loving yourself abundantly: Relationship of the narcissistic personality to self- and other perceptions of workplace deviance, leadership, and task and contextual performance. *The Journal of Applied Psychology*, 91(4), 762–776. https://doi.org/10.1037/0021-9010.91.4.762

Kacmar K. M., Carlson D. S., & Bratton V. K. (2004). Situational and dispositional factors as antecedents of ingratiatory behaviors in organizational settings. *Journal of Vocational Behavior*, 65(2), 309–331. https://doi.org/10.1016/j.jvb.2003.09.002

Kim J. J., & Anderson R. (2024). CEO narcissism and the agency cost of debt. *Journal of Empirical Finance*, 77, 101477. https://doi.org/10.1016/j.jempfin.2024.101477

Kimbrough M. D., & Louis H. (2011). Voluntary disclosure to influence investor reactions to Merger Announcements: An examination of conference calls. *The Accounting Review*, 86(2), 637–667

Kuperman J. C. (2003). Using cognitive schema theory in the development of public relations strategy: Exploring the case of firms and financial analysts following acquisition announcements. *Journal of Public Relations Research*, 15(2), 117–150. https://doi.org/10.1207/S1532754XJPRR1502_2

Lammers F., & Pape U. (2024). The impact of powerful CFOs in M&A: Evidence from U.S. acquisitions. *Review of Managerial Science*. https://doi.org/10.1007/s11846-024-00803-8

Lee G., Cho S. Y., Arthurs J. D., & Lee E. K. (2020). Celebrity CEO, identity threat, and impression management: Impact of celebrity status on corporate social responsibility. *Journal of Business Research*, 111, 69–84. https://doi.org/10.1016/j.jbusres.2020.01.015

Lehn K. M., & Zhao M. (2006). CEO turnover after acquisitions: Are bad bidders fired? *The Journal of Finance*, 61(4), 1759–1811

Li F. (2008). Annual report readability, current earnings, and earnings persistence. *Journal of Accounting and Economics*, 45(2-3), 221–247. https://doi.org/10.1016/j.jacceco.2008.02.003

Lovelace J. B., Bundy J., Hambrick D. C., & Pollock T. G. (2018). The shackles of CEO celebrity: Sociocognitive and behavioral role constraints on "Star" leaders. *Academy of Management Review*, 43(3), 419–444. https://doi.org/10.5465/amr.2016.0064

Malmendier U., & Tate G. (2008). Who makes acquisitions? CEO overconfidence and the market's reaction. *Journal of Financial Economics*, 89(1), 20–43. https://doi.org/10.1016/j.jfineco.2007.07.002

Malmendier U., & Tate G. (2009). Superstar CEOs. *The Quarterly Journal of Economics*, 124(4), 1593–1638

Marquez-Illescas G., Zebedee A. A., & Zhou L. (2019). Hear me write: Does CEO narcissism affect disclosure? *Journal of Business Ethics*, 159(2), 401–417. https://doi.org/10.1007/s10551-018-3796-3

Masulis R. W., Wang C., & Xie F. (2007). Corporate governance and acquirer returns. *The Journal of Finance*, 62(4), 1851–1889. https://doi.org/10.1111/j.1540-6261.2007.01259.x

McFarland L. A., Hendricks J. L., & Ward W. B. (2023). A contextual framework for understanding impression management. *Human Resource Management Review*, 33(1), 100912. https://doi.org/10.1016/j.hrmr.2022.100912

Miller J. D., Hoffman B. J., Gaughan E. T., Gentile B., Maples J., & Keith Campbell W. (2011). Grandiose and vulnerable narcissism: a nomological network analysis. *Journal of personality*, 79(5), 1013–1042. https://doi.org/10.1111/j.1467-6494.2010.00711.x

Narita K., Tena J. D., & Detotto C. (2023). Causal inference with observational data: A tutorial on propensity score analysis. *The Leadership Quarterly*, 34(3), 101678. https://doi.org/10.1016/j.leaqua.2023.101678

Noh J., & Zhou D. (2022). Executives' Blaming External Factors and Market Reactions: Evidence from Earnings Conference Calls. *Journal of Banking & Finance*, 134(106358)

Olsen K. J., Young S. M., & Dworkis K. K. (2014). CEO narcissism and accounting: A picture of profits. *Journal of Management Accounting Research*, 26(2), 243–267. https://doi.org/10.2139/ssrn.2115067

O'Reilly C. A., Doerr B., Caldwell D. F., & Chatman J. A. (2014). Narcissistic CEOs and executive compensation. *The Leadership Quarterly*, 25(2), 218–231. https://doi.org/10.1016/j.leaqua.2013.08.002

Park J.-H., Kim C., & Sung Y.-D. (2014). Whom to dismiss? CEO celebrity and management dismissal. *Journal of Business Research*, 67(11), 2346–2355. https://doi.org/10.1016/j.jbusres.2014.01.010

Patel P. C., & Cooper D. (2014). The harder they fall, the faster they rise: Approach and avoidance focus in narcissistic CEOs. *Strategic Management Journal*, 35, 1528–1540

Petrenko O. V., Aime F., Ridge J., & Hill A. (2016). Corporate social responsibility or CEO narcissism? CSR motivations and organizational performance. *Strategic Management Journal*, 37(2), 262–279

Raskin R. N., & Hall C. S. (1979). A narcissistic personality inventory. *Psychological Reports*, 45(2), 590

Reeb D., Sakakibara M., & Mahmood I. P. (2012). From the editors: Endogeneity in international business research. *Journal of International Business Studies*, 43(3), 211–218

Reina C. S., Zhang Z., & Peterson S. J. (2014). CEO grandiose narcissism and firm performance: The role of organizational identification. *The Leadership Quarterly*, 25(5), 958–971. https://doi.org/10.1016/j.leaqua.2014.06.004

Renneboog L., & Vansteenkiste C. (2019). Failure and success in mergers and acquisitions. *Journal of Corporate Finance*, 58, 650–699. https://doi.org/10.1016/j.jcorpfin.2019.07.010

Rijsenbilt A., & Commandeur H. (2013). Narcissus enters the courtroom: CEO narcissism and fraud. *Journal of Business Ethics*, 117(2), 413–429. https://doi.org/10.1007/s10551-012-1528-7

Rosenbaum P. R., & Rubin D. B. (1983). The central role of the propensity score in observational studies for causal effects. *Biometrika*, 70(1), 41–55

Rosenthal S. A., & Pittinsky T. L. (2006). Narcissistic leadership. *The Leadership Quarterly*, 17(6), 617–633. https://doi.org/10.1016/j.leaqua.2006.10.005

Rubin D. B. (2001). Using propensity scores to help design observational studies: Application to the tobacco litigation. *Health Services & Outcomes Research Methodology*, 2, 169–188. https://doi.org/10.1017/CBO9780511810725.030

Schmid S., Altfeld F., & Dauth T. (2018). Americanization as a driver of CEO pay in Europe: The moderating role of CEO power. *Journal of World Business*, 53(4), 433–451. https://doi.org/10.1016/j.jwb.2017.12.002

Schmidt B. (2015). Costs and benefits of friendly boards during mergers and acquisitions. *Journal of Financial Economics*, 117(2), 424–447. https://doi.org/10.1016/j.jfineco.2015.02.007

Tang Y., Mack D. Z., & Chen G. (2018). The differential effects of CEO narcissism and hubris on corporate social responsibility. *Strategic Management Journal*, 39, 1370–1387

Tsileponis N., Stathopoulos K., & Walker M. (2020). Do corporate press releases drive media coverage? *The British Accounting Review*, 52, 100881. https://doi.org/10.1016/j.bar.2020.100881

Tyler J. M., Connaughton S. L., Desrayaud N., & Fedesco H. N. (2012). Organizational impression management: Utilizing anticipatory tactics. *Basic and Applied Social Psychology*, 34(4), 336–348. https://doi.org/10.1080/01973533.2012.693449

van Iddekinge C. H., McFarland L. A., & Raymark P. H. (2007). Antecedents of impression management use and effectiveness in a structured interview. *Journal of Management*, 33(5), 752–773. https://doi.org/10.1177/0149206307305563

Wales W. J., Patel P. C., & Lumpkin G. T. (2013). In pursuit of greatness: CEO narcissism, entrepreneurial orientation, and firm performance variance. *Journal of Management Studies*, 50(6), 1041–1069. https://doi.org/10.1111/joms.12034

Wang G., Holmes R. M., Jr., Oh I.-S., & Zhu W. (2016). Do CEOs matter to firm strategic actions and firm performance? A meta-analytic investigation based on upper echelons theory. *Personnel Psychology*, 69(4), 775–862. https://doi.org/10.1111/peps.12140

Wangrow D. B., Schepker D. J., & Barker V. L. (2015). Managerial Discretion. *Journal of Management*, 41(1), 99–135. https://doi.org/10.1177/0149206314554214

Washburn M., & Bromiley P. (2014). Managers and analysts: An examination of mutual influence. *Academy of Management Journal*, 57(3), 849–868. https://doi.org/10.5465/amj.2011.0420

Welch X., Pavićević S., Keil T., & Laamanen T. (2019). The pre-deal phase of Mergers and Acquisitions: A review and research agenda. *Journal of Management*, 46(6), 843–878

Westphal J. D., & Clement M. (2008). Socialpolitical dynamics in relations between top managers and security analysts: Favor rendering, reciprocity, and analyst stock recommendations. *Academy of Management Journal*, 51(5), 873–897

Westphal J. D., & Deephouse D. L. (2011). Avoiding bad press: Interpersonal influence in relations between CEOs and journalists and the consequences for press reporting about firms and their leadership. *Organization Science*, 22(4), 1061–1086

Westphal J. D., & Graebner M. (2010). A matter of appearances: How corporate leaders manage the impressions of financial analysts about the conduct of their boards. *Academy of Management Journal*, 53(1), 15–43. https://doi.org/10.5465/amj.2010.48036721

Zorn D. M. (2004). Here a chief, there a chief: The rise of the CFO in the American firm. *American Sociological Review*, 69(1), 345–364

Research Manuscript 3 6

CEO Narcissism and Linguistic Complexity in Earnings Conference Calls

Abstract

Existing research shows that firms leverage linguistic complexity in corporate communication to obscure negative information and shape audience perception. In this study, we examine the impact of CEO narcissism on the strategic use of linguistic complexity during earnings conference calls. Driven by strong (weak) motivation for impression management in image-enhancing (threatening) scenarios, narcissistic CEOs are expected to employ less complex language when reporting favorable (unfavorable) performance. Utilizing a narcissism index comprising fifteen indicators, we find a significant negative relationship between CEO narcissism and linguistic complexity in the question-and-answer (Q&A) sections of these calls.

This chapter is based on the article: Lammers F., & Pape U. (2025). CEO Narcissism and Linguistic Complexity in Earnings Conference Calls. Accounting & Finance, 65(3), 3081–3106.
DOI: https://doi.org/10.1111/acfi.70031. Reproduced with permission from John Wiley & Sons; with minor modifications.

Supplementary Information The online version contains supplementary material available at https://doi.org/10.1007/978-3-658-51855-4_6.

F. Lammers, *The Role of Executive Characteristics in Financial Decision-Making*, Studies in Finance and Accounting, https://doi.org/10.1007/978-3-658-51855-4_6

6.1 Introduction

A substantial body of literature recognizes the valuation relevance of narrative disclosures conveyed through various corporate communication dimensions (e.g., Allee, 2015; Bamber et al., 2010; Brochet et al., 2015). Linguistic attributes such as tone, the presence or absence of boilerplate, and the use of euphemisms have been associated with the decision-making of crucial stakeholders, including investors (Bushee and Huang, 2024), financial analysts (Lehavy et al., 2011), and rating agencies (Bonsall and Miller, 2017). Given their potential influence, it is unsurprising that firms strategically employ linguistic attributes to shape audience perceptions of their actions and achievements (Brennan et al., 2009). Linguistic complexity has proven particularly effective in this respect, being central to accurately extracting and evaluating the information presented (Loughran and McDonald, 2016). Indeed, recognizing the importance of clear and concise language, regulators such as the Securities and Exchange Commission (SEC) have made substantial efforts to promote transparency in corporate disclosures, emphasizing the need to avoid linguistic complexity that could obscure critical information (SEC, 2013, 1998). The role of linguistic complexity as an impression management technique has also sparked significant scholarly interest in exploring the factors that drive its use in corporate disclosures. However, while much of this research has focused on firm-level determinants, increasing attention is being drawn to the underexplored influence of executives, prompting repeated calls for further examination into their role in shaping such practices (e.g., Gamache et al., 2019; Graffin et al., 2011). Given the effectiveness and subtle nature of strategically employing linguistic complexity, it appears crucial to better understand the factors influencing its use in corporate communication. Expanding on this, we examine whether chief executive officers' (CEOs) strategic use of complex language during conference calls is linked to their narcissistic personality. This focus is particularly relevant because intangible decisions, such as employing linguistic complexity in speech, are highly influenced by executives' psychological characteristics. Such actions often arise in situations where outcomes are uncertain, and probabilities cannot be easily calculated (Petrenko et al., 2016). Moreover, the frequent presence of narcissistic personalities in top management positions (Campbell et al., 2011) underscores the importance of better understanding how these traits might influence strategic corporate communication.

Narcissism has increasingly been used to explain behaviors in organizations, including risk-taking (Buyl et al., 2019), performance (Wales et al., 2013), and acquisition behavior (Aktas et al., 2016). As a personality trait, it is characterized by an exaggerated desire for self-enhancement, driving narcissists to pursue opportunities that underscore their superiority and enable them to receive adoration. Although these traits are often assumed to encourage efforts towards positive self-presentation, recent research indicates a more complex dynamic (Hart et al., 2017; Hart et al., 2019). Accordingly, narcissists are particularly motivated to manage impressions in image-enhancing situations, where they encounter promising opportunities to actively shape and promote their desired persona. Conversely, they show little motivation to engage in such behavior during image-threatening events, as evidenced—for example—by reduced hedging behavior (Buyl et al., 2019; Patel and Cooper, 2014). This motivational pattern is expected to manifest in earnings conference calls, with more narcissistic CEOs being less inclined to strategically use linguistic complexity to shape audience perception. Since disclosing poor earnings constitutes an image-threatening scenario with minimal potential for self-enhancement, we expect narcissistic CEOs to be less motivated to obscure unfavorable information through linguistic complexity. Conversely, reporting positive financial performance is ideal for narcissistic CEOs to reinforce their perceived superiority. Thus, these CEOs are likely incentivized to use clear and direct language to ensure their achievements are fully understood by their audience (Bushee and Huang, 2024). Ultimately, we conjecture that CEO narcissism negatively relates to linguistic complexity during earnings conference calls, even after controlling for firm performance.

We assess CEO narcissism using a fifteen-item index based on Rijsenbilt and Commandeur (2013) and employ the Gunning Fog Index (Gunning, 1952) to measure the linguistic complexity of CEOs' speech during both the scripted presentation and the more spontaneous question-and-answer (Q&A) part of each call. To more accurately capture the intent to convey a specific narrative through complex language, we follow Bushee et al. (2017) in decomposing complex language into its obfuscation and information components. Using a large sample of 3,931 U.S. firm-quarter observations from 2010 to 2018, we document that CEO narcissism is significantly negatively associated with using obfuscatory complexity during the Q&A section of conference calls. These results proof robust against alternative specifications for linguistic complexity and the use of a stacked difference-in-differences (DiD) analysis.

This study contributes to the existing literature in several ways. First, it advances the ongoing debate on the consequences of CEO narcissism for organizational outcomes. While prior research predominantly emphasizes narcissism's "dark side" (Borgholthaus et al., 2023), linking it to detrimental managerial decisions such as overinvestment (Ham et al., 2018), fraud (Rijsenbilt and Commandeur, 2013), and excessive compensation claims (O'Reilly et al., 2014), our findings offer a different perspective. Specifically, we show that CEO narcissism is positively associated with greater disclosure transparency during earnings conference call Q&A sessions, which are widely regarded as one of the most important channels for corporate communication (Matsumoto et al., 2011). In doing so, we add to an emerging perspective on potential benefits of narcissistic traits in the business context (Al-Shammari et al., 2019; Cragun et al., 2020).

Second, we contribute to the broader literature on impression management within organizational contexts. To the best of our knowledge, this study provides initial evidence on the relationship between CEOs' psychological traits and their strategic use of linguistic complexity in earnings conference calls. Although prior research highlights the effectiveness of linguistic complexity in shaping audience perception across various settings, its antecedents remain underexplored, with existing studies primarily focusing on firm-level characteristics. This gap is particularly notable given that manager-specific factors play a crucial role in shaping linguistic attributes of corporate communication (Davis et al., 2015). Against this background, our study responds to recurring calls for integrating an upper echelons perspective to better understand the drivers of impression management techniques (Gamache et al., 2019; Graffin et al., 2011).

Finally, we add to research on linguistic attributes. The majority of existing work in this domain focuses on written disclosure formats such as annual reports (Li, 2008), letters to shareholders (Amernic et al., 2010), and press releases (Davis et al., 2012). While these sources are often more accessible, they are typically drafted and refined by multiple individuals (Larcker and Zakolyukina, 2012), potentially biasing efforts to examine the influence of individual executives (Amicis et al., 2021). We utilize earnings conference calls as a more personalized disclosure channel, allowing individual executives to share information and directly engage with financial analysts' inquiries (Bae et al., 2023). This live interrogation provides a more authentic reflection of how personal traits shape linguistic attributes in corporate communication (Mayew and Venkatachalam, 2012; Burgoon et al., 2016). Relatedly, conference calls represent a particularly appealing opportunity to examine the impact of narcissism on firms' disclosure behavior due to their unique role in satisfying narcissistic CEOs' desire to continually reaffirm their superiority (Chatterjee and Hambrick, 2007). Conference calls are usually scheduled quarterly, followed by analysts, and garner substantial media coverage (Amernic and Craig, 2010), providing an ideal context for narcissistic traits to manifest.

6.2 Background

6.2.1 Linguistic Complexity of Corporate Disclosures

Linguistic attributes in firm communication convey incremental information, shaping how content is processed and influencing audience decision-making (Huang et al., 2014; Li, 2008). We focus on linguistic complexity, which has been consistently recognized as particularly impactful. Linguistic complexity is widely regarded as a broad construct encompassing various features, such as the use of technical jargon and abstract language. Despite its recognized significance, however, there is limited consensus on its precise components. Aligning with existing research, we adopt a comprehensive approach to linguistic complexity rather than isolating individual attributes, conceptualizing it as the broader challenge of whether the receiver can accurately interpret and reconstruct the intended message (Loughran and McDonald, 2016). Building on this, a more complex presentation of information makes it less accessible to audiences, creating confusion concerning what conclusion can be drawn from the disclosed information (Bloomfield, 2002; Fabrizio and Kim, 2019).

Prior studies suggest that linguistic complexity influences critical firm outcomes and stakeholder responses across diverse disclosure outlets. For example, in the context of CSR reporting, Gao et al. (2023) find that investors read and process CSR and financial information differently based on the complexity level in the disclosures. Focusing on remuneration disclosures, Hemmings et al. (2020) document that when CEO compensation levels are clearly excessive, reduced readability of the compensation discussion and analysis section leads to a higher likelihood of shareholder dissent. In their international study on the economic consequences of linguistic attributes, Lang and Stice-Lawrence (2015) document that more complex annual reports are associated with fewer analysts following and lower institutional ownership. This aligns with results obtained by Lehavy et al. (2011), which indicate that less readable 10-K filings lead to greater dispersion in analyst forecasts and lower accuracy. Bonsall et al. (2017) observe that firms with more complex annual reports experience greater post-filing stock return volatility, while Li (2008) demonstrates an inverse relationship between a company's reported earnings and the complexity of its annual reports. Furthermore, several studies highlight the negative effect of increased financial disclosure complexity on investment decisions, indicating that individuals invest less when disclosures are longer and more difficult to process (Elliott et al., 2014; Lawrence, 2013; Miller, 2010; Aghamolla and Smith, 2023).

Given such evidence emphasizing the valuation significance of linguistic complexity, researchers have begun exploring whether firms strategically employ those attributes to shape the interpretation of presented content and ultimately influence audience actions (Bloomfield, 2002; Merkl-Davies and Brennan, 2007). In this context, a firm's performance has been identified as a crucial factor incentivizing executives to shape audience perceptions through strategic linguistic narratives. Using an experimental design, Asay et al. (2018) find that negative earnings disclosures contain more passive voice and fewer self-references than positive ones. Similarly, Bushee and Huang (2024) document that managers strategically use increased linguistic complexity in earnings conference calls to obscure the true nature of poor firm performance, while employing less complex language and providing clear and informative technical disclosures when reporting positive firm performance. Matsumoto et al. (2011) suggest that managers provide less financial and more future-oriented disclosures in the presentation segment of conference calls when firm performance is poor. Kim et al. (2019) indicate that firms with persistent negative earnings obscure negative information by using complex financial reports, leading to stock price crashes when the accumulated bad news eventually reaches a critical tipping point. Indeed, Fabrizio and Kim (2019) suggest that this relationship extends beyond financial performance measures, demonstrating that companies reporting negative environmental information tend to use more complex language in their disclosures than those revealing positive environmental news. Moreover, literature indicates that conversations between analysts and executives provide valuable market information, and executives are more likely to refrain from answering performance-related questions during conference calls when the performance news is unfavorable (Rennekamp et al., 2022; Gow et al., 2021). Focusing on macro-level factors, recent studies provide evidence that political corruption (Chourou et al., 2024) and political uncertainty (Mekhaimer et al., 2024) are positively associated with the strategic use of obfuscatory language in conference calls.

6.2.2 Influence of Executive Characteristics on Corporate Disclosure

Recognizing that firm- and macro-level factors alone do not fully explain the strategic use of linguistic attributes, research increasingly employs an upper-echelons perspective to better understand executive behavior in corporate communication. The Upper Echelons Theory suggests that individual differences among executives—shaped by personal values, experiences, and cognitive styles—influence managerial decision-making processes, which is ultimately reflected in corporate outcomes (Hambrick and Mason, 1984). These differences are assumed to be evident in observable characteristics such as age, education, or functional background. In support of this, a substantial body of literature consistently demonstrates the impact of executive characteristics and traits on firm outcomes. In the context of corporate communication and disclosure, Davis et al. (2015) examine the influence of managerial fixed effects—reflecting individual management styles—on the use of tone in earnings conference calls, highlighting that "measures of tone do not simply reflect the current and anticipated economic events of the firm but also the way managers choose to describe these events" (p. 642). Echoing this view, Bamber et al. (2010) further demonstrate that managerial fixed effects can explain a significantly larger portion of the variation in linguistic disclosure choices than firm-specific factors, while managers' disclosure styles are related to demographic factors such as functional background and age. Hasan (2020) documents that managerial ability is inversely related to the extent to which managers' firms obfuscate their actual performance through complex language. Amicis et al. (2021) indicate that female executives use a more positive and less ambiguous tone than their male counterparts during conference calls. Similarly, Nadeem (2022) provides evidence of a positive relationship between board gender diversity and the linguistic complexity of 10-K reports. Other manager-specific traits found to influence linguistic attributes in corporate disclosure include overconfidence (Gong, 2023), tenure (Bochkay et al., 2019), and executive individualisms (Jiang et al., 2024).

In summary, existing literature suggests that executives can shape audience perceptions and evaluations of firms' financial disclosures through specific linguistic attributes. Linguistic complexity is particularly impactful and frequently used strategically by firms to influence audience perceptions. While an increasing number of studies explore the role of managers in this context, the extent to which individual characteristics contribute to these strategies remains poorly understood. Corroborating Upper Echelons Theory, we propose that a CEO's strategic use of complex language is partly a function of their narcissistic traits.

6.2.3 Narcissism

While clinical literature defines narcissism as a mental disorder that presents as "a pervasive pattern of grandiosity (in fantasy or behavior), need for admiration, and lack of empathy" (American Psychiatric Association, 2013, p. 669), we subscribe to the widespread view that it is not a mental disorder but rather a multidimensional personality trait encompassing a set of psychological characteristics that can be measured on a continuous scale (Chatterjee and Hambrick, 2007; Aktas et al., 2016). Research has identified two main subtypes of this trait: grandiose narcissism is characterized by attention-seeking behavior, a sense of grandiosity, a desire for dominance, and a tendency to exploit others, while those exhibiting vulnerable narcissism experience low self-esteem, feelings of restriction, and difficulty forming social connections (Miller et al., 2011; Dickinson and Pincus, 2003). Given that most existing research conceptualizes narcissism at the CEO level primarily in terms of grandiosity rather than vulnerability (e.g., Chatterjee and Hambrick, 2007; Kim and Anderson, 2024; Reina et al., 2014), our study focuses on the former subtype. This also aligns with studies suggesting that grandiose narcissism is more prevalent in high-status occupations compared to vulnerable narcissism (Campbell et al., 2011; O'Reilly et al., 2014). Therefore, in subsequent mentions of CEO narcissism, we refer to its grandiose form.[1]

Narcissists demonstrate grandiose expressions of self-importance, leading to a pronounced belief in their own superiority (American Psychiatric Association, 2013). This is reflected by high self-ratings on various agentic dimensions (Chatterjee and Hambrick, 2011), including leadership skills (Judge et al., 2006), intelligence (Campbell et al., 2002), creativity (Farwell and Wohlwend-Lloyd, 1998), and competence (Anderson and Kilduff, 2009). Fueled by their need for self-enhancement, narcissists have been found to engage in highly visible actions that reinforce their inflated sense of self-worth, such as pursuing large acquisitions (Capalbo et al., 2017; Buchholz et al., 2020; Chatterjee and Hambrick, 2007). When narcissists find themselves in the spotlight, they actively pursue performance opportunities aimed at receiving validation through the admiration of others (Amernic and Craig, 2010). While narcissism is typically associated with increased efforts concerning positive self-presentation, recent research suggests a more nuanced dynamic in this regard (Hart et al., 2017; Hart et al., 2019). Accordingly, narcissists are especially motivated to manage their impressions in situations where they can actively shape and promote their desired image. Their preoccupation with personal superiority drives them to invest maximum effort when encountering opportunities for self-enhancement (Wallace and Baumeister, 2002). For instance, existing research finds that when experiencing success,

[1] We acknowledge that various other psychological traits have recently gained scholarly interest, including overconfidence (Aktas et al., 2016; Galasso and Simcoe, 2011), hubris (Akstinaite et al., 2020; Tang et al., 2018), and individualism (Jiang et al., 2024). For a recent review on the influence of prominent traits and their differences, see Borgholthaus et al. (2023).

narcissists use linguistic strategies such as boasting about their achievements to satisfy their desire for self-enhancement and reaffirm their sense of superiority (Buss and Chiodo, 1991; Nathan DeWall et al., 2011). Similarly, in the organizational context, studies document that narcissistic CEOs seek to reinforce their grandiose self-image by promoting favorable media coverage (Aabo et al., 2022) or pursuing product innovations (Kashmiri et al., 2017).

By contrast, when facing image-threatening situations that offer limited potential for self-enhancement, narcissists might not exhibit increased motivation to employ strategies aimed at promoting their self-image. In this context, Hart et al. (2017) highlight that "grandiose narcissists do not seem to experience negative social emotions that signal image threat and motivate remediation to the same extent as non-narcissists" (p. 49). Psychological literature suggests that grandiose narcissism is inversely related to emotional responses that typically signal increased motivation towards impression management in threatening situations, including depression, feelings of vulnerability, social anxiety, and susceptibility to shame (Watson and Biderman, 1993; Lyons et al., 2019; Rose, 2002; Hendin and Cheek, 1997). Consistent with this, management studies show that when confronted with economic threats, narcissistic CEOs are less likely to adopt risk-mitigating behaviors, such as hedging or closely monitoring the market's behavior (Patel and Cooper, 2014; Buyl et al., 2019). Collectively, literature suggests that narcissists exhibit a strong tendency to proactively shape and promote their desired identity in situations that offer promising opportunities to do so, while showing little sensitivity to mitigate or prevent damage from image-threatening events (Hart et al., 2018). Building on the above discussion, we conjecture more narcissistic CEOs use less complex language during earnings conference calls. As noted in Section 2.1, previous literature has documented that executives are especially incentivized to use complex, obfuscating language to mitigate the risk of adverse stakeholder reactions. Reporting poor performance is likely to invite criticism of the CEO, creating a significant threat where narcissists see limited potential for self-enhancement and maintaining a positive image (Wallace and Baumeister, 2002). Considering narcissistic CEOs' low motivation to engage in impression management under threatening situations that do not provide opportunities for self-enhancement, we expect them to be less inclined to employ obfuscatory complex language.

On the other hand, reporting positive earnings provides an ideal situation for narcissistic CEOs to have their sense of superiority and positive self-image reinforced. In such cases, more narcissistic CEOs are expected to use clear, straightforward, and easy-to-understand language, effectively highlighting their success and ensuring broad recognition, fulfilling their desire for admiration and validation (Bushee and Huang, 2024). Moreover, recent research documents that executives with higher management abilities will likely employ less complex language in corporate disclosures to effectively reveal their superior performance (Hasan, 2020). Since narcissistic CEOs hold an inflated self-view, believing in their exceptional management skills (Judge et al., 2006), CEOs with higher levels of narcissism might adopt more straightforward and accessible language to project an image of superior performance. We present our reasoning visually in Fig. 6.1.

Building on the preceding discussion, we propose the following hypothesis:

Hypothesis 1: CEOs with greater narcissistic tendencies use less complex language during earnings conference calls to obfuscate information.

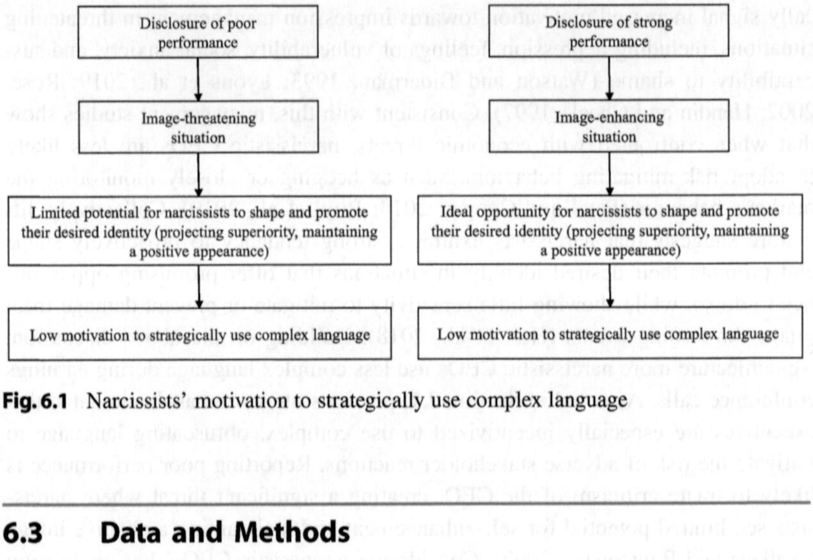

Fig. 6.1 Narcissists' motivation to strategically use complex language

6.3 Data and Methods

6.3.1 CEO Narcissism

Due to the multifaceted nature of personality traits such as narcissism and the fact that some aspects are difficult to directly observe, we leverage archival data rather than self-reported measures. This approach mitigates the potential biases that might arise from a CEO's reluctance, availability, or self-perception when responding to surveys (Buchholz et al., 2018). We construct our narcissism measure based on Rijsenbilt and Commandeur (2013), who introduced an index comprising fifteen indicators. To our knowledge, this measure utilizes the largest available set of indicators to assess CEO narcissism, offering enhanced measurement accuracy compared to other proxies by relying on a more concise set of dimensions (Buchholz et al., 2020; Cragun et al., 2020). The items reflect the four dimensions of (1) compensation, (2) public exposure, (3) managerial power, and (4) acquisition behavior.

The compensation dimension comprises five indicators relating to a narcissistic individual's overly developed sense of self-importance. Chatterjee and Hambrick (2007) highlight that "the highly narcissistic CEO believes he or she is far more valuable than anyone else in the firm, and this then becomes reflected in the CEO's compensation relative to others" (p. 364). First, we include the CEO's cash (salary + bonus) and total compensation in absolute terms, using data from Compustat Execucomp. We also include the CEO's cash compensation and total compensation relative to the company's second-highest-paid executive. Finally, we create an ordinal measure reflecting the CEO's cash compensation rank compared to all other executives. Higher ranks on this scale refer to higher levels of narcissism.

The second dimension measures CEOs' public exposure through five indicators. A CEO's public exposure refers to information highlighting the firm's leader, emphasizing personality traits that reinforce the myth of an exceptional leader and savior (Rijsenbilt and Commandeur, 2013). Highly narcissistic CEOs address their need for self-reinforcement and public acclaim through public exposure, such as by seeking enhanced media coverage (Chatterjee and Pollock, 2017; Aabo et al., 2022). The first indicator measures the prominence of the CEO's photograph in the company's annual report, with a score of 1 assigned if the report shows no CEO photograph, 2 if the CEO is shown with one or more fellow executives, 3 if the photograph shows the CEO alone and occupies less than half a page, and 4 if the photograph shows the CEO alone and occupies more than half a page (Chatterjee and Hambrick, 2007). We utilize the Marquis Who's Who database to count the number of awards and lines in the CEO's biography, constituting the second and third indicators, respectively. The fourth indicator represents the number of times that the CEO is mentioned jointly with the firm's name in major U.S. business outlets, measured using the Dow Jones Factiva database. We scale the number of mentions by the number of tenure years to derive the average annual number of publications per CEO. Finally, we include data from the annual DEF 14 A proxy statement on the value of CEOs' personal use of corporate aircraft as a fifth indicator. Perquisites such as the personal use of corporate aircraft reinforce the CEO's status within an organization, satisfying a narcissistic CEO's constant desire to display status and grandiosity (Rijsenbilt and Commandeur, 2013).

As the managerial power of top management team members is crucial to their ability to influence decisions and outcomes (Chin et al., 2013), highly narcissistic CEOs will seek to centralize decision-making power to satisfy their desire for self-importance. Our measure captures the managerial power dimension using three indicators: the number of role titles as indicated in the Execucomp database; CEO duality as a binary variable equal to 1 if the CEO is also chair of the board and 0 otherwise; and the organization's score in the London Stock Exchange Group (LSEG; formerly Refinitiv) Governance index, which measures shareholder rights in a firm.

Regarding the acquisition behavior dimension, we apply a final set of indicators to capture a narcissistic CEO's need for superiority (Chatterjee and Hambrick, 2007). For this purpose, we collect the number and value of acquisitions during a CEO's tenure using the LSEG Eikon database, including all deals with a value of at least 10 million USD where 50% or more of the target firm is acquired. These two variables are scaled by the firm's market value and subsequently divided by the CEO's tenure years.

Table 6.1 reports the correlation matrix for the fifteen items. Notably, we observe a similar pattern as reported by Rijsenbilt and Commandeur (2013), who based their work on CEOs of S&P 500 companies from 1992 to 2008. We employ principal component analysis to derive an overall measure of CEO narcissism (*Narcissism*). Consistent with prior studies using this approach for assessing narcissism, we extract four components with eigenvalues ranging from 1.25 to 2.02 (Buchholz et al., 2018; Buchholz et al., 2020; Rijsenbilt and Commandeur, 2013). Table 6.2 presents the factor loadings (> 0.20) for the fifteen items. To enhance the validity of our CEO narcissism measure, we also construct a narcissism index based on Chatterjee and Hambrick's (2007) method, which is widely recognized as the most frequently used and consistently validated approach for measuring CEO narcissism (Cragun et al., 2020). Our analysis indicates a significant positive correlation ($r = 0.52$, $p < 0.001$) between the two measures.

Table 6.1 Pearson's correlation matrix

Variable	(1)	(2)	(3)	(4)	(5)	(6)	(7)	(8)	(9)	(10)	(11)	(12)	(13)	(14)	(15)
(1) Cash compensation	1.000														
(2) Total compensation	**0.421**	1.000													
(3) Cash compensation ratio	**0.318**	−0.009	1.000												
(4) Total compensation ratio	−0.012	**0.215**	**0.374**	1.000											
(5) Cash compensation rank	**−0.057**	**0.076**	**−0.549**	**−0.208**	1.000										
(6) Photography size	**−0.139**	−0.025	−0.023	**0.033**	−0.002	1.000									
(7) No. of awards	**0.217**	**0.139**	**0.038**	**−0.147**	0.005	**−0.074**	1.000								
(8) Biography lines	**0.045**	**0.119**	−0.028	−0.023	0.008	0.003	**0.324**	1.000							
(9) Publicity	**0.208**	**0.166**	0.004	**−0.205**	**0.181**	**−0.033**	**0.407**	**0.154**	1.000						
(10) Jet use	**0.300**	**0.283**	**0.074**	−0.009	0.008	**−0.106**	**0.159**	**0.075**	**0.049**	1.000					
(11) No. of titles	**−0.045**	**−0.061**	−0.028	**0.037**	0.030	**−0.067**	**0.045**	0.025	**−0.046**	0.007	1.000				
(12) Duality	**0.166**	**0.110**	**0.140**	**0.046**	**−0.045**	**0.155**	**0.091**	**0.222**	**−0.054**	**0.139**	**−0.092**	1.000			
(13) Governance	**−0.069**	**−0.044**	0.022	0.019	**−0.046**	**0.045**	−0.012	0.022	**0.052**	**−0.104**	**0.038**	**0.036**	1.000		
(14) Number of M&A	**0.159**	**0.271**	**0.061**	**0.033**	0.009	−0.028	**−0.048**	−0.011	0.028	**0.071**	**−0.122**	−0.018	**−0.070**	1.000	
(15) Value of M&A	−0.005	0.004	−0.024	**−0.049**	−0.023	**−0.077**	**−0.032**	−0.025	−0.031	−0.008	**0.055**	**−0.061**	**0.041**	0.010	1.000

This table presents the Pearson correlation matrix for the individual items used to construct the CEO narcissism measure. Correlation coefficients in bold are significant at the 5% level. Full variable definitions are provided in Table 1 of Appendix C in the electronic supplementary material

Our sample comprises firms that were consistently part of the S&P 500 from 2010 to 2018. After identifying this initial set of 349 companies, we collect their quarterly earnings conference call transcripts from LSEG Eikon. We focus on conference calls that follow earnings announcements, specifically those held on the day of or following the announcement (Chen et al., 2013). We obtain 14,041 raw transcripts and identify a firm's CEO by parsing the corporate participant's part of each call. A typical conference call comprises a prepared presentation segment essentially reiterating the content of the earnings press release (Price et al., 2012), followed by a more spontaneous Q&A session during which analysts can ask questions. We separately extract the CEO's speech during the company's presentation of the results and the subsequent Q&A session. Next, we merge the conference call data with the CEO narcissism data, excluding observations where the CEO's name from the conference call transcript does not match the name provided by the Compustat data. In line with previous literature on CEO narcissism, observations for a CEO's first year are omitted to avoid potential biases arising from CEO turnover and succession (Olsen et al., 2014; Buchholz et al., 2020; Chatterjee and Hambrick, 2007). We also only retain observations where the CEO's intervention in the presentation and Q&A comprises at least 200 words (Amicis et al., 2021). Our final sample includes 203 unique firms and 3,931 firm-quarter observations.

Table 6.2 Factor loadings

Variable	Component 1	Component 2	Component 3	Component 4
Cash compensation		0.553		
Total compensation		0.555		
Cash compensation ratio	0.607			
Total compensation ratio	0.465			
Cash compensation rank	−0.571			
Photography size				0.622
No. of awards			0.600	
Biography lines			0.584	
Publicity	−0.218	0.214	0.332	
Jet use		0.330		

(continued)

Table 6.2 (continued)

Variable	Component 1	Component 2	Component 3	Component 4
No. of titles				−0.518
Duality			0.240	0.447
Governance				
Number of M&A		0.366	−0.214	
Value of M&A				−0.290
Eigenvalues	**2.012**	**1.926**	**1.376**	**1.248**

This table displays the factor loadings for the fifteen components of CEO narcissism. Blank cells indicate absolute loadings < 0.2. Full variable definitions are provided in Table 1 of Appendix C in the electronic supplementary material

6.3.2 Linguistic Complexity

Following recent literature on linguistic complexity in conference calls (e.g., Bushee et al., 2017; Bushee and Huang, 2024; Mekhaimer et al., 2024; Chourou et al., 2024), we employ the Gunning Fog Index (Gunning, 1952) to measure the complexity of CEOs' and analysts' speech during the conference calls. The Gunning Fog Index captures linguistic complexity as a function of the average sentence length (in words) and the percentage of complex words (words with three syllables or more):

$$FogIndex = \left[\left(\frac{words}{sentences}\right) + 100\left(\frac{complexwords}{words}\right)\right]0.4 \quad (6.1)$$

The index value indicates the years of formal education required to understand the given text on a first read, with a higher score indicating a more complex text.

In establishing the association between CEO narcissism and the use of linguistic complexity, we encounter what Leuz and Wysocki (2016) describe as the "fundamental problem" of readability measures, namely distinguishing between informative and obfuscatory complexity. Indeed, while previous research has often assumed that complex language is used as an intentional strategy to obscure information, it might simply be required to accurately describe a firm's operations or financial situation. Building upon this argument, Bushee et al. (2017) illustrate how language complexity can be decomposed into two components: "The information component represents linguistic complexity attributable to informative technical disclosure about the business. The obfuscation component represents linguistic complexity intended to reduce the informativeness of the disclosure" (p. 86). Following Bushee et al. (2017), we isolate the latent obfuscation component by using the linguistic complexity of analysts attending the conference call as a benchmark for the inherent level of informative technical disclosure, i.e., the information component. Specifically, we estimate the following regression model:

$$Fog(.)_{iq} = \beta_0 + \beta_1 Fog(Analysts)_{iq} + \delta Controls_{iq} + \varepsilon_{iq} \tag{6.2}$$

where *Fog*(.) refers to either *Fog*(*Pres*) or *Fog*(*QA*), representing the complexity of the CEO's speech in the presentation and Q&A sections of the call, respectively. *Fog*(*Analysts*) captures the complexity of the analysts' speech during the call. δ*Controls* includes a set of control variables—as suggested by Bushee et al. (2017)—that might not be reflected in the complexity of the analysts' speech. These controls include firm size (*Size*), leverage (*Leverage*), book-to-market ratio (*BTM*), capital intensity (*Capital intensity*), capital expenditures (*Capex*), acquisition value (*Acquisitions*), stock and debt issuance (*Financing*), goodwill impairment (*Goodwill*), research and development expenditures (*R&D*), restructuring charges (*Restructuring*), the standard deviation of operating cash flows (σ*CFO*), and stock returns (*Return*). The fitted values from the estimation represent the information component, *Info*(*Pres*) and *Info*(*QA*). The residual captures the obfuscatory element of the CEO's narrative disclosure, which we use to construct our dependent variables of interest, *Obf* (*Pres*) and *Obf* (*QA*). . We apply industry and time fixed effects and adjust standard errors by clustering observations at the firm level and by conference call date (Chourou et al., 2024).

Table 6.3 presents the regression estimation results for the presentation and Q&A segments of the call, respectively. Consistent with Bushee et al. (2017), we observe a significant positive relationship between CEO and analyst use of complex language in both the presentation and Q&A sections.

Table 6.3 Decomposition of information and obfuscation components in complex language

	(1) Fog(Pres)	(2) Fog(QA)
Fog(Analysts)	0.188**	0.527***
	(0.082)	(0.062)
Size	−0.284**	−0.058
	(0.116)	(0.082)
Leverage	0.222	0.665
	(0.844)	(0.471)
BTM	−0.585	0.093
	(0.363)	(0.256)
Capital intensity	−0.856	−0.334
	(0.795)	(0.449)
Capex	−12.978	−0.616
	(11.719)	(8.834)
Acquisitions	0.924	2.245*
	(2.557)	(1.216)
Financing	−0.407	−0.373
	(2.292)	(0.699)
Goodwill	−0.088	−0.199
	(0.323)	(0.163)
R&D	3.251	0.542
	(2.664)	(1.975)
Restructuring	0.054	−0.186
	(0.212)	(0.117)
σCFO	0.300	3.555
	(9.350)	(5.182)
Return	−0.000	−0.000
	(0.003)	(0.002)
Constant	17.374***	6.609***
	(1.365)	(0.971)

(continued)

Table 6.3 (continued)

	(1) Fog(Pres)	(2) Fog(QA)
N	3,979	3,979
Industry FE	Yes	Yes
Time FE	Yes	Yes
Adj. R-squared	12.61	15.62

This table presents the estimation results of the regression used to decompose the information and obfuscation components of complex language, following the approach developed by Bushee et al. (2017). The dependent variables in Models 1 and 2—Fog(Pres) and Fog(QA)—represent the complexity of the CEO's speech during the presentation and Q&A portions of the call, as measured by the Gunning Fog Index. Fog(Analysts) denotes the complexity of the analysts' speech during the call. Additional variables serve as controls to account for effects potentially influencing speech complexity beyond the analysts' language. Full variable definitions are provided in Table 1 of Appendix C in the electronic supplementary material. Robust standard errors clustered at the firm and date level are provided in parentheses. *** p<0.01, ** p<0.05, * p<0.1

6.3.3 Controls

For our main analysis, we include several control variables that have been found to influence firms' narrative disclosures. The first set of control variables aims to capture the effect on linguistic attributes of a firm's current performance and future outlook. As executives have been frequently found to employ more complex language when reporting negative earnings news (Li, 2008), we include an indicator variable *Loss*, equal to 1 for quarters with negative earnings and 0 otherwise. We further measure a firm's *Sales growth*, calculated as the change in sales from the same quarter of the previous year (Davis et al., 2015). *Return on assets* represents quarterly earnings before extraordinary items divided by total assets. In addition to these accounting-based measures, we include the firm's *Stock return* calculated over the quarterly period.

We also include control variables related to the complexity of the financial disclosures, stemming from the firm's operations. We incorporate the number of business segments (*No. business segments*) and geographic segments (*No. geographical segments*) a firm operates into our analyses to address the influence of a firm's business complexity on its executives' usage of linguistic complexity (Huang et al., 2014). As previous studies document that the complexity of financial disclosures increases with firm size, we include *Size*, calculated as the logged value of the firm's quarterly market value (Franco et al., 2015). Additionally, *Leverage* controls for effects associated with the possibility that executives of firms with more equity financing might be more sensitive to shareholders' reactions, potentially incentivizing them to conduct impression management through linguistic complexity (Allee, 2015). Given that a firm's level of institutional ownership has been found to positively influence the complexity of financial disclosures (Lang and Stice-Lawrence, 2015), we control for the percentage of institutional ownership (*Inst. ownership*). Furthermore, as existing studies suggest that firms' growth opportunities are associated with using complex language in financial disclosures (Hasan, 2020), we seek to control for this effect by including a firm's book-to-market ratio (*BTM*), calculated as the book value of equity divided by the market value of equity.

Since financial analysts are a crucial audience for earnings conference calls, their role might incentivize CEOs to employ more complex language through various mechanisms. The control variable *Earnings surprise* is included to represent the difference between reported earnings per share and the latest analyst mean forecast. *Forecast missed* equals 1 if *Earnings surprise* is negative and 0 otherwise. As a proxy for investors' interest in a firm, we control for *Analysts following*, defined as the number of analysts contributing to the latest analysts' consensus before the conference call date. As managers might be inclined to use more complex language when uncertainty about the firm is high, we include *Forecast dispersion*, measured as the standard deviation of analyst forecasts (Allee, 2015).

Following prior research on the influence of manager-specific components on the complexity of earnings conference calls (Davis et al., 2015), we control for *CEO age*, *CEO gender*, and *CEO tenure*. Moreover, given that managers' incentives to deliberately use complex language might also be related to their equity incentives (Li, 2008), we include the logged value of unexercised but exercisable stock options (*CEO options unexercised*) and the logged value of the percentage of shares held by the CEO (*CEO shares*). Finally, we control for the length of the CEO's speech in each section by including the logged number of words, represented as *No. of words (Pres)* and *No. of words (QA)*, respectively (Nguyen, 2021).

6.4 Results

6.4.1 Descriptive Statistics

Panel A of Table 4 reports summary statistics for the variables employed. The mean narcissism score in our sample is – 0.1, with a standard deviation of 2.05, in line with the results observed by Buchholz et al. (2020) in their sample of S&P 500 CEOs ($\overline{x} = 0$, $\sigma = 2.71$). CEO speech complexity is greater in the prepared presentation part than in the less scripted Q&A session, as reflected by mean Fog Index scores of 16 for presentations and 11 for the Q&A. As residual values, the obfuscation components Obf(Pres) and Obf(QA) have means around zero by construction. The means of Info(Pres) and Info(QA) are 15.91 and 11.20, respectively, consistent with values reported in prior research using the same model specification for decomposing complex language (e.g., Mekhaimer et al., 2024). The firms in our sample average 20,090 million USD in size, with a mean BTM ratio of 0.45 and 6.6% annual sales growth. On average, CEOs hold their positions for seven years, with the majority being men and the full sample having an average age of 57 years.

Panel B of Table 6.4 shows the distribution of conference call observations across our 203 sample firms. For approximately half of the firms, transcripts (along with all other relevant data) are available for at least twenty quarters, with an overall average of 27 conference calls per firm.

Panel C of Table 6.4 presents univariate tests for high-narcissism CEOs (top decile) compared to a control group (Deciles 1–9). We observe a significantly higher Fog Index in the control group (CEOs with lower narcissism) across both the presentation and Q&A sections of the conference calls. Additionally, for both sections, on average the obfuscation and information components are significantly lower in firms led by highly narcissistic CEOs. Consistent with existing studies, we also find that firms led by highly narcissistic CEOs are larger and operate across more geographical and business segments (Buchholz et al., 2018). Additionally, we observe that institutional ownership is lower in firms with highly narcissistic CEOs. Furthermore, more narcissistic CEOs tend to have significantly longer tenures and are more heavily invested in the company than their less narcissistic counterparts.

Table 6.4 Summary statistics and univariate analysis

Panel A: Descriptive statistics

				Percentiles				
	N	**Mean**	**SD**	**10th**	**25th**	**50th**	**75th**	**90th**
Narcissism	3931	−0.097	2.051	−2.593	−1.558	0.012	1.095	2.289
Fog(Pres)	3931	15.908	1.887	13.475	14.797	16.005	17.145	18.185
Fog(QA)	3931	11.202	1.399	9.563	10.281	11.115	12.003	12.920
Obf(Pres)	3931	0	1.752	−2.183	−1.051	0.076	1.162	2.147
Obf(QA)	3931	−0.002	1.275	−1.502	−0.802	−0.069	0.732	1.545
Info(Pres)	3931	15.909	0.522	15.17	15.568	15.956	16.27	16.534
Info(QA)	3931	11.203	0.531	10.563	10.832	11.154	11.525	11.883
Return on assets	3931	0.016	0.018	0.002	0.005	0.013	0.024	0.036
Size	3931	9.908	0.949	8.823	9.201	9.804	10.497	11.198
Leverage	3931	0.656	0.204	0.421	0.531	0.655	0.782	0.890
BTM	3931	0.446	0.353	0.113	0.209	0.363	0.599	0.904
Loss	3931	0.071	0.258	0	0	0	0	0
Sales growth	3931	0.066	0.182	−0.078	−0.009	0.049	0.114	0.227
Stock return	3931	2.923	12.592	−12.044	−4.228	3.260	10.506	16.817
No. geographical segments	3931	1.338	0.476	0.693	1	1.099	1.609	1.946

(continued)

Table 6.4 (continued)

No. business segments	3931	1.390	0.459	0.693	1	1.386	1.792	1.946
Analysts following	3931	17.666	7.269	9	12	17	22	28
Forecast dispersion	3931	0.043	0.048	0.010	0.020	0.030	0.050	0.090
Earnings surprise	3931	0.039	0.129	−0.050	0	0.020	0.070	0.140
Forecast missed	3931	0.224	0.417	0	0	0	0	1
Inst. ownership	3931	0.797	0.136	0.627	0.722	0.816	0.890	0.941
CEO age	3931	57.133	5.292	51	54	57	61	63
CEO tenure	3931	6.980	4.594	2.263	3.485	5.797	9.499	13.156
CEO gender	3931	0.969	0.174	1	1	1	1	1
CEO shares	3931	0.278	0.357	0.032	0.081	0.160	0.332	0.614
CEO options unexercised	3931	7.090	4.092	0	5.736	8.671	10.061	10.98
No. of words (Pres)	3931	7.057	0.513	6.410	6.711	7.080	7.433	7.701
No. of words (QA)	3931	7.511	0.656	6.572	7.143	7.631	7.976	8.258

(continued)

Table 6.4 (continued)

Panel B: Frequency distribution of conference calls			
No. of conference calls	**No. of firms**	**Percentage**	**Cum.**
< = 19	92	45.32%	45.32%
20	10	4.93%	50.25%
21	7	3.45%	53.69%
22	14	6.90%	60.59%
23	5	2.46%	63.05%
24	11	5.42%	68.47%
25	8	3.94%	72.41%
26	13	6.40%	78.82%
27	11	5.42%	84.24%
28	5	2.46%	86.70%
29	9	4.43%	91.13%
30	4	1.97%	93.10%
31	5	2.46%	95.57%
32	1	0.49%	96.06%
33	4	1.97%	98.03%
34	1	0.49%	98.52%
35	3	1.48%	100.00%
Total	**203**	**100%**	

(continued)

Table 6.4 (continued)

Panel C: Univariate analysis

	10th decile	**Control sample**	**Difference (means)**
Narcissism	3.696	−0.515	4.211***
Fog(Pres)	15.275	15.978	−0.703***
Fog(QA)	10.833	11.242	−0.409***
Obf(Pres)	−0.402	0.044	−0.446***
Obf(QA)	−0.250	0.025	−0.276***
Info(Pres)	15.829	15.918	−0.089***
Info(QA)	11.076	11.216	−0.141***
Return on assets	0.018	0.015	0.003***
Size	10.686	9.822	0.864***
Leverage	0.688	0.652	0.036***
BTM	0.361	0.455	−0.094***
Loss	0.036	0.075	−0.040***
Sales growth	0.053	0.067	−0.014
Stock return	2.712	2.946	−0.234
No. geographical segments	1.462	1.324	0.138***
No. business segments	1.514	1.377	0.137***
Analysts following	20.269	17.379	2.890***
Forecast dispersion	0.038	0.043	−0.006**
Earnings surprise	0.043	0.038	0.005

(continued)

Table 6.4 (continued)

Forecast missed	0.159	0.231	−0.072***
Inst. ownership	0.719	0.805	−0.087***
CEO age	59.926	56.825	3.101***
CEO tenure	8.312	6.833	1.479***
CEO gender	0.867	0.980	−0.113***
CEO shares	0.321	0.273	0.047**
CEO options unexercised	7.564	7.038	0.526
No. of words (Pres)	6.967	7.067	−0.100***
No. of words (QA)	7.557	7.506	0.051

This table provides descriptive statistics for the variables used in the estimation (Panel A). Panel B shows the distribution of conference call observations across sample firms. Panel C presents results from a univariate analysis comparing highly narcissistic CEOs (10th decile) with a control group (deciles 1–9). Full variable definitions are provided in Table 1 of Appendix C in the electronic supplementary material. *** $p<0.01$, ** $p<0.05$, * $p<0.1$

6.4.2 CEO Narcissism and Linguistic Complexity in Earnings Conference Calls

We estimate the following model to examine the influence of CEO narcissism on the strategic use of complex language:

$$Obf\,(.)_{iq} = \beta_0 + \beta_1 Narcissism_{iq} + \beta_2 \delta Controls_{iq} + \vartheta_t + \varphi_i + \varepsilon_{iq} \tag{6.3}$$

where *Obf* (.) refers to the obfuscation component of the presentation or Q&A sections of the call, *Narcissism* is the level of CEO narcissism, and δ*Controls* refer to the list of control variables described in Section 3.3. ϑ_t represents time fixed effects and φ_i denotes firm fixed effects.

In Model 1 of Table 6.5, we present estimation results where the dependent variable is Obf(Pres), our measure of linguistic obfuscation used by the CEO during the presentation segment of a conference call. The coefficient for our narcissism variable is negative but statistically insignificant, indicating that more narcissistic CEOs do not exhibit less obfuscatory language in the presentation portion of conference calls compared to their less narcissistic counterparts. We explore the relationship between CEO narcissism and the information component of a conference call in Model 2. As expected, the narcissism coefficient remains statistically insignificant as the information component reflects the inherent complexity of the firm's operations, which should not be easily influenced by executive personality traits.

In Model 3, the dependent variable Obf(QA) captures the CEO's degree of obfuscation during the Q&A portion of the call. Consistent with our hypothesis, the results suggest that more narcissistic CEOs engage in significantly less obfuscatory language in the Q&A session. This effect is also economically meaningful, as a one-standard-deviation increase in narcissism is associated with a 9.69% standard deviation reduction in obfuscation (calculated as (−0.060*2.051)/1.275)). Finally, Model 4 in Table 5 shows that the narcissism coefficient remains insignificant when using Info(QA) as the dependent variable.

We examine the moderating effect of reported firm performance in Models 5 and 6 to further validate our findings. The statistically insignificant coefficients on the interaction term in both models suggest that CEOs are equally likely to use obfuscatory language regardless of their firms' performance. These findings remain robust when employing *Forecast missed* as an alternative measure of firm performance.

Table 6.5 Effect of CEO narcissism on the use of obfuscatory language during conference calls

	(1) Obf(Pres)	(2) Info(Pres)	(3) Obf(QA)	(4) Info(QA)	(5) Obf(Pres)	(6) Obf(QA)
Narcissism	−0.022	−0.001	−0.060**	−0.011	−0.022	−0.062**
	(0.031)	(0.004)	(0.027)	(0.009)	(0.031)	(0.028)
Loss	0.263***	−0.027	0.087	−0.052	0.263***	0.093
	(0.097)	(0.017)	(0.081)	(0.033)	(0.097)	(0.082)
Narcissism x Loss					0.001 (0.051)	0.014 (0.042)
Return on assets	6.190***	−0.519	2.192*	−1.313*	6.190***	2.188*
	(1.968)	(0.394)	(1.277)	(0.750)	(1.964)	(1.278)
Size	−0.038	−0.195***	−0.185	0.018	−0.038	−0.184
	(0.195)	(0.028)	(0.152)	(0.053)	(0.195)	(0.152)
Leverage	0.141	0.274***	−0.123	0.406***	0.141	−0.125
	(0.369)	(0.057)	(0.298)	(0.118)	(0.367)	(0.299)
BTM	0.019	−0.236***	−0.257	0.142**	0.019	−0.257
	(0.201)	(0.053)	(0.190)	(0.060)	(0.201)	(0.190)
Sales growth	−0.073	0.036	−0.001	0.011	−0.073	−0.001
	(0.150)	(0.024)	(0.106)	(0.049)	(0.150)	(0.105)
Stock return	0.000	0.001*	0.000	−0.001	0.000	0.000
	(0.002)	(0.000)	(0.001)	(0.001)	(0.002)	(0.001)
No. geographical segments	0.382 (0.252)	0.003 (0.030)	0.055 (0.185)	0.027 (0.060)	0.382 (0.252)	0.055 (0.185)
No. business segments	0.331	−0.007	0.088	0.103	0.331	0.090
	(0.351)	(0.044)	(0.203)	(0.090)	(0.351)	(0.203)
Analysts following	0.011	0.001	−0.003	0.002	0.011	−0.003
	(0.013)	(0.002)	(0.009)	(0.003)	(0.013)	(0.009)
Forecast dispersion	0.777	−0.085	0.419	−0.072	0.777	0.420
	(0.870)	(0.093)	(0.648)	(0.236)	(0.870)	(0.649)

(continued)

Table 6.5 (continued)

	(1) Obf(Pres)	(2) Info(Pres)	(3) Obf(QA)	(4) Info(QA)	(5) Obf(Pres)	(6) Obf(QA)
Earnings surprise	−0.240	0.056*	0.222	0.096	−0.240	0.222
	(0.192)	(0.029)	(0.183)	(0.067)	(0.192)	(0.183)
Forecast missed	0.021	−0.004	0.020	−0.007	0.020	0.020
	(0.054)	(0.008)	(0.051)	(0.021)	(0.054)	(0.051)
Inst. ownership	−0.040	0.018	0.351	0.042	−0.040	0.353
	(0.381)	(0.049)	(0.273)	(0.129)	(0.381)	(0.272)
CEO age	−0.017	0.002	−0.026	0.001	−0.017	−0.026
	(0.026)	(0.003)	(0.020)	(0.004)	(0.026)	(0.020)
CEO tenure	−0.017	−0.004*	0.015	−0.007	−0.017	0.015
	(0.023)	(0.003)	(0.019)	(0.006)	(0.023)	(0.019)
CEO gender	0.010	0.022	−0.772	−0.046	0.010	−0.774
	(0.415)	(0.046)	(0.495)	(0.118)	(0.415)	(0.497)
CEO shares	−0.132	0.003	0.095	0.086	−0.132	0.096
	(0.284)	(0.032)	(0.192)	(0.068)	(0.284)	(0.191)
CEO options unexercised	0.002	0.001	0.009	0.002	0.002	0.009
	(0.014)	(0.002)	(0.011)	(0.004)	(0.014)	(0.011)
No. of words (Pres)	0.225*	0.008			0.225*	
	(0.115)	(0.013)			(0.116)	
No. of words (QA)			0.236***	0.040**		0.236***
			(0.069)	(0.020)		(0.069)
Constant	−1.475	17.580***	1.803	10.143***	−1.476	1.791
	(2.341)	(0.303)	(1.930)	(0.578)	(2.339)	(1.940)
N	3,931	3,931	3,931	3,931	3,931	3,931
Firm FE	Yes	Yes	Yes	Yes	Yes	Yes

(continued)

Table 6.5 (continued)

	(1) Obf(Pres)	(2) Info(Pres)	(3) Obf(QA)	(4) Info(QA)	(5) Obf(Pres)	(6) Obf(QA)
Time FE	Yes	Yes	Yes	Yes	Yes	Yes
Adj. R-squared	0.562	0.888	0.410	0.380	0.562	0.410

This table presents estimation results from the main analysis of the effect of CEO narcissism on the obfuscatory use of complex language. Obf(Pres) and Obf(QA) denote the obfuscation component of complex language in the presentation and Q&A sections of the call, respectively. Info(Pres) and Info(QA) represent the information components. Both components are extracted following the method developed by Bushee et al. (2017). Narcissism refers to our measure of CEO narcissism. Full variable definitions are provided in Table 1 of Appendix C in the electronic supplementary material. Robust standard errors clustered at the firm and date level are provided in parentheses. *** p<0.01, ** p<0.05, * p<0.1

6.5 Robustness

6.5.1 Alternative Measures for Linguistic Complexity

We re-estimate our models using three alternative linguistic complexity measures commonly adopted in prior research (e.g., Franco et al., 2015; Hasan, 2020; Laksmana et al., 2012; Xu et al., 2018). The Bog Index—introduced by Bonsall and Miller (2017)—closely aligns with the SEC's plain English requirements, with higher scores indicating greater complexity. The mean Bog Index for the presentation and Q&A parts are 55.08 and 33.43, respectively—both lower than those reported in previous studies on written disclosure outlets (Bonsall and Miller, 2017; Hasan, 2020; Nguyen, 2021). The Flesch score rates text complexity on a scale of 0 to 100, with higher scores reflecting simpler text. Finally, the Simple Measure of Gobbledygook (SMOG) Index estimates the years of education necessary to fully comprehend a text (Mc Laughlin, 1969). We observe a mean Flesch Index of 41.43 for the presentation and 65.89 for the Q&A sections of the call, as well as a mean SMOG score of 13.22 for the presentation and 11.07 for the Q&A part. We extract the information and obfuscation components from these alternative measures of linguistic complexity, following the procedure outlined in Section 3.2. The results with the obfuscation components as dependent variables are presented in Table 6. Across all model specifications, the results are consistent with our main analysis, suggesting a negative association between

CEO narcissism and the obfuscatory use of complex language in the Q&A part of conference calls.

6.5.2 Stacked Difference-in-Differences Analysis

We conduct a stacked difference-in-differences analysis to strengthen the robustness of our findings. Emerging research highlights that traditional DiD regressions might yield biased estimates when treatment timing varies across units (e.g., Baker et al., 2022). A stacked DiD approach mitigates the bias in standard DiD that arises when treatment timing varies across units by structuring the data into multiple two-group, two-period comparisons (Babenko et al., 2024). Unlike the conventional DiD approach, which pools all treatment groups together under a single specification, a stacked DiD conducts separate comparisons for each cohort of treated units and then combines the results, ensuring that the relative timing of treatment is properly aligned, leading to unbiased effect estimates. This approach enables us to examine how the appointment of a more narcissistic CEO—compared to a less narcissistic predecessor—influences the use of obfuscatory language, with narcissism levels defined by the median score of each CEO. Specifically, we estimate the following model:

$$Obf(.)_{iq} = \beta_0 + \beta_1 Treated_{iq} + \beta_2 Post_{iq} + \beta_3 Treated_{iq} \times Post_{iq} + \beta_4 \delta Controls_{iq} + \vartheta_t + \varphi_i + \varepsilon_{iq} \quad (6.4)$$

where, $Treated_{iq}$ is a binary indicator set to 1 if the firm transitions from a less narcissistic CEO to a more narcissistic one. $Post_{iq}$ is a binary indicator equal to 1 for periods q following the appointment of a more narcissistic CEO.

The results are presented in Models 7 and 8 of Table 6. We use *NarcInc* to represent $Treated_{iq} \times Post_{iq}$, which equals 1 for periods following a firm's transition from a less narcissistic to a more narcissistic CEO, and zero otherwise. In support of our main findings, we observe an insignificant coefficient for *NarcInc* when using Obf(Pres) as the dependent variable, but a significant negative coefficient when analyzing obfuscatory language in the Q&A section of the call. These results indicate that CEOs use less complex language during the Q&A section of conference calls in firms that transitioned from a less narcissistic CEO to a more narcissistic one compared to firms without such a change.

Table 6.6 Robustness tests

	Obfuscation							
	(1) Bog (Pres)	(2) Bog (QA)	(3) Flesch (Pres)	(4) Flesch (QA)	(5) Smog (Pres)	(6) Smog (QA)	(7) Obf (Pres)	(8) Obf (QA)
Narcissism	−0.115 (0.208)	−0.620** (0.265)	0.044 (0.136)	0.282** (0.123)	−0.021 (0.020)	−0.044* (0.023)		
NarcInc							−0.510 (0.412)	−0.480* (0.253)
N	3,931	3,930	3,931	3,931	3,931	3,931	1,913	1,913
Controls	Yes	Yes	Yes	Yes	Yes	Yes	Yes	Yes
Firm FE	Yes	Yes	Yes	Yes	Yes	Yes	Yes	Yes
Time FE	Yes	Yes	Yes	Yes	Yes	Yes	Yes	Yes
Adj. R-squared	0.588	0.371	0.631	0.445	0.555	0.437	0.567	0.290

This table presents the estimation results using alternative metrics for assessing linguistic obfuscation during conference calls (Models 1–6), alongside results from a stacked difference-in-differences (DiD) analysis (Models 7–8). In Models 1–6, the dependent variable is the obfuscation component of complex language, measured using the Bog Index, Flesch Index, and SMOG Index, respectively. The obfuscation component is derived following the method of Bushee et al. (2017). The *Narcissism* variable represents the measure of CEO narcissism. In Models 7–8, the dependent variable is the obfuscation component measured using the Gunning Fog Index. Utilizing a stacked DiD approach, these models investigate how appointing a more narcissistic CEO—relative to a less narcissistic predecessor—influences the use of obfuscatory language. CEO narcissism levels are categorized based on the median score of each CEO. *NarcInc* is a binary indicator set to 1 for periods following a firm's transition from a less narcissistic to a more narcissistic CEO, and zero otherwise. All model specifications include the same control variables used in the baseline regression. Full variable definitions are provided in Table 1 of Appendix C in the electronic supplementary material. Robust standard errors clustered at the firm and date level are provided in parentheses. *** p<0.01, ** p<0.05, * p<0.1

6.5.3 Exclusion of Financial Firms

Existing studies emphasize the unique nature of firms operating in the financial industry with respect to their disclosures (Lim et al., 2018; Price et al., 2012). To mitigate the risk that factors related to this uniqueness might bias our findings, we exclude all firms counted as financial firms according to the Fama–French twelve-industry classification system, with the results of this (untabulated) analysis corroborating our findings from the main analysis.

6.6 Supplementary Analyses

6.6.1 CEO Narcissism and the Tone of Conference Calls

Previous literature suggests that their positive expectancy bias might drive more narcissistic CEOs to employ an abnormally positive tone during certain written disclosures, including earnings announcements (Marquez-Illescas et al., 2019) and 10-K filings (Buchholz et al., 2018). In this section, we describe additional tests conducted to determine whether this also holds for the tone employed during earnings conference calls. We capture this by counting the number of positive and negative words used in the presentation and Q&A section based on the predominantly used Loughran and McDonald (2011) dictionary. Using a large sample of 10-K filings, Loughran and McDonald (2011) compiled a word list that they demonstrated to be more suitable for labeling positive and negative tones in financial documents than other commonly used sources for word classification, such as the Harvard Psychosociological Dictionary. We create our tone measure by taking the total number of positive words minus the total number of negative words scaled by the total number of words used in a CEO's speech (Huang et al., 2014). We account for negations and do not count a positive word if it is preceded in a three-word range by a negating word (*no*, *not*, *none*, *neither*, *never*, *nobody*) (Loughran and McDonald, 2011). In addition, we do not classify "good" as a positive word if it appears as part of the phrase *good question* or in the context of the conference call's opening and closing phrases (e.g., *Good morning*, *Good afternoon*, *Have a good day*). Finally, following Allee (2015), we do not count *effective* as positive if it was followed by *income*, *tax*, or *rate*.

Table 6.7 presents estimation results where the dependent variable is the CEO's speech tone during the conference call's presentation (Model 1) and Q&A (Model 2). We find that performance-related firm-level characteristics such as sales growth, stock return, and earnings surprise are significantly positively associated with tone during the scripted presentation part of the call, echoing previous findings by Huang et al. (2014) and Allee (2015). By contrast, our CEO narcissism measure shows an insignificant association with the tone used during earnings conference calls for both the presentation and Q&A parts. These findings contradict Marquez-Illescas et al. (2019) and Buchholz et al. (2018), who observe a significant positive association between CEO narcissism and tone in written disclosure contexts such as earnings announcements and 10-K filings. One potential explanation for these contradicting results is that the human voice conveys considerable information beyond the literal meaning of verbal content (Caffi and Janney, 1994). Indeed, vocal cues or expressions have been found to play a crucial role in drawing inferences about both positive affective states (e.g., happiness, excitement, and enjoyment) and negative affective states (e.g., fear, tension, and anxiety) (Mayew and Venkatachalam, 2012). Thus, the presence of vocal cues in spoken communication may alter the way narcissistic tendencies manifest in tone, potentially diminishing the relationship observed in written disclosures.

6.6.2 CEO Narcissism and Blaming

In this section, we examine the relationship between CEOs' narcissistic personality and their willingness to take responsibility for negative outcomes. Research suggests that narcissistic individuals blame external, uncontrollable causes when confronted with unfavorable outcomes (Bettman and Weitz, 1983; Chatterjee and Pollock, 2017; Emmons, 1987). Specifically, we test whether more narcissistic CEOs tend to attribute poor performance to external rather than internal factors on a more frequent basis than their less narcissistic peers. We apply the blame measurement introduced by Noh and Zhou (2022) and split CEOs' speech into individual sentences based on punctuation in the transcripts. We then determine whether each sentence describes the state of the economy or industry based on the keywords proposed by Noh and Zhou (2022) (i.e., *economic growth*, *economic condition*, *economy*, and *industry*, as well as their respective plural forms). We assess the tone of each sentence identified as such a description using the Loughran and McDonald (2011) dictionary. If the sentence contains more negative than positive words, it is assumed to express a negative description of the economic situation and thus classified as a "blame sentence." Finally, we calculate the ratio of blame sentences to all sentences to construct the blame measure. The *Narcissism x Loss* interaction term is used to represent the combined variable of CEO narcissism and reported performance. The estimation results for the presentation part of the call in Model 3 of Table 6.7 show that CEOs tend to use fewer blame sentences when reported sales growth or stock returns are higher. Notably, we observe a positive and significant coefficient on *Narcissism x Loss*, suggesting that more narcissistic CEOs exhibit greater blaming behavior during the presentation part of the call when reporting financial losses. However, we do not find evidence of such a relationship in the Q&A session of the conference calls (Model 4).

Table 6.7 Supplementary analyses

	(1) Tone(Pres)	(2) Tone(QA)	(3) Blame(Pres)	(4) Blame(QA)
Narcissism	−0.033	0.004	−0.015	−0.007
	(0.022)	(0.014)	(0.015)	(0.008)
Loss	0.086	−0.039	−0.003	0.017
	(0.071)	(0.048)	(0.051)	(0.034)
Narcissism x Loss			0.051*	0.018
			(0.026)	(0.021)
Return on assets	3.418**	1.171	0.048	−0.853
	(1.616)	(1.198)	(0.809)	(0.594)
Size	−0.085	0.057	−0.167**	−0.055
	(0.123)	(0.086)	(0.078)	(0.034)
Leverage	−0.104	0.066	−0.124	−0.062
	(0.237)	(0.346)	(0.200)	(0.069)
BTM	−0.185	−0.070	−0.050	−0.112*
	(0.129)	(0.143)	(0.103)	(0.060)
Sales growth	0.384***	0.057	−0.148**	−0.018
	(0.141)	(0.076)	(0.075)	(0.039)
Stock return	0.007***	0.002**	−0.004***	−0.000
	(0.001)	(0.001)	(0.001)	(0.001)
No. geographical segments	0.265 (0.205)	−0.080 (0.107)	0.060 (0.087)	−0.001 (0.052)
No. business segments	0.126 (0.187)	0.033 (0.134)	0.078 (0.080)	0.076 (0.053)
Analysts following	−0.016**	−0.006	0.005	0.003
	(0.008)	(0.006)	(0.005)	(0.003)
Forecast dispersion	−0.618	−0.046	0.137	−0.249
	(0.492)	(0.488)	(0.459)	(0.202)
Earnings surprise	0.580***	0.151	−0.102	0.017
	(0.159)	(0.117)	(0.111)	(0.064)
Forecast missed	−0.127***	−0.106***	0.062	−0.000
	(0.043)	(0.032)	(0.040)	(0.022)

(continued)

Table 6.7 (continued)

	(1) Tone(Pres)	(2) Tone(QA)	(3) Blame(Pres)	(4) Blame(QA)
Inst. ownership	−0.351	0.001	0.170	0.060
	(0.314)	(0.215)	(0.180)	(0.118)
CEO age	0.012	−0.011	0.003	−0.002
	(0.013)	(0.009)	(0.009)	(0.005)
CEO tenure	−0.034**	−0.016	−0.004	0.010**
	(0.015)	(0.011)	(0.009)	(0.005)
CEO gender	0.387	−0.009	0.029	−0.041
	(0.478)	(0.166)	(0.144)	(0.069)
CEO shares	0.111	0.036	0.128	0.068
	(0.170)	(0.114)	(0.131)	(0.065)
CEO options unexercised	0.004 (0.010)	0.010 (0.007)	0.000 (0.005)	−0.009** (0.004)
No. of words (Pres)	−0.295***		−0.016	
	(0.080)		(0.044)	
No. of words (QA)		−0.166***		0.015
		(0.043)		(0.022)
Constant	4.239***	2.457**	1.555*	0.637
	(1.592)	(1.119)	(0.909)	(0.546)
N	3,931	3,931	3,931	3,931
Firm FE	Yes	Yes	Yes	Yes
Time FE	Yes	Yes	Yes	Yes
Adj. R-squared	0.476	0.386	0.0932	0.0840

This table presents supplementary analyses. In Models 1–2, the dependent variables are the tone of the CEO's speech in the presentation and Q&A sections of the call, respectively. Tone is calculated as the difference between the total number of positive words and the total number of negative words, scaled by the total number of words in the CEO's speech. The counts of positive and negative words are determined using the Loughran and McDonald (2011) dictionary. In Models 3–4, the dependent variables represent the blame measure introduced by Noh and Zhou (2022). Narcissism refers to our measure of CEO narcissism. Full variable definitions are provided in Table 1 of Appendix C in the electronic supplementary material. Robust standard errors clustered at the firm and date level are provided in parentheses. *** $p<0.01$, ** $p<0.05$, * $p<0.1$

6.6.3 Linguistic Complexity and Analysts' Behavior

Building on previous literature suggesting an influence of linguistic complexity in corporate disclosure on financial analysts (Lehavy et al., 2011; Bushee and Huang, 2024; Lee, 2016), we next examine how analysts respond to the linguistic complexity of CEO speech during conference calls. Specifically, we test whether the number of analysts following a firm and the dispersion of their forecasts are associated with the informative and obfuscating components of complex language. We measure the number of analysts following a firm as the count of those providing an earnings forecast for year $t + 1$ in the first consensus following a conference call. Forecast dispersion is calculated as the standard deviation of individual analyst forecasts in this initial consensus, scaled by the beginning-of-quarter price (Lehavy et al., 2011).

The results of the presentation and Q&A section are presented in Table 8. The findings from Models 1 and 2 indicate that the information or the obfuscation component in CEO speeches during presentations and Q&A sessions does not significantly influence the number of analysts covering a firm. One potential explanation is the inherent prominence and market significance of S&P 500 companies, which naturally attract substantial analyst attention. Thus, analysts might be compelled to follow these firms due to their substantial impact on the market and investor portfolios, making the nuances of CEO speech less critical in determining analyst coverage. In Models 3 and 4, the dependent variable is analysts' forecast dispersion. The coefficients for the obfuscation and information components in the presentation speech (Model 3) are statistically insignificant, suggesting that linguistic complexity during the presentation does not significantly influence the variability in analysts' forecasts. However, focusing on the Q&A section, we find that the information component is statistically significant and positive, indicating that increased informational content in this segment is associated with greater dispersion in analysts' forecasts. These findings mirror prior research demonstrating that the Q&A portion of earnings calls tends to be more informative than the presentation segment (Matsumoto et al., 2011; Price et al., 2012). The heightened informativeness of the Q&A section might stem from its interactive nature, allowing analysts to probe management on specific concerns and leading to the disclosure of information not covered in the prepared presentation. This dynamic can result in a broader range of interpretations and opinions among analysts, thereby increasing forecast dispersion.

Table 6.8 Impact of linguistic complexity on analyst behavior

	(1) Analysts foll.	(2) Analysts foll.	(3) Forecast disp.	(4) Forecast disp.
Obf(Pres)	−0.009		0.000	
	(0.065)		(0.000)	
Info(Pres)	0.388		0.000	
	(0.371)		(0.000)	
Obf(QA)		−0.082		0.000
		(0.065)		(0.000)
Info(QA)		0.040		0.001**
		(0.140)		(0.000)
Loss	−0.361	−0.416	0.001***	0.002**
	(0.271)	(0.270)	(0.000)	(0.001)
Return on assets	1.353	0.549	−0.011	−0.004
	(5.788)	(5.843)	(0.010)	(0.010)
Size	1.348**	1.340**	−0.002***	−0.003***
	(0.560)	(0.552)	(0.001)	(0.001)
Leverage	−0.174	0.143	0.003**	0.003*
	(1.224)	(1.212)	(0.001)	(0.002)
BTM	1.146*	1.039*	0.004***	0.006***
	(0.629)	(0.609)	(0.001)	(0.001)
Sales growth	−0.769*	−0.787*	0.000	−0.000
	(0.419)	(0.408)	(0.000)	(0.001)
Stock return	−0.013**	−0.013**	0.000***	0.000***
	(0.006)	(0.006)	(0.000)	(0.000)
No. geographical segments	−0.299 (0.653)	−0.387 (0.645)	0.000 (0.001)	0.001 (0.001)
No. business segments	−0.951 (1.079)	−0.986 (1.100)	−0.000 (0.001)	−0.001 (0.001)
Analysts following			0.000	0.000
			(0.000)	(0.000)
Forecast dispersion	−0.830	−0.657		
	(1.604)	(1.620)		

(continued)

Table 6.8 (continued)

	(1) Analysts foll.	(2) Analysts foll.	(3) Forecast disp.	(4) Forecast disp.
Earnings surprise	0.181	0.269	0.001	0.002
	(0.427)	(0.428)	(0.000)	(0.002)
Forecast missed	−0.146	−0.158	0.000***	0.001**
	(0.146)	(0.146)	(0.000)	(0.000)
Inst. ownership	−0.993	−1.050	0.001	0.002
	(1.285)	(1.279)	(0.001)	(0.001)
CEO age	0.042	0.060	0.000	0.000
	(0.054)	(0.053)	(0.000)	(0.000)
CEO tenure	−0.098	−0.101*	−0.000	−0.000
	(0.061)	(0.057)	(0.000)	(0.000)
CEO gender	0.592	0.371	0.000	−0.000
	(1.006)	(0.940)	(0.001)	(0.001)
CEO shares	−0.303	−0.405	−0.000	0.000
	(0.560)	(0.578)	(0.001)	(0.001)
CEO options unexercised	0.045 (0.037)	0.041 (0.037)	−0.000 (0.000)	−0.000* (0.000)
No. of words (Pres)	−0.315		0.000**	
	(0.248)		(0.000)	
No. of words (QA)		0.641***		−0.000
		(0.163)		(0.000)
Constant	1.811	−0.137	0.008	0.016**
	(9.775)	(7.231)	(0.009)	(0.006)
N	3,931	3,931	3,928	3,929
Firm FE	Yes	Yes	Yes	Yes
Time FE	Yes	Yes	Yes	Yes
Adj. R-squared	0.844	0.845	0.566	0.577

This table presents estimation results of analyses examining analyst behavior in response to linguistic complexity. In Models 1–2, the dependent variable is the number of analysts following a firm, defined as the number of analysts providing an earnings forecast for year t + 1 in the first consensus following a conference call. In Models 3–4, the dependent variable is the dispersion of analysts' forecasts, measured as the standard deviation of individual analyst forecasts within this initial consensus, scaled by the beginning-of-quarter price. Narcissism refers to our measure of CEO narcissism. Full variable definitions are provided in Table 1 of Appendix C in the electronic supplementary material. Robust standard errors clustered at the firm and date level are provided in parentheses. *** $p<0.01$, ** $p<0.05$, * $p<0.1$

6.7 Summary

A growing body of literature recognizes the effectiveness of various linguistic strategies that executives employ to shape audience perception during financial disclosures. However, despite consistent evidence of their impact, the antecedents of these techniques remain largely unexplored. Drawing on insights from Upper Echelons Theory, this study complements existing research by examining the association between CEOs' narcissistic traits and their use of complex language during earnings conference calls. Building on the idea that narcissistic CEOs have weaker (stronger) motivation to engage in impression management in image-threatening (image-enhancing) situations, we hypothesize that more narcissistic CEOs are less likely to use complex language to convey a desired narrative during earnings conference calls. We adopt the approach pioneered by Bushee et al. (2017) to decompose complex language into its inherent obfuscation and informational components, enabling a more nuanced analysis of its strategic use. Utilizing a large sample of S&P 500 firms, we find that the speech of more narcissistic CEOs during the Q&A sessions of earnings conference calls exhibits significantly lower obfuscatory language than that of their less narcissistic counterparts. Our results remain robust when employing alternative measures of obfuscatory language and applying a stacked DiD approach. We do not find evidence of this relationship in the presentation portion of the conference call. The lack of significant results for the presentation part might be attributed to its structured and controlled nature, which could dilute the influence of executive personal traits. Prior research supports this, showing that this segment is often carefully scripted and reviewed by external parties, such as communication specialists and legal advisors (Chen et al., 2013; Chourou et al., 2024; Flam et al., 2023). By contrast, psychological traits such as narcissism might be more likely to manifest in the unscripted, spontaneous flow of speech characteristic of the Q&A section (Larcker and Zakolyukina, 2012). This aligns with Burgoon et al. (2016), who highlight the differences in linguistic behavior between rehearsed statements and spontaneous responses in conference calls. Further analysis indicates that findings from prior studies on written disclosures do not necessarily apply to the context of spoken language. Specifically, we find no association between CEO narcissism and the tone employed during earnings conference calls, contradicting findings from the literature on written disclosures suggesting that highly narcissistic CEOs introduce a positive tonal bias in financial reporting (Marquez-Illescas et al., 2019). Consistent with findings in psychology research that highly narcissistic individuals tend to attribute failures to external factors beyond their control, we document weak evidence of a positive association between CEO narcissism and the tendency to blame external factors for poor performance during a conference call's presentation part. Our findings indicate that the CEO's use of complex language during conference calls does not influence the number of analysts following a firm. This might be attributed to the substantial market relevance and established visibility of the S&P 500 firms in our sample, which potentially diminishes the impact of linguistic complexity on analyst interest. Finally, we observe that forecast dispersion is positively associated with the information component inherent in complex language during the Q&A session.

This study has several limitations, which open avenues for future research. First, while archival measures for psychological traits are well-established, they have limitations in fully capturing complex constructs like narcissism (Borgholthaus et al., 2023). Although self-report methods such as the Narcissistic Personality Inventory (NPI) pose data collection challenges—particularly for upper echelons—they could offer deeper insights into how narcissistic traits influence managerial behavior and corporate communication (Cragun et al., 2020). Second, our focus on CEOs does not capture the broader role of top management teams in shaping corporate communication. Future research could explore how other executives contribute to linguistic strategies, given their active role in conference calls. For instance, CFOs play a pivotal role in corporate disclosures and may shape linguistic complexity, as suggested by recent studies (Abdulsalam, 2022). Third, while our findings do not indicate that CEO narcissism's influence depends on firm performance, other factors may shape its manifestation. Situational factors, such as media coverage, have been shown to affect narcissistic behavior (Aabo et al., 2022). Future research could explore conditions that amplify or mitigate such traits, providing a more nuanced understanding of their impact. Finally, we focus on S&P 500 firms due to the availability of rich CEO- and firm-level data. However, as narcissism's influence varies across cultural and organizational contexts (Chatterjee and Pollock, 2017), future studies should investigate whether these findings generalize to smaller or non-U.S. firms.

Despite these limitations, our study offers practical implications. Our findings align with growing research highlighting the significant role individual executives play in shaping verbal corporate disclosure (e.g., Amicis et al., 2021). Regulatory bodies like the SEC may consider developing best practices for verbal disclosures, particularly during earnings calls, to ensure that executive language remains clear yet sufficiently detailed. While existing initiatives, such as the SEC's Plain English Disclosure Rule (SEC, 1998), provide explicit guidance for written reports, they do not necessarily extend to verbal communication (Mayew and Venkatachalam, 2012). Establishing a regulatory framework for spoken disclosures could improve consistency and transparency for stakeholders while also assisting firms in strengthening governance mechanisms to mitigate executive-driven biases in corporate communication. Indeed, well-enforced governance practices appear crucial to maintain the integrity of financial reporting and ensure unbiased, accessible information for stakeholders (Ernstberger and Grüning, 2013). Finally, analysts and investors should critically assess corporate disclosure narratives, recognizing the dual function of complex language—both informative and obfuscatory. By distinguishing between these elements, they can enhance the accuracy of their evaluations and make more informed decisions.

References

Aabo, T., Jacobsen, M. L., Stendys, K., 2022. Pay me with fame, not mammon: CEO narcissism, compensation, and media coverage, *Finance Research Letters* 46. https://doi.org/10.1016/j.frl.2021.102495.

Abdulsalam, K. A., 2022. CFO power and financial reporting readability, *Working paper*, https://ssrn.com/abstract=4315865.

Aghamolla, C. and Smith, K., 2023. Strategic complexity in disclosure, *Journal of Accounting and Economics* 76, 101635. https://doi.org/10.1016/j.jacceco.2023.101635.

Akstinaite, V., Robinson, G., Sadler-Smith, E., 2020. Linguistic markers of CEO hubris, *Journal of Business Ethics* 167, 687–705. https://doi.org/10.1007/s10551-019-04183-y.

Aktas, N., Bodt, E. de, Bollaert, H., Roll, R., 2016. CEO narcissism and the takeover process: From private initiation to deal completion, *Journal of Financial and Quantitative Analysis* 51, 113–137. https://doi.org/10.1017/S0022109016000065.

Allee, K. D., 2015. The structure of voluntary disclosure narratives: Evidence from tone dispersion, *Journal of Accounting Research* 53, 241–274. https://doi.org/10.1111/1475-679X.12072.

Al-Shammari, M., Rasheed, A., Al-Shammari, H. A., 2019. CEO narcissism and corporate social responsibility: Does CEO narcissism affect CSR focus?, *Journal of Business Research* 104, 106–117. https://doi.org/10.1016/j.jbusres.2019.07.005.

American Psychiatric Association, 2013. Diagnostic and statistical manual of mental disorders (5th ed.), Washington D.C.

Amernic, J., R. Craig, and D. Tourish, 2010. Measuring and assessing tone at the top using annual report CEO letters. *The Institute of Chartered Accountants of Scotland,* Edinburgh.

Amernic, J. H. and Craig, R. J., 2010. Accounting as a facilitator of extreme narcissism, *Journal of Business Ethics* 96, 79–93. https://doi.org/10.1007/s10551-010-0450-0.

Amicis, C. de, Falconieri, S., Tastan, M., 2021. Sentiment analysis and gender differences in earnings conference calls, *Journal of Corporate Finance* 71, 101809. https://doi.org/10.1016/j.jcorpfin.2020.101809.

Anderson, C. and Kilduff, G. J., 2009. Why do dominant personalities attain influence in face-to-face groups? The competence-signaling effects of trait dominance, *Journal of Personality and Social Psychology* 96, 491–503. https://doi.org/10.1037/a0014201.

Asay, H. S., Libby, R., Rennekamp, K., 2018. Firm performance, reporting goals, and language choices in narrative disclosures, *Journal of Accounting and Economics* 65, 380–398. https://doi.org/10.1016/j.jacceco.2018.02.002.

Babenko, I., Bennett, B., Wang, Z., 2024. Does better access to disclosure curb CEO pay? Evidence from a modern information technology improvement, *Working paper*, https://ssrn.com/abstract=4523306.

Bae, J., Yu Hung, C., van Lent, L., 2023. Mobilizing text as data, *European Accounting Review* 32, 1085–1106. https://doi.org/10.1080/09638180.2023.2218423.

Baker, A. C., Larcker, D. F., Wang, C. C., 2022. How much should we trust staggered difference-in-differences estimates?, *Journal of Financial Economics* 144, 370–395. https://doi.org/10.1016/j.jfineco.2022.01.004.

Bamber, L. S., Jiang, J., Wang, I. Y., 2010. What's my style? The influence of top managers on voluntary corporate financial disclosure, *The Accounting Review* 85, 1131–1162. https://doi.org/10.2308/accr.2010.85.4.1131.

Bettman, J. R. and Weitz, B. A., 1983. Attributions in the board room: Causal reasoning in corporate annual reports, *Administrative Science Quarterly* 28, 165–183. https://doi.org/10.2307/2392616.

Bloomfield, R. J., 2002. The "Incomplete Revelation Hypothesis" and financial reporting, *Accounting Horizons* 16, 233–243. https://doi.org/10.2308/acch.2002.16.3.233.

Bochkay, K., Chychyla, R., Nanda, D., 2019. Dynamics of CEO disclosure style, *The Accounting Review* 94, 103–140. https://doi.org/10.2308/accr-52281.

Bonsall, S. B., Leone, A. J., Miller, B. P., Rennekamp, K., 2017. A plain English measure of financial reporting readability, *Journal of Accounting and Economics* 63, 329–357. https://doi.org/10.1016/j.jacceco.2017.03.002.

Bonsall, S. B. and Miller, B. P., 2017. The impact of narrative disclosure readability on bond ratings and the cost of debt, *Review of Accounting Studies* 22, 608–643. https://doi.org/10.1007/s11142-017-9388-0.

Borgholthaus, C. J., White, J. V., Harms, P. D., 2023. CEO dark personality: A critical review, bibliometric analysis, and research agenda, *Personality and Individual Differences* 201, 111951. https://doi.org/10.1016/j.paid.2022.111951.

Brennan, N. M., Guillamon-Saorin, E., Pierce, A., 2009. Impression management: Developing and illustrating a scheme of analysis for narrative disclosures—A methodological note, *Accounting, Auditing & Accountability Journal* 22, 789–832. https://doi.org/10.1108/09513570910966379.

Brochet, F., Loumioti, M., Serafeim, G., 2015. Speaking of the short-term: Disclosure horizon and managerial myopia, *Review of Accounting Studies* 20, 1122–1163. https://doi.org/10.1007/s11142-015-9329-8.

Buchholz, F., Jaeschke, R., Lopatta, K., Maas, K., 2018. The use of optimistic tone by narcissistic CEOs, *Accounting, Auditing & Accountability Journal* 31, 531–562. https://doi.org/10.1108/AAAJ-11-2015-2292.

Buchholz, F., Lopatta, K., Maas, K., 2020. The deliberate engagement of narcissistic CEOs in earnings management, *Journal of Business Ethics* 167, 663–686. https://doi.org/10.1007/s10551-019-04176-x.

Burgoon, J., Mayew, W. J., Giboney, J. S., Elkins, A. C., Moffitt, K., Dorn, B., Byrd, M., Spitzley, L., 2016. Which spoken language markers identify deception in high-stakes

settings? Evidence from earnings conference calls, *Journal of Language and Social Psychology* 35, 123–157. https://doi.org/10.1177/0261927X15586792.
Bushee, B. J., Gow, I. D., Taylor, D. J., 2017. Linguistic complexity in firm disclosures: Obfuscation or information?, *Journal of Accounting Research* 56, 85–121. https://doi.org/10.1111/1475-679X.12179.
Bushee, B. J. and Huang, Y., 2024. Do analysts and investors efficiently respond to managerial linguistic complexity during conference calls?, *The Accounting Review* 99, 143–168. https://doi.org/10.2308/TAR-2019-0358.
Buss, D. M. and Chiodo, L. M., 1991. Narcissistic acts in everyday life, *Journal of Personality* 59, 179–215. https://doi.org/10.1111/j.1467-6494.1991.tb00773.x.
Buyl, T., Boone, C., Wade, J. B., 2019. CEO narcissism, risk-taking, and resilience: An empirical analysis in U.S. commercial banks, *Journal of Management* 45, 1372–1400. https://doi.org/10.1177/0149206317699521.
Caffi, C. and Janney, R. W., 1994. Toward a pragmatics of emotive communication, *Journal of Pragmatics* 22, 325–373. https://doi.org/10.1016/0378-2166(94)90115-5.
Campbell, W. K., Hoffman, B. J., Campbell, S. M., Marchisio, G., 2011. Narcissism in organizational contexts, *Human Resource Management Review* 21, 268–284. https://doi.org/10.1016/j.hrmr.2010.10.007.
Campbell, W. K., Rudich, E. A., Sedikides, C., 2002. Narcissism, self-esteem, and the positivity of self-views: Two portraits of self-love, *Personality & Social Psychology Bulletin* 28, 358–368. https://doi.org/10.1177/0146167202286007.
Capalbo, F., Frino, A., Lim, M. Y., Mollica, V., Palumbo, R., 2017. The impact of CEO narcissism on earnings management, *Abacus* 54, 210–226. https://doi.org/10.1111/abac.12116.
Chatterjee, A. and Hambrick, D. C., 2007. It's all about me: Narcissistic Chief Executive Officers and their effects on company strategy and performance, *Administrative Science Quarterly* 52, 351–386. https://doi.org/10.2189/asqu.52.3.351.
Chatterjee, A. and Hambrick, D. C., 2011. Executive personality, capability cues, and risk taking, *Administrative Science Quarterly* 56, 202–237. https://doi.org/10.1177/0001839211427534.
Chatterjee, A. and Pollock, T. G., 2017. Master of puppets: How narcissistic CEOs construct their professional worlds, *Academy of Management Review* 42, 703–725. https://doi.org/10.5465/amr.2015.0224.
Chen, J., Demers, E., Lev, B., 2013. Oh what a beautiful morning! The time of day effect on the tone and market impact of conference calls, *Working paper*, https://ideas.repec.org/p/unm/umagsb/2013038.html.
Chin, M. K., Hambrick, D. C., Treviño, L. K., 2013. Political ideologies of CEOs, *Administrative Science Quarterly* 58, 197–232. https://doi.org/10.1177/0001839213486984.
Chourou, L., Hossain, A. T., Jha, A., 2024. U.S. political corruption and quarterly conference calls, *Journal of Banking & Finance* 161, 107108. https://doi.org/10.1016/j.jbankfin.2024.107108.
Cragun, O. R., Olsen, K. J., Wright, P. M., 2020. Making CEO narcissism research great: A review and meta-analysis of CEO narcissism, *Journal of Management* 46, 908–936. https://doi.org/10.1177/0149206319892678.

Davis, A. K., Ge, W., Matsumoto, D., Zhang, J. L., 2015. The effect of manager-specific optimism on the tone of earnings conference calls, *Review of Accounting Studies* 20, 639–673. https://doi.org/10.1007/s11142-014-9309-4.

Davis, A. K., Piger, J. M., Sedor, L. M., 2012. Beyond the numbers: Measuring the information content of earnings press release language, *Contemporary Accounting Research* 29, 845–868. https://doi.org/10.1111/j.1911-3846.2011.01130.x.

Dickinson, K. and Pincus, A. L., 2003. Interpersonal analysis of grandiose and vulnerable narcissism, *Journal of Personality Disorders* 17, 188–207. https://doi.org/10.1521/pedi.17.3.188.22146.

Elliott, W. B., Rennekamp, K. M., White, B. J., 2014. Does concrete language in disclosures increase willingness to invest?, *Review of Accounting Studies* 20, 839–865. https://doi.org/10.1007/s11142-014-9315-6.

Emmons, R. A., 1987. Narcissism: Theory and measurement, *Journal of Personality and Social Psychology* 52, 11–17. https://doi.org/10.1037/0022-3514.52.1.11.

Ernstberger, J. and Grüning, M., 2013. How do firm- and country-level governance mechanisms affect firms' disclosure?, *Journal of Accounting and Public Policy* 32, 50–67. https://doi.org/10.1016/j.jaccpubpol.2013.02.003.

Fabrizio, K. R. and Kim, E.-H., 2019. Reluctant disclosure and transparency: Evidence from environmental disclosures, *Organization Science* 30, 1207–1231. https://doi.org/10.1287/orsc.2019.1298.

Farwell, L. and Wohlwend-Lloyd, R., 1998. Narcissistic processes: Optimistic expectations, favorable self-evaluations, and self-enhancing attributions, *Journal of Personality* 66, 65–83. https://doi.org/10.1111/1467-6494.00003.

Flam, R. W., Green, J., Lee, J. A., Sharp, N. Y., 2023. Ethnic minority analysts' participation in public earnings conference calls, *Journal of Accounting Research* 61, 1591–1631. https://doi.org/10.1111/1475-679X.12504.

Franco, G. de, Hope, O.-K., Vyas, D., Zhou, Y., 2015. Analyst report readability, *Contemporary Accounting Research* 32, 76–104. https://doi.org/10.1111/1911-3846.12062.

Galasso, A. and Simcoe, T. S., 2011. CEO Overconfidence and Innovation, *Management Science* 57, 1469–1484. https://doi.org/10.1287/mnsc.1110.1374.

Gamache, D. L., McNamara, G., Graffin, S. D., Kiley, J., Haleblian, J., Devers, C. E., 2019. Impression offsetting as an early warning signal of low CEO confidence in acquisitions, *Academy of Management Journal* 62, 1307–1332. https://doi.org/10.5465/amj.2017.0158.

Gao, J., Hartmann, F., Zhang, M., Chen, Y., 2023. The impact of CSR performance and CSR disclosure readability on investors' earnings estimates, *Accounting & Finance* 63, 1157–1186. https://doi.org/10.1111/acfi.12938.

Gong, R., 2023. CEO overconfidence and the tone of press release, *Accounting & Finance* 63, 2081–2108. https://doi.org/10.1111/acfi.12950.

Gow, I. D., Larcker, D. F., Zakolyukina, A. A., 2021. Non-answers during conference calls, *Journal of Accounting Research* 59, 1349–1384. https://doi.org/10.1111/1475-679X.12371.

Graffin, S. D., Carpenter, M. A., Boivie, S., 2011. What's all that (strategic) noise? Anticipatory impression management in CEO succession, *Strategic Management Journal* 32, 748–770. https://doi.org/10.1002/smj.906.

Gunning, R., 1952. The technique of clear writing. *McGraw-Hill,* New York, N.Y.

Ham, C., Seybert, N., Wang, S., 2018. Narcissism is a bad sign: CEO signature size, investment, and performance, *Review of Accounting Studies* 23, 234–264. https://doi.org/10.1007/s11142-017-9427-x.

Hambrick, D. C. and Mason, P. A., 1984. Upper echelons: The organization as a reflection of its top managers, *The Academy of Management Journal* 9, 193–206. https://doi.org/10.2307/258434.

Hart, W., Adams, J., Burton, K. A., Tortoriello, G. K., 2017. Narcissism and self-presentation: Profiling grandiose and vulnerable Narcissists' self-presentation tactic use, *Personality and Individual Differences* 104, 48–57. https://doi.org/10.1016/j.paid.2016.06.062.

Hart, W., Richardson, K., Tortoriello, G. K., Breeden, C. J., 2019. Revisiting profiles and profile comparisons of grandiose and vulnerable narcissism on self-presentation tactic use, *Personality and Individual Differences* 151, 109523. https://doi.org/10.1016/j.paid.2019.109523.

Hart, W., Tortoriello, G. K., Richardson, K., Breeden, C. J., 2018. Profiles and profile comparisons between dark triad constructs on self-presentation tactic usage and tactic beliefs, *Journal of Personality* 87, 501–517. https://doi.org/10.1111/jopy.12411.

Hasan, M. M., 2020. Readability of narrative disclosures in 10-K reports: Does managerial ability matter?, *European Accounting Review* 29, 147–168. https://doi.org/10.1080/09638180.2018.1528169.

Hemmings, D., Hodgkinson, L., Williams, G., 2020. It's OK to pay well, if you write well: The effects of remuneration disclosure readability, *Journal of Business Finance & Accounting* 47, 547–586. https://doi.org/10.1111/jbfa.12431.

Hendin, H. M. and Cheek, J. M., 1997. Assessing hypersensitive narcissism: A reexamination of Murray's narcissm scale, *Journal of Research in Personality* 31, 588–599. https://doi.org/10.1006/jrpe.1997.2204.

Huang, X., Teoh, S. H., Zhang, Y., 2014. Tone management, *The Accounting Review* 89, 1083–1113. https://doi.org/10.2308/accr-50684.

Jiang, W., Shi, C., Li, Y., Xie, S., 2024. Executive individualism and the tone of firms' annual reports, *Accounting & Finance*. https://doi.org/10.1111/acfi.13284.

Judge, T. A., LePine, J. A., Rich, B. L., 2006. Loving yourself abundantly: Relationship of the narcissistic personality to self- and other perceptions of workplace deviance, leadership, and task and contextual performance, *The Journal of Applied Psychology* 91, 762–776. https://doi.org/10.1037/0021-9010.91.4.762.

Kashmiri, S., Nicol, C. D., Arora, S., 2017. Me, myself, and I:Influence of CEO narcissism on firms' innovation strategy and the likelihood of product-harm crises, *Journal of the Academy of Marketing Science* 45, 633–656. https://doi.org/10.1007/s11747-017-0535-8.

Kim, C. F., Wang, K., Zhang, L., 2019. Readability of 10-K reports and stock price crash risk, *Contemporary Accounting Research* 36, 1184–1216. https://doi.org/10.1111/1911-3846.12452.

Kim, J. J. and Anderson, R., 2024. CEO narcissism and the agency cost of debt, *Journal of Empirical Finance* 77, 101477. https://doi.org/10.1016/j.jempfin.2024.101477.

Laksmana, I., Tietz, W., Yang, Y.-W., 2012. Compensation discussion and analysis (CD&A): Readability and management obfuscation, *Journal of Accounting and Public Policy* 31, 185–203. https://doi.org/10.1016/j.jaccpubpol.2011.08.003.

Lang, M. and Stice-Lawrence, L., 2015. Textual analysis and international financial reporting: Large sample evidence, *Journal of Accounting and Economics* 60, 110–135. https://doi.org/10.1016/j.jacceco.2015.09.002.

Larcker, D. F. and Zakolyukina, A. A., 2012. Detecting deceptive discussions in conference calls, *Journal of Accounting Research* 50, 495–540. https://doi.org/10.1111/j.1475-679X.2012.00450.x.

Lawrence, A., 2013. Individual investors and financial disclosure, *Journal of Accounting and Economics* 56, 130–147. https://doi.org/10.1016/j.jacceco.2013.05.001.

Lee, J., 2016. Can investors detect managers' lack of spontaneity? Adherence to predetermined scripts during earnings conference calls, *The Accounting Review* 91, 229–250. https://doi.org/10.2308/accr-51135.

Lehavy, R., Li, F., Merkley, K., 2011. The effect of annual report readability on analyst following and the properties of their earnings forecasts, *The Accounting Review* 86, 1087–1115. https://doi.org/10.2308/accr.00000043.

Leuz, C. and Wysocki, P. D., 2016. The economics of disclosure and financial reporting regulation: Evidence and suggestions for future research, *Journal of Accounting Research* 54, 525–622. https://doi.org/10.1111/1475-679X.12115.

Li, F., 2008. Annual report readability, current earnings, and earnings persistence, *Journal of Accounting and Economics* 45, 221–247. https://doi.org/10.1016/j.jacceco.2008.02.003.

Lim, E. K., Chalmers, K., Hanlon, D., 2018. The influence of business strategy on annual report readability, *Journal of Accounting and Public Policy* 37, 65–81. https://doi.org/10.1016/j.jaccpubpol.2018.01.003.

Loughran, T. and McDonald, B., 2011. When is a liability not a liability? Textual analysis, dictionaries, and 10Ks, *The Journal of Finance* 66, 35–65. https://doi.org/10.1111/j.1540-6261.2010.01625.x.

Loughran, T. and McDonald, B., 2016. Textual analysis in accounting and finance: A survey, *Journal of Accounting Research* 54, 1187–1230. https://doi.org/10.1111/1475-679X.12123.

Lyons, M., Evans, K., Helle, S., 2019. Do "dark" personality features fuffer against adversity? The associations between cumulative life stress, the dark triad, and mental distress, *Sage Open* 9. https://doi.org/10.1177/2158244018822383.

Marquez-Illescas, G., Zebedee, A. A., Zhou, L., 2019. Hear me write: Does CEO narcissism affect disclosure?, *Journal of Business Ethics* 159, 401–417. https://doi.org/10.1007/s10551-018-3796-3.

Matsumoto, D., Pronk, M., Roelofsen, E., 2011. What makes conference calls useful? The information content of managers' presentations and analysts' discussion sessions, *The Accounting Review* 86, 1383–1414. https://doi.org/10.2308/accr-10034.

Mayew, W. J. and Venkatachalam, M., 2012. The Power of Voice: Managerial Affective States and Future Firm Performance, *The Journal of Finance* 67. https://doi.org/10.1111/j.1540-6261.2011.01705.x.

Mc Laughlin, H. G., 1969. SMOG Grading: A new readability formula, *Journal of Reading* 12.

Mekhaimer, M., Soliman, M., Zhang, W., 2024. Does political uncertainty obfuscate narrative disclosure?, *The Accounting Review* 99, 367–394. https://doi.org/10.2308/TAR-2021-0884.

Merkl-Davies, D. M. and Brennan, N. M., 2007. Discretionary disclosure strategies in corporate narratives: Incremental information or impression management?, *Journal of Accounting Literature* 27, 116–196.

Miller, B. P., 2010. The effects of reporting complexity on small and large investor trading, *The Accounting Review* 85, 2107–2143. https://doi.org/10.2308/accr.00000001.

Miller, J. D., Hoffman, B. J., Gaughan, E. T., Gentile, B., Maples, J., Keith Campbell, W., 2011. Grandiose and vulnerable narcissism: A nomological network analysis, *Journal of Personality* 79, 1013–1042. https://doi.org/10.1111/j.1467-6494.2010.00711.x.

Nadeem, M., 2022. Board gender diversity and managerial obfuscation: Evidence from the readability of narrative disclosure in 10-K reports, *Journal of Business Ethics* 179, 153–177. https://doi.org/10.1007/s10551-021-04830-3.

Nathan DeWall, C., Buffardi, L. E., Bonser, I., Keith Campbell, W., 2011. Narcissism and implicit attention seeking: Evidence from linguistic analyses of social networking and online presentation, *Personality and Individual Differences* 51, 57–62. https://doi.org/10.1016/j.paid.2011.03.011.

Nguyen, J. H., 2021. Tax avoidance and financial statement readability, *European Accounting Review* 30, 1043–1066. https://doi.org/10.1080/09638180.2020.1811745.

Noh, J. and Zhou, D., 2022. Executives' blaming external factors and market reactions: Evidence from earnings conference calls, *Journal of Banking and Finance* 134. https://doi.org/10.1016/j.jbankfin.2021.106358.

Olsen, K. J., Young, S. M., Dworkis, K. K., 2014. CEO narcissism and accounting: A picture of profits, *Journal of Management Accounting Research* 26, 243–267. https://doi.org/10.2139/ssrn.2115067.

O'Reilly, C. A., Doerr, B., Caldwell, D. F., Chatman, J. A., 2014. Narcissistic CEOs and executive compensation, *The Leadership Quarterly* 25, 218–231. https://doi.org/10.1016/j.leaqua.2013.08.002.

Patel, P. C. and Cooper, D., 2014. The harder they fall, the faster they rise: Approach and avoidance focus in narcissistic CEOs, *Strategic Management Journal* 35, 1528–1540.

Petrenko, O. V., Aime, F., Ridge, J., Hill, A., 2016. Corporate social responsibility or CEO narcissism? CSR motivations and organizational performance, *Strategic Management Journal* 37, 262–279. https://doi.org/10.1002/smj.2348.

Price, S. M., Doran, J. S., Peterson, D. R., Bliss, B. A., 2012. Earnings conference calls and stock returns: The incremental informativeness of textual tone, *Journal of Banking & Finance* 36, 992–1011. https://doi.org/10.1016/j.jbankfin.2011.10.013.

Reina, C. S., Zhang, Z., Peterson, S. J., 2014. CEO grandiose narcissism and firm performance: The role of organizational identification, *The Leadership Quarterly* 25, 958–971. https://doi.org/10.1016/j.leaqua.2014.06.004.

Rennekamp, K. M., Sethuraman, M., Steenhoven, B. A., 2022. Engagement in earnings conference calls, *Journal of Accounting and Economics* 74, 101498. https://doi.org/10.1016/j.jacceco.2022.101498.

Rijsenbilt, A. and Commandeur, H., 2013. Narcissus enters the courtroom: CEO narcissism and fraud, *Journal of Business Ethics* 117, 413–429. https://doi.org/10.1007/s10551-012-1528-7.

Rose, P., 2002. The happy and unhappy faces of narcissism, *Personality and Individual Differences* 33, 379–391. https://doi.org/10.1016/S0191-8869(01)00162-3.

Security Exchange Commission (SEC), 1998. A plain English handbook: How to create clear SEC disclosure, http://www.sec.gov/pdf/handbook.pdf.

Security Exchange Commission (SEC), 2013. The path forward on disclosure, https://www.sec.gov/news/speech/spch101513mjw.

Tang, Y., Mack, D. Z., Chen, G., 2018. The differential effects of CEO narcissism and hubris on corporate social responsibility, *Strategic Management Journal* 39, 1370–1387.

Wales, W. J., Patel, P. C., Lumpkin, G. T., 2013. In pursuit of greatness: CEO narcissism, entrepreneurial orientation, and firm performance variance, *Journal of Management Studies* 50, 1041–1069. https://doi.org/10.1111/joms.12034.

Wallace, H. M. and Baumeister, R. F., 2002. The performance of narcissists rises and falls with perceived opportunity for glory, *Journal of Personality and Social Psychology* 82, 819–834. https://doi.org/10.1037//0022-3514.82.5.819.

Watson, P. J. and Biderman, M. D., 1993. Narcissistic personality inventory factors, splitting, and self-consciousness, *Journal of Personality Assessment* 61, 41–57. https://doi.org/10.1207/s15327752jpa6101_4.

Xu, Q., Fernando, G. D., Tam, K., 2018. Executive age and the readability of financial reports, *Advances in Accounting* 43, 70–81. https://doi.org/10.1016/j.adiac.2018.09.004.

7 Discussion

Abstract

This chapter synthesizes the contributions of the three research manuscripts and situates them within the broader landscape of Upper Echelons Theory (UET) and corporate finance research. The discussion identifies distinct contributions across the subfields of M&A, organizational impression management, and strategic corporate communication, while highlighting shared theoretical advancements. Practical implications are outlined for investors, boards, and regulators, emphasizing how awareness of executive psychological traits can improve governance and the critical evaluation of corporate disclosures. The chapter concludes by acknowledging key limitations of this work.

Researchers and practitioners have an enduring concern with gaining a comprehensive understanding of the strategic choices made by organizations (Bromiley & Rau, 2016; Cristofaro et al., 2024). Significant progress in this endeavor arises from acknowledging human behavior in all its dimensions (e.g., cognitions, values, and perceptions), a focus that has steadily expanded since recognizing the limitations inherent in economic models based solely on expected utility paradigms (Abatecola & Cristofaro, 2018; Carpenter, 2011; Finkelstein et al., 2009). Today, this behavioral perspective has flourished alongside the rapid and extensive diffusion of the UET across various disciplines (White & Borgholthaus, 2022), enriching our understanding of decision-making processes by integrating psychological insights into traditional economic analyses (Abatecola & Cristofaro, 2018).

F. Lammers, *The Role of Executive Characteristics in Financial Decision-Making*, Studies in Finance and Accounting, https://doi.org/10.1007/978-3-658-51855-4_7

However, while the notion that TMT characteristics can influence corporate behavior is broadly acknowledged across various economic disciplines, traditional financial research has generally been cautious about incorporating the role of individual managerial differences, often viewing them as outside the narrow scope of its rather parochial models (Bamber et al., 2010; Bertrand & Schoar, 2003; Hertrampf et al., 2025). This conceptual limitation has reinforced an overreliance on rational economic self-interest as the primary explanatory variable for managerial behavior, an assumption increasingly acknowledged as a significant flaw in conventional financial thinking (Wowak et al., 2017). To address this research gap, the present dissertation seeks to integrate the UET into the field of corporate finance. By explicitly incorporating a UET perspective into the analysis of strategic decision-making, the research enhances both theoretical frameworks and empirical insights, contributing to a more nuanced and realistic understanding of managerial influence in financial contexts.

7.1 Contributions to Literature

While the three manuscripts share a common theoretical grounding in UET, they contribute to distinct streams of literature by addressing unique research questions within the broader field of corporate finance. Specifically, each manuscript deepens the understanding of executive influence on strategic choices by shedding light on the particular conditions and contexts in which these decisions unfold, thereby enriching the existing literature in their respective subfields.

Research manuscript 1 is embedded within the context of M&A, which constitute some of the most impactful financial decisions undertaken by companies (DePamphilis, 2019). Although existing scholars extensively document the influence of CEOs on various acquisition outcomes, including firm performance (Aktas et al., 2016; Custódio & Metzger, 2013), target premium (Hayward & Hambrick, 1997), and acquisition frequency (El-Khatib et al., 2015), the roles played by other TMT members remain comparatively underexplored (Iskandar-Datta & Shekhar, 2020). This gap is particularly notable concerning CFOs, whose financial expertise has frequently been identified, both in academic literature (Rorem et al., 2013) and among practitioners (Agrawal et al., 2020), as essential for effectively navigating through the complex dynamics of acquisition processes. Examining the influence of powerful CFOs throughout various stages of the acquisition process, this study contributes to the M&A literature by providing a more nuanced understanding of how their financial expertise shapes deal-making dynamics and outcomes. Furthermore, by differentiating among various sources from which CFOs derive managerial power, the study sheds light on their relative significance, thereby enriching the broader discussion on managerial power and its strategic implications for corporate decision-making (Wangrow et al., 2015).

Research manuscript 2 advances the emerging literature on organizational impression management, a domain that has recently gained considerable momentum due to growing evidence of its effectiveness in steering stakeholder perceptions across a wide range of corporate strategic decisions (Blankespoor & deHaan, 2020; Bolino et al., 2016; Gamache et al., 2019). Building on this, the study expands the relatively sparse body of research on the antecedents of such strategies by investigating the influence of CEO narcissism on organizational impression management around large M&A announcements. Developing a deeper understanding of the motivations driving top managers to engage in impression management during M&A activities appears particularly important, as existing research consistently highlights the negative market reactions commonly observed following acquisition announcements (Renneboog & Vansteenkiste, 2019), thereby creating fertile ground for impression management (Graffin et al., 2016). As such, this study also contributes to the ongoing debate within the broader M&A literature regarding the determinants of negative market reactions following acquisition announcements (Moeller et al., 2005). Furthermore, by incorporating CEO reputation and managerial power as moderating factors, this study directly addresses recent calls in the CEO narcissism literature to identify specific contextual conditions that either amplify or constrain situational narcissism (Cragun et al., 2020).

Research manuscript 3 investigates the influence of CEO narcissism on the strategic use of complex language in corporate communication. By focusing on earnings conference calls, this study moves beyond the traditional scope of impression management literature, which has largely centered on written disclosure formats such as annual reports (Lehavy et al., 2011) or press releases (Marquez-Illescas et al., 2019). Compared to these more curated and collaboratively prepared formats (Larcker & Zakolyukina, 2012), earnings calls provide a less biased setting to examine the influence of executive psychological traits, as they require more direct, spontaneous communication between executives and financial analysts (Bae et al., 2023; Price et al., 2012). Furthermore, utilizing spoken language from conference calls enables the application of recent advances in the quantification of strategic linguistic complexity (Bushee et al., 2017), thereby facilitating a more direct and robust assessment of complex language as a tool for impression management. In addition to its theoretical contributions, this manuscript enhances methodological rigor within the CEO narcissism literature. By adopting one of the most comprehensive altruism-based measures of

CEO narcissism currently available (Cragun et al., 2020), a method that has seen limited use to date, the study offers greater precision and deeper insight into the altruistic dimension of narcissistic leadership.

7.2 Theoretical Contributions

Beyond contributing to the specific literature streams in which the individual research manuscripts are situated, this dissertation further adds to the theoretical advancements of upper- echelons research outlined in Sect. 2.3. Research manuscript 1 advances UET by engaging with one of its core and long-debated elements: the appropriate unit of analysis. While UET fundamentally conceptualizes the TMT as the firm's dominant coalition, there remains a lack of consensus regarding which executives should be included in the scope of analysis (Mithani & O'Brien, 2021; Nielsen, 2010). This ambiguity is especially salient given the increasing recognition that the pervasive CEO-centric perspective offers an incomplete account of how strategic decisions are shaped (van Doorn et al., 2022). Responding to calls for a broader conceptualization of executive influence (Bedard et al., 2014; Welch et al., 2020), Manuscript 1 underscores the strategic role of the CFO, thereby extending the analytical lens beyond the CEO. In doing so, the study not only deepens our understanding of how multiple senior executives contribute to firm-level outcomes, but also promotes a more nuanced and balanced theoretical articulation of executive influence within the TMT. This shift represents a valuable step forward in the continued evolution of UET.

Furthermore, research Manuscripts 1 and 2 contribute to the ongoing discourse in upper- echelons research related to the critical role of contextual contingencies in the theory's explanatory power. While early work rested on relatively deterministic assumptions, theoretical advancements emphasized the importance of situational factors, positioning UET as a more context-sensitive framework of strategic leadership (Carpenter et al., 2004; Crossland & Hambrick, 2011). This evolution reflects growing recognition that executive effects do not operate in isolation but are embedded within and conditioned by broader contextual environments. In line with calls from scholars for a deeper understanding of the boundary conditions under which executive characteristics translate into organizational outcomes (e.g., Busenbark et al., 2016; Graffin et al., 2013; Wang et al., 2016), both manuscripts respond with theoretically grounded and empirically robust examinations of moderating variables. By doing so, this dissertation advances a more nuanced understanding of the conditions under which executive effects manifest, which is essential for the continued theoretical development and practical relevance of UET (Neely et al., 2020).

Moreover, manuscripts 2 and 3 extend upper-echelons research by moving beyond traditional demographic proxies such as executive age, tenure, and experience, and instead adopting direct and theoretically grounded measures of executive psychological attributes to investigate strategy-related outcomes (Wowak et al., 2017). By providing rigorous conceptual justification for the use of unobtrusive measures, these studies address prior criticisms regarding the misalignment between empirical indicators and the underlying constructs they purport to represent (Neely et al., 2020). Furthermore, while executive personality traits have garnered increased scholarly attention, the impact of many of these traits remains ambiguous, as emphasized by Bromiley and Rau (2016): "While we know that different dimensions of CEO personality significantly influence organizational outcomes, whether these dimensions have positive or negative effects on organizations needs more examination" (p. 192). By specifically examining CEO narcissism, a trait typically considered detrimental (Cragun et al., 2020), these studies contribute valuable insights into the nuanced and potentially ambiguous effects of executive psychological characteristics within UET.

7.3 Practical Implications

This dissertation also provides practical implications that can enhance strategic decision-making in different contexts. Reinforcing practitioners' recognition of the finance function's strategic importance in corporate takeovers (Agrawal et al., 2020; Fuhrer et al., 2017), Manuscript 1 offers empirical evidence that greater managerial decision power allocated to acquiring firms' CFOs can benefit deal outcomes through a set of distinct mechanisms. While this impact might not become evident in every stage of a deal, it emphasizes the value of empowering CFOs as strategic leaders whose influence extends beyond financial stewardship to shaping the overall success and value creation potential of corporate acquisitions. Moreover, the study highlights the particular importance of a CFO's prior M&A experience, which emerges as the most consistently associated factor with improved deal outcomes. This finding reinforces the notion that task-specific expertise plays a critical role in shaping acquisition success (Custódio & Metzger, 2013; Field & Mkrtchyan, 2017), suggesting that seasoned CFOs can draw on their experiential knowledge to navigate complex transactions more effectively and deliver greater value to the firm.

Manuscripts 2 and 3 add to a more advanced understanding of the antecedents of impression management around high-stakes corporate events, holding significant value for a broad range of stakeholders, including investors, analysts, and regulators. By uncovering the psychological and contextual drivers behind how firms strategically shape external narratives, stakeholders are better positioned to critically assess the credibility and intent behind corporate disclosures. This, in turn, supports more informed decision-making and enhances the overall transparency and accountability of executive communication strategies. These insights are also relevant for boards and directors, as they underscore the importance of recognizing how psychological traits can influence strategic messaging and stakeholder perceptions. By equipping directors with this understanding, organizations can foster more critical evaluations of executive behavior and communication, ultimately supporting more balanced and informed governance practices. Raising awareness of the heuristics and potential biases associated with such traits is crucial, especially in light of prior research showing that individuals can mitigate the impact of cognitive and behavioral biases when they are made consciously aware of them (Graffin et al., 2013; Ross et al., 1975).

7.4 Limitations and Future Research Avenues

As with any scientific work, this dissertation is subject to limitations stemming from the theories and models employed. Nonetheless, these constraints also highlight fruitful directions for future research. A primary limitation concerns the omission of potential effects arising from interactions among TMT members on strategic decision-making processes. This is attributable to the consistent application of an "executives-in-isolation" model across the manuscripts (van Doorn et al., 2022). While this approach offers analytical clarity and is well-established in the literature (Carpenter et al., 2004), it inherently overlooks team-level dynamics such as collective decision-making, power asymmetries, intra-team conflict, and cohesion (Papagiannidis, 2022). Recent scholarship increasingly addresses these complexities by adopting multilevel models that consider both CEO-level and team-level influences, collecting primary data on TMT interactions, and applying variance partitioning techniques to disentangle individual from collective effects (Wowak et al., 2017). Nevertheless, the interactional dynamics within TMTs, particularly the interplay among different members, remain an underexplored but theoretically rich domain (Harrison et al., 2023), and thus represent a compelling avenue for future inquiry (Hodgkinson et al., 2023).

Another limitation inherent to this dissertation is its exclusive geographical focus on U.S. firms, potentially restricting the generalizability of the findings. Prior research suggests that external factors such as national culture (Han et al., 2010), institutional norms (Sine & Lee, 2009), and environmental interdependencies (Casciaro & Piskorski, 2005) can significantly shape TMT structures and decision-making mechanisms (Wowak et al., 2017), thereby impacting the explanatory power of UET. Accordingly, future research would benefit from systematically examining how varying institutional and cultural environments affect upper-echelon dynamics and strategic outcomes.

A related limitation pertains to the composition of the empirical samples used across the manuscripts, which are predominantly drawn from large publicly listed firms. While this sampling strategy enhances data availability and quality, it narrows the scope of inference. Prior studies indicate that the mechanisms and predictive validity of UET may differ in alternative organizational settings, particularly in family-owned enterprises—an area of growing scholarly interest. Given the substantial economic relevance of family firms (Carney et al., 2015), future research should explore how these distinctive contexts, shaped by unique ownership structures, succession norms, and relational dynamics, may influence TMT behavior and its implications.

Finally, research on the influence of TMT on corporate outcomes is inherently susceptible to endogeneity-related concerns (Cuypers et al., 2022), and the studies underlying this dissertation are no exception. Endogeneity is a central challenge in UET, as failure to adequately address it often casts doubt on the validity of causal interpretations drawn from empirical findings. While all three studies included in this dissertation employ appropriate econometric techniques to mitigate potential endogeneity biases, caution remains warranted when making inferences about the direction of causality. Advancing this line of research calls for more rigorous methodological approaches that can better isolate causal mechanisms. A promising avenue lies in the integration of experimental or quasi-experimental designs, to more directly and convincingly test the theorized causal pathways between TMT attributes and organizational outcomes (Neely et al., 2020).

References

Aabo, T., Jacobsen, M. L., & Stendys, K. (2022). Pay me with fame, not mammon: CEO narcissism, compensation, and media coverage. *Finance Research Letters*, *46*, Article 102495. https://doi.org/10.1016/j.frl.2021.102495

Abatecola, G., & Cristofaro, M. (2018). Hambrick and Mason's "Upper Echelons Theory": Evolution and open avenues. *Journal of Management History*, *26*(1), 116–136. https://doi.org/10.1108/JMH-02-2018-0016

Agrawal, A., Kim, E., Dinneen, B., & Uhlaner, R. (2020). *The one task the CFO should not delegate: Integrations.* https://www.mckinsey.com/business-functions/m-and-a/our-insights/the-one-task-the-cfo-should-not-delegate-integrations

Aharoni, Y., Tihanyi, L., & Connelly, B. L. (2011). Managerial decision-making in international business: A forty-five-year retrospective. *Journal of World Business*, *46*(2), 135–142. https://doi.org/10.1016/j.jwb.2010.05.001

Aktas, N., Bodt, E. de, Bollaert, H., & Roll, R. (2016). CEO narcissism and the takeover process: From private initiation to deal completion. *Journal of Financial and Quantitative Analysis*, *51*(1), 113–137. https://doi.org/10.1017/S0022109016000065

Ali, R., Rehman, R. U., Suleman, S., & Ntim, C. G. (2022). CEO attributes, investment decisions, and firm performance: New insights from upper echelons theory. *Managerial and Decision Economics*, *43*(2), 398–417. https://doi.org/10.1002/mde.3389

Allee, K. D. (2015). The structure of voluntary disclosure narratives: Evidence from tone dispersion. *Journal of Accounting Research*, *53*(2), 241–274. https://doi.org/10.1111/1475-679X.12072

Alphabet Inc. (2024). *Form 10-K: Annual report.* https://abc.xyz/assets/77/51/9841ad5c4fbe85b4440c47a4df8d/goog-10-k-2024.pdf

Amason, A. C. (1996). Distinguishing the effects of functional and dysfunctional conflict on strategic decision making: Resolving a paradox for top management teams. *Academy of Management Journal*, *39*(1), 123–148. https://doi.org/10.2307/256633

Amicis, C. de, Falconieri, S., & Tastan, M. (2021). Sentiment analysis and gender differences in earnings conference calls. *Journal of Corporate Finance*, *71*, Article 101809. https://doi.org/10.1016/j.jcorpfin.2020.101809

Ang, S. H., Benischke, M. H., & Doh, J. P. (2015). The interactions of institutions on foreign market entry mode. *Strategic Management Journal*, *36*(10), 1536–1553. https://doi.org/10.1002/smj.2295

F. Lammers, *The Role of Executive Characteristics in Financial Decision-Making*, Studies in Finance and Accounting, https://doi.org/10.1007/978-3-658-51855-4

Apple Inc. (2009). *Form 10-K: Annual report*. https://d1lge852tjjqow.cloudfront.net/CIK-0000320193/5dfc8604-cbdc-448b-ba04-700a22a37909.pdf

Apple Inc. (2024). *Form 10-K: Annual report*. https://d18rn0p25nwr6d.cloudfront.net/CIK-0000320193/c87043b9-5d89-4717-9f49-c4f9663d0061.pdf

Augier, M. (2010). Cyert, March, and the Carnegie School. In P. G. Klein (Ed.), *The Elgar companion to transaction cost economics* (pp. 49–58). Edward Elgar.

Augier, M., & March, J. G. (2008). A retrospective look at A Behavioral Theory of the Firm. *Journal of Economic Behavior & Organization*, *66*(1), 1–6. https://doi.org/10.1016/j.jebo.2008.01.005

Augier, M., & Teece, D. J. (2009). Dynamic capabilities and the role of managers in business strategy and economic performance. *Organization Science*, *20*(2), 410–421. https://doi.org/10.1287/orsc.1090.0424

Bae, J., Yu Hung, C., & van Lent, L. (2023). Mobilizing text as data. *European Accounting Review*, *32*(5), 1085–1106. https://doi.org/10.1080/09638180.2023.2218423

Bamber, L. S., Jiang, J., & Wang, I. Y. (2010). What's my style? The influence of top managers on voluntary corporate financial disclosure. *The Accounting Review*, *85*(4), 1131–1162. https://doi.org/10.2308/accr.2010.85.4.1131

Bardmann, M. (2011). *Grundlagen der allgemeinen Betriebswirtschaftslehre*. Gabler.

Barrick, M. R., & Mount, M. K. (1991). The big five personality dimensions and job performance: A meta-analysis. *Personnel Psychology*, *44*(1), 1–26. https://doi.org/10.1111/j.1744-6570.1991.tb00688.x

Bartlett, C. A., & Ghoshal, S. (1993). Beyond the M-form: Toward a managerial theory of the firm. *Strategic Management Journal*, *14*(2), 23–46. https://doi.org/10.1002/smj.4250141005

Baumol, W. J. (1968). Entrepreneurship in economic theory. *The American Economic Review*, *58*(2), 64–71.

Bedard, J., Hoitash, R., & Hoitash, U. (2014). Chief Financial Officers as inside directors. *Contemporary Accounting Research*, *31*(3), 787–817. https://doi.org/10.1111/1911-3846.12045

Bendickson, J., Muldoon, J., Liguori, E., & Davis, P. E. (2016). Agency theory: The times, they are a-changin'. *Management Decision*, *54*(1), 174–193. https://doi.org/10.1108/MD-02-2015-0058

Ben-Shahar, D., Carmeli, A., Sulganik, E., & Weiss, D. (2023). Power and dominant coalitions in family business. *The Academy of Management Review*, *48*(3), 530–555. https://doi.org/10.5465/amr.2021.0007

Bertrand, M., & Schoar, A. (2003). Managing with style: The effect of managers on firm policies. *The Quarterly Journal of Economics*, *118*(4), 1169–1208. https://doi.org/10.1162/003355303322552775

Bidwell, M. J. (2012). Politics and firm boundaries: How organizational structure, group interests, and resources affect outsourcing. *Organization Science*, *23*(6), 1622–1642. https://doi.org/10.1287/orsc.1120.0772

Blankespoor, E., & deHaan, E. (2020). Strategic disclosure and CEO media visibility. *Journal of Financial Reporting*, *5*(1), 25–50. https://doi.org/10.2308/jfr-2018-0004

Boivie, S., Lange, D., McDonald, M. L., & Westphal, J. D. (2011). Me or we: The effects of CEO organizational identification on agency costs. *Academy of Management Journal*, *54*(3), 551–576. https://doi.org/10.5465/amj.2011.61968081

Bolino, M. C., Long, D., & Turnley, W. (2016). Impression management in organizations: Critical questions, answers, and areas for future research. *Annual Review of Organizational Psychology and Organizational Behavior*, *3*(1), 377–406. https://doi.org/10.1146/annurev-orgpsych-041015-062337

Bonsall, S. B., & Miller, B. P. (2017). The impact of narrative disclosure readability on bond ratings and the cost of debt. *Review of Accounting Studies*, *22*(2), 608–643. https://doi.org/10.1007/s11142-017-9388-0

Borgholthaus, C. J., White, J. V., & Harms, P. D. (2023). CEO dark personality: A critical review, bibliometric analysis, and research agenda. *Personality and Individual Differences*, *201*, Article 111951. https://doi.org/10.1016/j.paid.2022.111951

Bosse, D. A., & Phillips, R. A. (2016). Agency theory and bounded self-interest. *The Academy of Management Review*, *41*(2), 276–297. https://doi.org/10.5465/amr.2013.0420

Brand, V. (2009). Empirical business ethics research and paradigm analysis. *Journal of Business Ethics*, *86*(4), 429–449. https://doi.org/10.1007/s10551-008-9856-3

Brauer, M., & Vandepoele, L. (2023). Managing the "downside" of downsizing: Firms' impression offsetting around downsizing announcements. *Journal of Management Studies*, *61*(8), Article joms.13024, 3684–3716. https://doi.org/10.1111/joms.13024

Bromiley, P., & Rau, D. (2016). Social, behavioral, and cognitive influences on upper echelons during strategy process. *Journal of Management*, *42*(1), 174–202. https://doi.org/10.1177/0149206315617240

Bruneel, J., Clarysse, B., Staessens, M., & Weemaes, S. (2020). Breaking with the past: The need for innovation in the governance of nonprofit social enterprises. *Academy of Management Perspectives*, *34*(2), 209–225. https://doi.org/10.5465/amp.2017.0176

Burrel, G., & Morgan, G. (1979). *Sociological paradigms and organisational analysis: Elements of the sociology of corporate life*. Heinemann.

Busenbark, J. R., Krause, R., Boivie, S., & Graffin, S. D. (2016). Toward a configurational perspective on the CEO. *Journal of Management*, *42*(1), 234–268. https://doi.org/10.1177/0149206315618448

Bushee, B. J., Gow, I. D., & Taylor, D. J. (2017). Linguistic complexity in firm disclosures: Obfuscation or information? *Journal of Accounting Research*, *56*(1), 85–121. https://doi.org/10.1111/1475-679X.12179

Bushee, B. J., & Huang, Y. (2024). Do analysts and investors efficiently respond to managerial linguistic complexity during conference calls? *The Accounting Review*, *99*(4), 143–168. https://doi.org/10.2308/TAR-2019-0358

Buyl, T., Boone, C., & Wade, J. B. (2019). CEO narcissism, risk-taking, and resilience: An empirical analysis in U.S. commercial banks. *Journal of Management*, *45*(4), 1372–1400. https://doi.org/10.1177/0149206317699521

Camerer, C., Loewenstein, G., & Rabin, M. (Eds.). (2004). *Advances in behavioral economics*. Russell Sage Foundation; Princeton University Press.

Campbell, R. J., Jeong, S.-H., & Graffin, S. D. (2019). Born to Take Risk? The Effect of CEO Birth Order on Strategic Risk Taking. *Academy of Management Journal*, *62*(4), 1278–1306. https://doi.org/10.5465/amj.2017.0790

Campling, J., Glancey, K. S., & McQuaid, R. (Eds.). (2000). *Entrepreneurial economics*. Palgrave Macmillan. https://doi.org/10.1057/9780333981245

Carney, M., van Essen, M., Gedajlovic, E. R., & Heugens, P. (2015). What do we know about private family firms? A meta–analytical review. *Entrepreneurship Theory and Practice, 39*(3), 513–544. https://doi.org/10.1111/etap.12054

Carpenter, M. A. (Ed.). (2011). *Handbook of research on top management teams.* Edward Elgar. https://doi.org/10.4337/9780857933201

Carpenter, M. A., Geletkanycz, M. A., & Sanders, W. G. (2004). Upper echelons research revisited: Antecedents, elements, and consequences of top management team composition. *Journal of Management, 30*(6), 749–778. https://doi.org/10.1016/j.jm.2004.06.001

Casciaro, T., & Piskorski, M. J. (2005). Power imbalance, mutual dependence, and constraint absorption: A closer look at resource dependence theory. *Administrative Science Quarterly, 50*(2), 167–199. https://doi.org/10.2189/asqu.2005.50.2.167

Chin, M. K., Hambrick, D. C., & Treviño, L. K. (2013). Political Ideologies of CEOs. *Administrative Science Quarterly, 58*(2), 197–232. https://doi.org/10.1177/0001839213486984

Coase, R. H. (1937). The nature of the firm. *Economica, 4*(16), 386–405. https://doi.org/10.1111/j.1468-0335.1937.tb00002.x

Coase, R. H. (1988). The nature of the firm: Influence. *Journal of Law, Economics, & Organization, 4*(1), 33–47. https://doi.org/10.1093/oxfordjournals.jleo.a036947

Colbert, A. E., Barrick, M. R., & Bradley, B. H. (2014). Personality and leadership composition in top management teams: Implications for organizational effectiveness. *Personnel Psychology, 67*(2), 351–387. https://doi.org/10.1111/peps.12036

Comte, A. (1865). *A general view of positivism.* Cambridge University Press. https://doi.org/10.1017/CBO9780511692888

Conyon, M. J., Haß, L. H., Vergauwe, S., & Zhang, Z. (2019). Foreign experience and CEO compensation. *Journal of Corporate Finance, 57*, 102–121. https://doi.org/10.1016/j.corpfin.2017.12.016

Corr, P., & Plagnol, A. C. (2023). *Behavioral economics: The basics* (2nd ed.). Routledge.

Cragun, O. R., Olsen, K. J., & Wright, P. M. (2020). Making CEO narcissism research great: A review and meta-analysis of CEO narcissism. *Journal of Management, 46*(6), 908–936. https://doi.org/10.1177/0149206319892678

Cristofaro, M., Augier, M., Lovallo, D., Abatecola, G., & Leoni, L. (2024). Behavioral strategy in evolution: A review and conceptual framework. *European Management Journal.* Advance online publication. https://doi.org/10.1016/j.emj.2024.10.002

Crossland, C., & Hambrick, D. C. (2007). How national systems differ in their constraints on corporate executives: A study of CEO effects in three countries. *Strategic Management Journal, 28*(8), 767–789. https://doi.org/10.1002/smj.610

Crossland, C., & Hambrick, D. C. (2011). Differences in managerial discretion across countries: How nation-level institutions affect the degree to which CEOs matter. *Strategic Management Journal, 32*(8), 797–819. https://doi.org/10.1002/smj.913

Crossland, C., Zyung, J., Hiller, N. J., & Hambrick, D. C. (2014). CEO career variety: Effects on firm-level strategic and social novelty. *Academy of Management Journal, 57*(3), 652–674. https://doi.org/10.5465/amj.2012.0469

Crotty, M. (1998). *The foundations of social research: Meaning and perspective in the research process.* SAGE Publications.

Custódio, C., & Metzger, D. (2013). How do CEOs matter? The effect of industry expertise on acquisition returns. *The Review of Financial Studies, 26*(8), 2007–2047. https://doi.org/10.1093/rfs/hht032

Cuypers, I. R. P., Patel, C., Ertug, G., Li, J., & Cuypers, Y. (2022). Top management teams in international business research: A review and suggestions for future research. *Journal of International Business Studies, 53*(3), 481–515. https://doi.org/10.1057/s41267-021-00456-9

Cyert, R. M., & March, J. G. (1963). *Behavioral theory of the firm.* Prentice Hall.

Delmas, M. A., & Toffel, M. W. (2008). Organizational responses to environmental demands: Opening the black box. *Strategic Management Journal, 29*(10), 1027–1055. https://doi.org/10.1002/smj.701

Demsetz, H. (1967). Toward a theory of property rights. *American Economic Review, 57*, 347–359.

DePamphilis, D. M. (2019). *Mergers, acquisitions, and other restructuring activities: An integrated approach to process, tools, cases and solutions* (10th ed.). Academic Press. https://doi.org/10.1016/B978-0-12-815075-7.00001-2

Desai, V. M. (2016). The behavioral theory of the (governed) firm: Corporate board influences on organizations' responses to performance shortfalls. *Academy of Management Journal, 59*(3), 860–879. https://doi.org/10.5465/amj.2013.0948

Drakopoulos, S. (2021). The relation of neoclassical economics to other disciplines: The case of physics and psychology (MPRA working paper no. 106597). Munich Personal RePEc Archive. https://mpra.ub.uni-muenchen.de/106597/1/MPRA_paper_106597.pdf

Earl, P. E. (2022). *Principles of behavioral economics: Bringing together old, new and evolutionary approaches* (1st ed.). Cambridge University Press.

Easterby-Smith, M., Thorpe, R., & Jackson, P. R. (2012). *Management research* (4th ed.). SAGE Publications.

El-Khatib, R., Fogel, K., & Jandik, T. (2015). CEO network centrality and merger performance. *Journal of Financial Economics, 116*(2), 349–382. https://doi.org/10.1016/j.jfineco.2015.01.001

Elnahas, A. M., & Kim, D. (2017). CEO political ideology and mergers and acquisitions decisions. *Journal of Corporate Finance, 45*, 162–175. https://doi.org/10.1016/j.jcorpfin.2017.04.013

Elsner, W., Heinrich, T., & Schwardt, H. (2015). *The microeconomics of complex economies: Evolutionary, institutional, neoclassical, and complexity perspectives.* Elsevier.

Endres, A. M., & Woods, C. R. (2006). Modern theories of entrepreneurial behavior: A comparison and appraisal. *Small Business Economics, 26*, 189–202. https://doi.org/10.1007/s11187-004-5608-7

Fang, C., Augier, M., & Rindova, V. P. (Eds.). (2018). *Behavioral strategy in perspective* (1st ed., Vol. 39). Emerald Publishing.

Field, L. C., & Mkrtchyan, A. (2017). The effect of director experience on acquisition performance. *Journal of Financial Economics, 123*(3), 488–511. https://doi.org/10.1016/j.jfineco.2016.12.001

Finkelstein, S. (1992). Power in top management teams: Dimensions, measurement, and validation. *Academy of Management Journal, 35*(3), 505–538. https://doi.org/10.2307/256485

Finkelstein, S., Hambrick, D. C., & Cannella, A. A., Jr. (2009). *Strategic leadership: Theory and research on executives, top management teams, and boards.* Oxford University Press.

Foss, N. J., & Mazzelli, A. (2025). Bringing managers and management back into strategy: Interfaces and dynamic managerial capabilities. *Journal of Business Research, 186*, Article 114947. https://doi.org/10.1016/j.jbusres.2024.114947

Frantz, R. S., Chen, S.-H., Dopfer, K., Heukelom, F., & Mousavi, S. (Eds.). (2017). *Routledge handbook of behavioral economics.* Routledge. https://doi.org/10.4324/9781315743479

Friedman, M. (1953). *Essays in positive economics.* University of Chicago Press.

Fuhrer, C., Liem, R., & Zwald, D. (2017). *Success factors in post-merger integration.* PwC. https://www.pwc.de/de/deals/success-factors-in-post-merger-integration.pdf

Gaba, V., & Joseph, J. (2013). Corporate structure and performance feedback: Aspirations and adaptation in m-form firms. *Organization Science, 24*(4), 1102–1119. https://doi.org/10.1287/orsc.1120.0788

Gamache, D. L., McNamara, G., Graffin, S. D., Kiley, J., Haleblian, J., & Devers, C. E. (2019). Impression offsetting as an early warning signal of low CEO confidence in acquisitions. *Academy of Management Journal, 62*(5), 1307–1332. https://doi.org/10.5465/amj.2017.0158

Gavetti, G., Greve, H. R., Levinthal, D. A., & Ocasio, W. (2012). The behavioral theory of the firm: Assessment and prospects. *Academy of Management Annals, 6*(1), 1–40. https://doi.org/10.5465/19416520.2012.656841

Gavetti, G., Levinthal, D. A., & Ocasio, W. (2007). Neo-carnegie: The carnegie school's past, present, and reconstructing for the future. *Organization Science, 18*(3), 523–536. https://doi.org/10.1287/orsc.1070.0277

Graffin, S. D., Boivie, S., & Carpenter, M. A. (2013). Examining CEO succession and the role of heuristics in early-stage CEO evaluation. *Strategic Management Journal, 34*(4), 383–403. https://doi.org/10.1002/smj.2019

Graffin, S. D., Haleblian, J., & Kiley, J. (2016). Ready, aim, acquire: Impression offsetting and acquisitions. *Academy of Management Journal, 59*(1), 232–252. https://doi.org/10.5465/amj.2013.0288

Greenwood, R., Hinings, C. R., & Whetten, D. A. (2014). Rethinking institutions and organizations. *Journal of Management Studies, 51*(7), 1206–1220. https://doi.org/10.1111/joms.12070

Greve, H. R. (2003). *Organizational learning from performance feedback.* Cambridge University Press. https://doi.org/10.1017/CBO9780511615139

Greve, H. R. (2008). A behavioral theory of firm growth: Sequential attention to size and performance goals. *Academy of Management Journal, 51*(3), 476–494. https://doi.org/10.5465/amj.2008.32625975

Greve, H. R., & Argote, L. (2015). Behavioral theories of organization. In N. J. Smelser & P. B. Baltes (Eds.), *International encyclopedia of the social & behavioral sciences* (pp. 481–486). Elsevier. https://doi.org/10.1016/B978-0-08-097086-8.73121-7

Guba, E. G., & Lincoln, Y. S. (1994). Competing paradigms in qualitative research. In N. K. Denzin & Y. S. Lincoln (Eds.), *Handbook of qualitative research* (pp. 105–117). SAGE Publications.

Hagen, M., Su, W., & Junge, S. (2024). 60th birthday of 'A Behavioral Theory of the Firm': A review of the relational concepts and recommendations for future research. *Management Review Quarterly, 74*(4), 2637–2682. https://doi.org/10.1007/s11301-023-00369-x

Hambrick, D. C. (1989). Guest editor's introduction: Putting top managers back in the strategy picture. *Strategic Management Journal, 10*(1), 5–15. https://doi.org/10.1002/smj.4250100703

Hambrick, D. C. (2007). Upper echelons theory: An update. *Academy of Management Journal, 32*(2), 334–343. https://doi.org/10.5465/AMR.2007.24345254

Hambrick, D. C. (2010). Top management teams. In F. Bournois, J. Duval-Hamel, S. Roussillon, & J.-L. Scaringella (Eds.), *Handbook of top management teams* (pp. 23–30). Palgrave Macmillan. https://doi.org/10.1057/9780230305335_2

Hambrick, D. C., & Finkelstein, S. (1987). Managerial discretion: A bridge between polar views of organizational outcomes. *Research in Organizational Behavior, 9*, 369–406.

Hambrick, D. C., & Mason, P. A. (1984). Upper echelons: The organization as a reflection of its top managers. *Academy of Management Journal, 9*(2), 193–206.

Hambrick, D. C., & Quigley, T. J. (2014). Toward more accurate contextualization of the CEO effect on firm performance. *Strategic Management Journal, 35*(4), 473–491. https://doi.org/10.1002/smj.2108

Han, S., Kang, T., Salter, S., & Yoo, Y. K. (2010). A cross-country study on the effects of national culture on earnings management. *Journal of International Business Studies, 41*(1), 123–141. https://doi.org/10.1057/jibs.2008.78

Harrison, J. S., Josefy, M. A., Kalm, M., & Krause, R. (2023). Using supervised machine learning to scale human-coded data: A method and dataset in the board leadership context. *Strategic Management Journal, 44*(7), 1780–1802. https://doi.org/10.1002/smj.3480

Hayward, M. L. A., & Hambrick, D. C. (1997). Explaining the premiums paid for large acquisitions: Evidence of CEO hubris. *Administrative Science Quarterly, 42*(1), 103. https://doi.org/10.2307/2393810

Hayward, M. L. A., Rindova, V. P., & Pollock, T. G. (2004). Believing one's own press: the causes and consequences of CEO celebrity. *Strategic Management Journal, 25*(7), 637–653. https://doi.org/10.1002/smj.405

Herrmann, P., & Datta, D. K. (2002). CEO successor characteristics and the choice of foreign market entry mode: An empirical study. *Journal of International Business Studies, 33*(3), 551–569. https://doi.org/10.1057/palgrave.jibs.8491031

Hertrampf, P., Brunner-Kirchmair, T. M., Hiebl, M. R. W., & Wiedemann, A. (2025). The relationship between CEO characteristics and banks' risk-taking: Review and research directions. *Schmalenbach Journal of Business Research, 77*(1), 127–178. https://doi.org/10.1007/s41471-024-00199-x

Hicks, J. R. (1939). *Value and capital: An inquiry into some fundamental principles of economic theory*. Oxford University Press.

Hiebl, M. R. W. (2014). Upper echelons theory in management accounting and control research. *Journal of Management Control, 24*(3), 223–240. https://doi.org/10.1007/s00187-013-0183-1

Hill, C. W. L., & Jones, T. M. (1992). Stakeholder-agency theory. *Journal of Management Studies, 29*(2), 131–154. https://doi.org/10.1111/j.1467-6486.1992.tb00657.x

Hodgkinson, G. P., Burkhard, B., Foss, N. J., Grichnik, D., Sarala, R. M., Tang, Y., & van Essen, M. (2023). The heuristics and biases of top managers: Past, present, and future. *Journal of Management Studies, 60*(5), 1033–1063. https://doi.org/10.1111/joms.12937

International Data Corporation. (2024). *Worldwide smartphone shipments grew 6.4% in 2024, despite macro challenges according to IDC*. https://www.idc.com/getdoc.jsp?containerId=prUS53072325

Iskandar-Datta, M., & Shekhar, S. (2020). Do insider CFOs deliver better acquisition performance? *Journal of Business Research, 118*(1), 240–252. https://doi.org/10.1016/j.jbusres.2020.06.040

Jensen, M. C., & Meckling, W. H. (1976). Theory of the firm: Managerial behavior, agency costs and ownership structure. *Journal of Financial Economics, 3*, 305–360. https://doi.org/10.1016/0304-405X(76)90026-X

Jensen, M. C., & Zajac, E. J. (2004). Corporate elites and corporate strategy: How demographic preferences and structural position shape the scope of the firm. *Strategic Management Journal, 25*(6), 507–524. https://doi.org/10.1002/smj.393

Jöhnk, C., Fuhrer, C., & Siemes, D. (2020). *Value creation in deals: Finance integration and separation*. PwC. https://www.pwc.de/en/deals/separation-and-integration/the-finance-function-as-the-key-to-successful-transactions.html

Judge, W. Q., Douglas, T. J., & Kutan, A. M. (2008). Institutional antecedents of corporate governance legitimacy. *Journal of Management, 34*(4), 765–785. https://doi.org/10.1177/0149206308318615

Kanihan, S. F., Hansen, K. A., Blair, S., Shore, M., & Myers, J. (2013). Communication managers in the dominant coalition. *Journal of Communication Management, 17*(2), 140–156. https://doi.org/10.1108/13632541311318747

King, B. G., Felin, T., & Whetten, D. A. (2010). Finding the organization in organizational theory: A meta-theory of the organization as a social actor. *Organization Science, 21*(1), 290–305. https://doi.org/10.1287/orsc.1090.0443

Kivunja, C., & Kuyini, A. B. (2017). Understanding and applying research paradigms in educational contexts. *International Journal of Higher Education, 6*(5), 26–41. https://doi.org/10.5430/ijhe.v6n5p26

Knight, F. H. (1921). *Risk, uncertainty, and profit*. Houghton Mifflin.

Langlois, R. N., & Cosgel, M. M. (1993). Frank Knight on risk, uncertainty, and the firm: A new interpretation. *Economic Inquiry, 31*(3), 456–465. https://doi.org/10.1111/j.1465-7295.1993.tb01305.x

Larcker, D. F., & Zakolyukina, A. A. (2012). Detecting deceptive discussions in conference calls. *Journal of Accounting Research, 50*(2), 495–540. https://doi.org/10.1111/j.1475-679X.2012.00450.x

Lather, P. (1986). Research as praxis. *Harvard Educational Review, 56*(3), 257–278. https://doi.org/10.17763/haer.56.3.bj2h231877069482

Leary, M. R. (1996). *Self-presentation*. Routledge. https://doi.org/10.4324/9780429497384

Leavy, P. (Ed.). (2014). *The Oxford handbook of qualitative research*. Oxford University Press. https://doi.org/10.1093/oxfordhb/9780199811755.001.0001

Lehavy, R., Li, F., & Merkley, K. (2011). The effect of annual report readability on analyst following and the properties of their earnings forecasts. *The Accounting Review, 86*(3), 1087–1115. https://doi.org/10.2308/accr.00000043

Love, E. G., Lim, J., & Bednar, M. K. (2017). The face of the firm: The influence of CEOs on corporate reputation. *Academy of Management Journal, 60*(4), 1462–1481. https://doi.org/10.5465/amj.2014.0862

Lovelace, J. B., Bundy, J., Hambrick, D. C., & Pollock, T. G. (2018). The shackles of CEO celebrity: Sociocognitive and behavioral role constraints on "star" leaders. *The Academy of Management Review*, *43*(3), 419–444. https://doi.org/10.5465/amr.2016.0064

Ma, S., Kor, Y. Y., & Seidl, D. (2022). Top management team role structure: A vantage point for advancing upper echelons research. *Strategic Management Journal*, *43*(8), 1–28. https://doi.org/10.1002/smj.3368

Mackenzie, N., & Knipe, S. (2006). Research dilemmas: Paradigms, methods and methodology. *Issues in Educational Research*, *16*(2), 193–205.

Mackey, A. (2008). The effect of CEOs on firm performance. *Strategic Management Journal*, *29*(12), 1357–1367. https://doi.org/10.1002/smj.708

Malmendier, U., & Tate, G. (2005). CEO overconfidence and corporate investment. *The Journal of Finance*, *60*(6), 2661–2700. https://doi.org/10.1111/j.1540-6261.2005.00813.x

March, J. G., & Simon, H. A. (1993). *Organizations* (2nd ed.). Blackwell Business.

Marquez-Illescas, G., Zebedee, A. A., & Zhou, L. (2019). Hear me write: Does CEO narcissism affect disclosure? *Journal of Business Ethics*, *159*(2), 401–417. https://doi.org/10.1007/s10551-018-3796-3

Menz, M. (2012). Functional top management team members. *Journal of Management*, *38*(1), 45–80. https://doi.org/10.1177/0149206311421830

Mertens, D. M. (1998). *Research methods in education and psychology: Integrating diversity with quantitative & qualitative approaches*. SAGE Publications.

Miller, K. D., & Lin, S.-J. (2010). Different truths in different worlds. *Organization Science*, *21*(1), 97–114. https://doi.org/10.1287/orsc.1080.0409

Miner, A. S., Gong, Y., & Baker, T. (2011). How does TMT prior experience shape strategy? A routine-based framework based on evidence from founding teams. In M. A. Carpenter (Ed.), *Handbook of research on top management teams*. Edward Elgar. https://doi.org/10.4337/9780857933201.00016

Mintzberg, H., Ahlstrand, B. W., & Lampel, J. (2009). *Strategy safari: The complete guide through the wilds of strategic management* (2nd ed.). Prentice Hall Financial Times.

Mitchell, R., & Meacheam, D. (2011). Knowledge worker control: Understanding via principal and agency theory. *The Learning Organization*, *18*(2), 149–160. https://doi.org/10.1108/09696471111103740

Mithani, M. A., & O'Brien, J. P. (2021). So what exactly is a "coalition" within an organization? A review and organizing framework. *Journal of Management*, *47*(1), 171–206. https://doi.org/10.1177/0149206320950433

Moeller, S., Schlingemann, F., & Stulz, R. (2005). Wealth destruction on a massive scale? A study of acquiring-firm returns in the recent merger wave. *The Journal of Finance*, *60*(2), 757–782. https://doi.org/10.1111/j.1540-6261.2005.00745.x

Mooney, A. C., & Amason, A. C. (2011). In search of the CEO's inner circle and how it is formed. In M. A. Carpenter (Ed.), *Handbook of research on top management teams* (pp. 35–48). Edward Elgar.

Morgan, G. (2006). *Images of organization* (Updated edition). SAGE Publications.

Nadkarni, S., & Herrmann, P. (2010). CEO personality, strategic flexibility, and firm performance: The case of the Indian business process outsourcing industry. *Academy of Management Journal*, *53*(5), 1050–1073. https://doi.org/10.5465/AMJ.2010.54533196

Neely, B. H., Lovelace, J. B., Cowen, A. P., & Hiller, N. J. (2020). Metacritiques of Upper Echelons Theory: Verdicts and recommendations for future research. *Journal of Management*, *46*(6), 1029–1062. https://doi.org/10.1177/0149206320908640

Nègre, E., Verdier, M.-A., Cho, C. H., & Patten, D. M. (2017). Disclosure strategies and investor reactions to downsizing announcements: A legitimacy perspective. *Journal of Accounting and Public Policy*, *36*(3), 239–257. https://doi.org/10.1016/j.jaccpubpol.2017.03.003

Nielsen, S. (2010). Top management team diversity: A review of theories and methodologies. *International Journal of Management Reviews*, *12*(3), 301–316. https://doi.org/10.1111/j.1468-2370.2009.00263.x

Noh, J., & Zhou, D. (2022). Executives' blaming external factors and market reactions: Evidence from earnings conference calls. *Journal of Banking & Finance*, *134*, Article 106358. https://doi.org/10.1016/j.jbankfin.2021.106358

North, D. C. (1990). *Institutions, institutional change and economic performance*. Cambridge University Press. https://doi.org/10.1017/CBO9780511808678

North, D. C. (1991). Institutions. *Journal of Economic Perspective*, *5*(1), 97–112.

Oliver, C. (1991). Strategic responses to institutional processes. *The Academy of Management Review*, *16*(1), 145–179. https://doi.org/10.2307/258610

Papagiannidis, S. (Ed.). (2022). *TheoryHub Book: A theory resource for students and researchers alike*. Newcastle University Business School.

Patel, P. C., & Cooper, D. (2014). The harder they fall, the faster they rise: Approach and avoidance focus in narcissistic CEOs. *Strategic Management Journal*, *35*(10), 1528–1540. https://doi.org/10.1002/smj.2162

Petrenko, O. V., Aime, F., Recendes, T., & Chandler, J. A. (2019). The case for humble expectations: CEO humility and market performance. *Strategic Management Journal*, *40*(12), 1938–1964. https://doi.org/10.1002/smj.3071

Phoenix, C., Osborne, N. J., Redshaw, C., Moran, R., Stahl-Timmins, W., Depledge, M. H., Fleming, L. E., & Wheeler, B. W. (2013). Paradigmatic approaches to studying environment and human health: (Forgotten) implications for interdisciplinary research. *Environmental Science & Policy*, *25*, 218–228. https://doi.org/10.1016/j.envsci.2012.10.015

Plöckinger, M., Aschauer, E., Hiebl, M. R. W., & Rohatschek, R. (2016). The influence of individual executives on corporate financial reporting: A review and outlook from the perspective of upper echelons theory. *Journal of Accounting Literature*, *37*(1), 55–75. https://doi.org/10.1016/j.acclit.2016.09.002

Popli, M., Ahsan, F. M., & Mukherjee, D. (2022). Upper echelons and firm internationalization: A critical review and future directions. *Journal of Business Research*, *152*, 505–521. https://doi.org/10.1016/j.jbusres.2022.07.048

Powell, T. C., Lovallo, D., & Fox, C. R. (2011). Behavioral strategy. *Strategic Management Journal*, *32*(13), 1369–1386. https://doi.org/10.1002/smj.968

Pretorius, L. (2024). Demystifying research paradigms: Navigating ontology, epistemology, and axiology in research. *The Qualitative Report*, *29*(10), 2698–2715. https://doi.org/10.46743/2160-3715/2024.7632

Price, S. M., Doran, J. S., Peterson, D. R., & Bliss, B. A. (2012). Earnings conference calls and stock returns: The incremental informativeness of textual tone. *Journal of Banking & Finance*, *36*(4), 992–1011. https://doi.org/10.1016/j.jbankfin.2011.10.013

Quan, X., Ke, Y., Qian, Y., & Zhang, Y. (2023). CEO foreign experience and green innovation: Evidence from China. *Journal of Business Ethics, 182*(2), 535–557. https://doi.org/10.1007/s10551-021-04977-z

Quigley, T. J., & Hambrick, D. C. (2015). Has the "CEO effect" increased in recent decades? A new explanation for the great rise in America's attention to corporate leaders. *Strategic Management Journal, 36*(6), 821–830. https://doi.org/10.1002/smj.2258

Renneboog, L., & Vansteenkiste, C. (2019). Failure and success in Mergers and Acquisitions. *Journal of Corporate Finance, 58*, 650–699. https://doi.org/10.1016/j.jcorpfin.2019.07.010

Rocha, V. C. (2012). The entrepreneur in economic theory: From an invisible man toward a new research field (RePEc working paper no. 459). University of Porto, School of Economics and Management. https://ideas.repec.org/p/por/fepwps/459.html

Rorem, R., Thomas, T., Lowrie, N., Rothman, H., Swaminathan, V., Gorr, C., Xu, J., & Velasquez, M. (2013). The role of CFO. In J. Roehl-Anderson (Ed.), *M&A information technology best practices* (321–343). John Wiley & Sons.

Ross, L., Lepper, M. R., & Hubbard, M. (1975). Perseverance in self-perception and social perception: Biased attributional processes in the debriefing paradigm. *Journal of Personality and Social Psychology, 32*(5), 880–892. https://doi.org/10.1037/0022-3514.32.5.880

Samuelson, P. A. (1947). *Foundations of economic analysis* (Enlarged edition). Harvard University Press.

Schlenker, B. R. (1980). *Impression management: The self-concept, social identity, and interpersonal relations*. Brooks/Cole Publishing.

Schneider, S. L. (1992). Framing and conflict: Aspiration level contingency, the status quo, and current theories of risky choice. *Journal of Experimental Psychology. Learning, Memory, and Cognition, 18*(5), 1040–1057. https://doi.org/10.1037/0278-7393.18.5.1040

Schnelker, D. L. (2006). The student-as-bricoleur: Making sense of research paradigms. *Teaching and Teacher Education, 22*(1), 42–57. https://doi.org/10.1016/j.tate.2005.07.001

Schreyögg, G., & Geiger, D. (2016). *Organisation: Grundlagen moderner Organisationsgestaltung. Mit Fallstudien* (6th ed.). Springer. https://doi.org/10.1007/978-3-8349-4485-6

Schumpeter, J. A. (1942). *Capitalism, socialism and democracy*. Harper.

Scotland, J. (2012). Exploring the philosophical underpinnings of research: Relating ontology and epistemology to the methodology and methods of the scientific, interpretive, and critical research paradigms. *English Language Teaching, 5*(9), 9–16. https://doi.org/10.5539/elt.v5n9p9

Scott, W. R. (2014). *Institutions and organizations: Ideas, interests and identities* (4th ed.). SAGE Publications.

Simon, H. A. (1957). *Models of man: Social and rational*. John Wiley & Sons.

Sine, W. D., & Lee, B. H. (2009). Tilting at windmills? The environmental movement and the emergence of the U.S. wind energy sector. *Administrative Science Quarterly, 54*(1), 123–155. https://doi.org/10.2189/asqu.2009.54.1.123

Smith, C. W., & Warner, J. B. (1979). On financial contracting. *Journal of Financial Economics, 7*(2), 117–161. https://doi.org/10.1016/0304-405X(79)90011-4

Stiglitz, J. E. (2011). Rethinking macroeconomics: What failed, and how to repair it. *Journal of the European Economic Association, 9*(4), 591–645. https://doi.org/10.1111/j.1542-4774.2011.01030.x

Suddaby, R., Elsbach, K. D., Greenwood, R., Meyer, J. W., & Zilber, T. B. (2010). Organizations and their institutional environments - Bringing meaning, values, and culture back. *Academy of Management Journal, 53*(6), 1234–1240. https://doi.org/10.2139/ssrn.2266086

Sugden, R. (2016). Ontology, methodological individualism, and the foundations of the social sciences. *Journal of Economic Literature, 54*(4), 1377–1389. https://doi.org/10.1257/jel.20151372

Surdu, I., Greve, H. R., & Benito, G. R. G. (2021). Back to basics: Behavioral theory and internationalization. *Journal of International Business Studies, 52*(6), 1047–1068. https://doi.org/10.1057/s41267-020-00388-w

Thaler, R. H. (2015). *Predictably unpredictable: Why we don't act like we should.* National Public Radio. https://www.npr.org/2016/01/12/462386252/richard-thaler-why-most-economists-might-as-well-be-studying-unicorns

Thaler, R. H. (2016). Behavioral economics: Past, present, and future. *American Economic Review, 106*(7), 1577–1600. https://doi.org/10.1257/aer.106.7.1577

Tsoulfidis, L., & Tsalikē, P. (2019). *Classical political economics and modern capitalism: Theories of value, competition, trade and long cycles.* Springer.

van Doorn, S., Heyden, M. L. M., Reimer, M., Buyl, T., & Volberda, H. W. (2022). Internal and external interfaces of the executive suite: Advancing research on the porous bounds of strategic leadership. *Long Range Planning, 55*(3), 102214. https://doi.org/10.1016/j.lrp.2022.102214

Waddingham, J. A., Chandler, J. A., Alexander, K. C., Zafar, S., & Anglin, A. (2025). The leisure paradox for entrepreneurs: A neo-institutional theory perspective of disclosing leisure activities in crowdfunding pitches. *Journal of Business Venturing, 40*(2), Article 106467. https://doi.org/10.1016/j.jbusvent.2024.106467

Wang, G., Holmes, R. M., Oh, I.-S., & Zhu, W. (2016). Do CEOs matter to firm strategic actions and firm performance? A meta-analytic investigation based on upper echelons theory. *Personnel Psychology, 69*(4), 775–862. https://doi.org/10.1111/peps.12140

Wangrow, D. B., Schepker, D. J., & Barker, V. L. (2015). Managerial discretion. *Journal of Management, 41*(1), 99–135. https://doi.org/10.1177/0149206314554214

Webb, J. W., Bruton, G. D., Tihanyi, L., & Ireland, R. D. (2013). Research on entrepreneurship in the informal economy: Framing a research agenda. *Journal of Business Venturing, 28*(5), 598–614. https://doi.org/10.1016/j.jbusvent.2012.05.003

Welch, X., Pavićević, S., Keil, T., & Laamanen, T. (2020). The pre-deal phase of Mergers and Acquisitions: A review and research agenda. *Journal of Management, 46*(6), 843–878. https://doi.org/10.1177/0149206319886908

Wheelen, T. L., Hunger, J. D., Hoffman, A. N., & Bamford, C. E. (2017). *Strategic management and business policy: Globalization, innovation and sustainability* (15th ed.). Pearson Education Limited.

Wheeler, G. (2024). Bounded rationality. In E. N. Zalta & U. Nodelman (Eds.), *The Stanford Encyclopedia of Philosophy.* https://plato.stanford.edu/archives/win2024/entries/bounded-rationality

White, J. V., & Borgholthaus, C. J. (2022). Who's in charge here? A bibliometric analysis of upper echelons research. *Journal of Business Research, 139*, 1012–1025. https://doi.org/10.1016/j.jbusres.2021.10.028

Whitler, K. A., Lee, B., Krause, R., & Morgan, N. A. (2021). Upper echelons research in marketing. *Journal of the Academy of Marketing Science, 49*(1), 198–219. https://doi.org/10.1007/s11747-020-00724-4

Williamson, O. E. (1975). *Markets and hierarchies: Analysis and antitrust implications: A study in the economics of internal organization.* Free Press; Collier Macmillan.

Wowak, A. J., Gomez-Mejia, L. R., & Steinbach, A. L. (2017). Inducements and motives at the top: A holistic perspective on the drivers of executive behavior. *Academy of Management Annals, 11*(2), 669–702. https://doi.org/10.5465/annals.2015.0121

Wowak, A. J., Mannor, M. J., Arrfelt, M., & McNamara, G. (2016). Earthquake or glacier? How CEO charisma manifests in firm strategy over time. *Strategic Management Journal, 37*(3), 586–603. https://doi.org/10.1002/smj.2346

Yamak, S., Nielsen, S., & Escribá-Esteve, A. (2014). The role of external environment in Upper Echelons Theory. *Group & Organization Management, 39*(1), 69–109. https://doi.org/10.1177/1059601113511663

Yeung, A. C. L., Lo, C. K. Y., & Cheng, T. C. E. (2011). Behind the iron cage: An institutional perspective on ISO 9000 adoption and CEO compensation. *Organization Science, 22*(6), 1600–1612. https://doi.org/10.1287/orsc.1110.0652

Zacharias, N. A., Six, B., Schiereck, D., & Stock, R. M. (2015). CEO influences on firms' strategic actions: A comparison of CEO-, firm-, and industry-level effects. *Journal of Business Research, 68*(11), 2338–2346. https://doi.org/10.1016/j.jbusres.2015.03.045

MIX
Papier aus verantwortungsvollen Quellen
Paper from responsible sources
FSC® C105338

If you have any concerns about our products,
you can contact us on
ProductSafety@springernature.com

In case Publisher is established outside the EU,
the EU authorized representative is:
Springer Nature Customer Service Center GmbH
Europaplatz 3, 69115 Heidelberg, Germany

Printed by Libri Plureos GmbH
in Hamburg, Germany